# TIGER WOODS
# THE CHAMPIONSHIP YEARS

Also by
TIM ROSAFORTE

# TIGER WOODS

## THE CHAMPIONSHIP YEARS

### TIM ROSAFORTE

**HEADLINE**

First published in 2000 by Thomas Dunne Books

First published in Great Britain in 2001
by HEADLINE BOOK PUBLISHING

All photographs provided by ALLSPORT UK, LTD

Tim Rosaforte would be happy to hear from readers with their comments on
the book at the following e-mail address: Rosaforte@aol.com

10 9 8 7 6 5 4 3 2

British Library Cataloguing in Publication Data

Rosaforte, Tim
    Tiger Woods: the championship years
    1.Woods, Tiger 2. Golfers – United States – Biography
    3.Afro-American golfers – Biography
    I.Title
    796.3'52'092

ISBN 0 7472 4980 6

Typeset by Letterpart Limited,
Reigate, Surrey

Printed and bound in Great Britain by
Mackays of Chatham plc, Chatham, Kent

HEADLINE BOOK PUBLISHING
A division of Hodder Headline
338 Euston Road
London NW1 3BH

www.headline.co.uk
www.hodderheadline.com

FOR GENEVIEVE, GENNA, MOLLY, AND MY FAMILY

# CONTENTS

# CONTENTS

# Acknowledgements

Thank You

—Tiger Woods, for producing four unbelievable years.
—Mark Steinberg and Bev Norwood of IMG, for taking the high road.
—Pete Wolverton, for being the Butch Harmon of this project, and Carolyn Dunkley, for being my Steve Williams.
—Frank Weimann and Scott Waxman, for putting this deal together.
—Geoff Russell for helping me raise the bar on my game.
—John Hawkins for pumping me up.
—Ron Sirak for mellowing me out.
—Jennifer Cole, Bob Verdi, Bill Fields, Tim Murphy, Mike Stachura, Ryan Herrington, John Huggan, John Strege, John Antonini, Lisa Vannais, Lisa Mickey, Steve Szurlej, Gary Newkirk, Rusty Jarrett and Larry Lambrecht for being so committed to the *Golf World* product.
—Terry Galvin, for a brand new start.
—Jerry Tarde, Bob Carney and the New York Times Company, for giving me permission to do this book.
—Craig Dolch, Jaime Diaz, Doug Ferguson, Cliff Brown, Dave Anderson, Dan Jenkins, Dave Kindred, Tom Callahan, Jeff Rude, Jimmy Roberts, Lorne Rubenstein, Melanie Hauser, Len Shapiro, Pete McDaniel, T. R. Reinman, Mark Soltau, Jim

## ACKNOWLEDGEMENTS

McCabe, Joe Gordon, Reid Hanley, Glenn Sheeley, Dave Shedloski, Jeff Babineau, Dave Lagarde, Hunki Yun, Matt Rudy, Bob Baptist, Helen Ross, David Owen, Michael Bamberger, S. L. Price, Alan Shipnuck, Robinson Holloway, Brad Townsend, Jimmy Burch, Eddie Sefko, Howard Richman, Ed Sherman, Gerry Dulac, Joe Juliano, Ron Green Jr., Mike Kern, Mark Cannizzaro, Hank Gola, Rick Remsnyder, Jeff Williams, Mike Purkey, Tom Bonk, Brian Hewitt, Marla Ridenour, George Sweda, Dave Hackenberg, Vartan Kupelian, Rick Dorsey, Bruce Berlet, Bob Harig, Mike Elliott, Randy Mell, Mike Mayo, Gary Smits, Bill Blighton, John Hopkins, Dai Davies, Mark Garrod, Derek Lawrenson, Colm Smith, Michael O'Malley, Craig Bestrom and Dermot Gilleece. If I wasn't there, you were.

—Alastair Johnston, Joel Hirsch, John Davis, Mike Harrigan, Mark Thaxton, Kel Devlin, Wally Uihlein, Bill Young, Doc Giffin, Rick Schloss, Jim Bell, Randy Reifers, Ed Sabo, Ray Kosowski, Craig Bowen, Bill O'Hara, Louis Wellen, Eddie Merrins, Scott Tolley, Davis Sezna, and Charles Pierce for taking me behind the scenes or enlightening me with a perspective I didn't have.

—Bert Yaeger, St. Martin's production-editor, for his advice.

—Peter Kessler, Scott Van Pelt, Lee Siegel, Eric Saperstein, Jeff Hymes, Danielle Williams, Mason Seay, Joy Henneberger, and all those at the Golf Channel who contributed to this project.

—To the staffs of Bob Combs (PGA Tour), Julius Mason (PGA of America), Marty Parkes (USGA) and Glenn Greenspan (Augusta National) for the tireless work you do for the Golf Writers Association of America.

—Angela Enright of the Four Seasons Resort in Irving, Texas, for Byron Nelson.

—Brad Martin (Cove Cottage at Blackberry Farm), Brad Quayle and Tony Dawson (Cordillera) and Ken Everett and Mark Acerni (Roaring Fork Club), for providing the settings.

—Larry Dorman, Kevin Murphy, Mark Mulvoy and Rick Goldsmith, for encouragement and guidance.

—Pastor Tom Mullins and Christ Fellowship Church, for showing me the way.

# FOREWORD

The first time I saw Tiger Woods, I was at Bel-Air Country Club in Los Angeles where Eddie Merrins is pro. My wife, Peggy, and I were there for a Friends of Golf Pro-Am honoring Jack Nicklaus in 1991. Eddie told me that Tiger was there. I had been reading about him, so Eddie gave us a cart, and we watched him play 14 holes. I was very much impressed with his swing, how well he hit the ball and how far he hit it. Even then he hit the ball a long way, even for a 15-year-old.

I saw Tiger play every year from then on until now, either in the juniors, as an amateur, or a pro. He won a junior tournament here at the TPC at Las Colinas in Irving, Texas, the AJGA Junior Championship. I went out to see him and told him, 'I'm glad to watch you play. I enjoyed watching you at Bel-Air.' In 1993, I wrote him a personal letter, inviting him to play in the GTE Byron Nelson Classic. He accepted, and I've been in touch with him ever since.

As a golfer, he has tremendous ability, and the great thing is, he is still learning. I admire him in a number of ways. One of the main things is, as well as he's been playing, he realizes to himself that he can play better. It's a trait all the great champions have.

Everybody talks about the way he hits the ball, but what impresses me even more is his ability as a putter. I think he reads a green better than anybody I've seen in 75 years of golf. He very seldom misses the line, and he's even money to make it from 15 feet in. Even a 30-to 40-foot putt; the feel he has is incredible. He has gone as much as 157 holes without three putting.

Could he become the greatest golfer who ever lived? At this stage of his life, I'd say he has the potential to, absolutely. You can never tell how well he is going to be able to perform the way he performs and for how long. The good Lord only knows that. He could hurt a wrist or his back, any golfer could. It could happen to him. But as far as his ability and desire and wanting to be the best player in the world: He doesn't just want to do it. He works at it.

The game is just so much different now than it was when I played. When I won 11-straight tournaments in 1945, I had one little bitsy endorsement. That was with Wheaties. There was no television and you had to go downtown to go on radio. You just can't believe how golf has grown. The best way I can explain it was last year, 1999, when Loren Roberts won our event, he said he never thought he'd made $540,000 from one tournament in his life. I told him, that's a lot of money, let me explain how much. In 1945 there were 32 tournaments. I played 30. Total prize money was only $520,000. That's how much it's grown, from the publicity on television, with President Eisenhower and Arnold Palmer, Jack Nicklaus and Tom Watson, Seve Ballesteros and Greg Norman, and now Tiger Woods. Every era has had one fine golfer. This era it's Tiger.

We were linked together earlier this year when he won his fifth and sixth straight PGA Tour events. I wrote him a note about it. I said, 'Tiger, I love watching you play on the TV, it's a lot of fun to watch you. If you do break my record, I'll be the first one to congratulate you. I had the record for 55 years. If you go ahead and break it, Merry Christmas.'

The unfortunate thing about this position, he doesn't have a life of his own. When I won the 11 in a row, nobody paid attention to me. I'm sure he can't go out to a restaurant and eat. That's difficult. But he is living with it wonderfully well. And he's improving himself all the time, I admire that. It must be tough. It must be difficult to live with. As long as he keeps the desire he has, he'll be fine. We had to play on our own. Now he can call his teacher, and Butch Harmon can come in to check him out. We didn't have that in our time. None.

People ask me if Tiger could win the Grand Slam. If anybody

could, he could. But it will be very difficult even for him. You're playing against the best players in the world in the majors and you have to be peaking at the right time, four times a year. So many other things enter into it. You can get a bad starting time, get caught in the wind. There are so many things that come into it other than an ability to play golf. I think it's remarkable that he won three.

I have a lot of fun watching him play. Everywhere I o I answer more questions about Tiger than about myself or the rest of the players combined. Whether it's Home Depot or the people at church, people ask me, 'What's Tiger going to do today? Do you think Tiger is going to win today?' It's amazing. People who have never played golf or viewed golf before ask me about Tiger.

I think the world of the young man. I just think he's great for the game.

– BYRON NELSON

# Introduction

The Golf Writers Association of America hosts its annual awards dinner at the Bell Auditorium in Augusta, Georgia, the night before the opening round of the Masters. On the eve of the 65th Masters, Tiger Woods was the featured speaker. He was scheduled to arrive just after the cocktail hour, receive his award as the male Player of the Year, and then leave just after his acceptance speech. He had a tournament to play the next day. The most important tournament in his life.

I had seen Tiger three weeks earlier, on the driving range at Isleworth County Club in Orlando. He had just come off a final-hole defeat to Thomas Bjorn in the Dubai Desert Classic, and had not seen the most recent *Golf World* cover, which pictured him, in the trees, slashing a recovery shot, behind the headline, 'What's wrong with Tiger Woods?' He went on to win that week at the Bay Hill Invitational, and I wrote the game story for *Golf World*, hooking it around the ridiculous notion that Tiger had been in a 'slump' because he hadn't won in eight-straight events. The story couldn't have been more objective, or positive.

The following week Tiger won again, at the Players Championship, and I had appeared on the Golf Channel for three nights at the TPC-Sawgrass in Ponte Vedra, Florida, and then, driving to the studios in Orlando following his Monday victory. While he claims not to read anything written about him, Woods does watch the Golf Channel. Rich Lerner, who hosted those Viewers' Forum shows from the TPC, asked me about the *Golf World* cover. I said it was justified in that Tiger had never double bogeyed the 72nd hole of a tournament to lose before, and, while it wasn't The Choke of Araby (as written in *Sports Illustrated*), it certainly was an example of the frustration Tiger was feeling over his winless streak.

None of us who cover golf regularly in the United States really understood how frustrated Tiger was with the word 'slump' until he appeared in an interview with NBC's Jimmy Roberts walking off the 18th green at the Players Championship. Roberts had diplomatically framed the 'slump question' during the third round at Bay Hill, and the mere mention of that word in a television interview set Tiger off. When Jimmy asked Tiger what a victory at the Players meant, Woods cut him off with a wise answer. 'Some slump,' Woods said. Roberts rephrased the question, asking Woods what it meant to win the Players. 'Means the slump is over,' he said. Roberts changed gears and tried again. Woods acknowledged that the Players was probably the fifth most important tournament in the world, but would not grant it major status. Roberts went into his wrap. It is common courtesy at this point for the athlete to stand there until the announcer is finished and the director has cut to another picture. Woods walked out in the middle of Roberts' sentence.

But that was history by the eve of the 65th Masters, when Tiger had won two straight and was riding the crest of momentum. When he walked past me and sat down at the GWAA dinner, I wanted to extend him a courtesy handshake, wish him well for the week, and, knowing he'd been wearing the game face, get in and out of his protective bubble in 10 seconds. Masters week was no place to get any quality time with Tiger Woods. I knew it, respected it, and understood it. But as soon as I got Tiger's attention, I knew something was different, that there was some bad feelings in the air.

'Hey Tiger, what's up?'

Instead of a smile, I got the cold death-stare he gave Roberts at the TPC, and a handshake that was a little firmer than usual. Like he was trying to deliver a message.

'Nothing wrong,' he said.

The rest of the conversation I'll never forget.

'What do you mean, nothing's wrong.'

'Nothing's wrong.'

'You mean nothing's wrong with you and Jimmy Roberts?'

'No, nothing's wrong with me.'

'I know nothing's wrong with you. What are you talking about?'

Finally, he let on.

'Your cover.'

'Oh, the cover . . . Yeah, we were going to follow up that Dubai headline, but Karrie [Webb] shot 59 . . .'

'You mean Annika [Sorenstam] shot 59.'

He was sitting. I was on my heels and squatting. A photographer from the *Augusta Chronicle* took our picture. I knew how the photograph would look: like I was sucking up. The whole scene was playing out exactly as Tiger wanted it to play out. I stood up, backed out, and realized this was no day to get into an argument with the world's most famous and powerful athlete. We'd deal with it some other time.

But I'm both hard-headed and overly sensitive enough that I just couldn't let it go. Tiger made his acceptance speech in a gracious and charming way. I introduced Tom Lehman, who was accepting the GWAA's Bartlett Award, given to the playing professional for his or her outstanding contributions to society. And then it was time for Tiger to bolt, which he did, right past me without making eye contact, in a hallway off the auditorium.

Of course, I followed. Down the hall, through the lobby, right to Tiger's car. His business manager, Mark Steinberg, was driving. Tiger was getting into the passenger seat.

'What was that all about?' I said.

He looked at me, and the cold, vacant stare melted into a mischievous smile.

'Man,' he said, 'I was just messing with you,' or words to that effect.

And with that he closed the door and drove away to his second Masters title, and his fourth straight major-championship victory.

Sure, he was messing with me, but he was mad about the cover because he felt that *Golf World*, of all publications, wouldn't do him like that. It was my job to take the heat for the magazine, which I did, and in my best interests not to take it personally, which I didn't. Reflecting on it, it was similar to some of the moments I had with Jack Nicklaus, when Jack would play his mind games with me just to maintain an upper hand in the relationship. Except now, the athlete wasn't 16 years older but 20 years younger than me, and incredibly more powerful.

If that wasn't clear before the Masters, it certainly was after it. In what seemed like a preordained passage in golf history, Woods went where no one had gone before. He won the Masters by two strokes, becoming the first player to hold all four professional major championships at the same time.

Tiger was right, of course. Nothing was wrong. Let this be a lesson. Nothing was wrong.

– TIM ROSAFORTE
Jupiter, Florida
April 15, 2001

# PREFACE

After he won the 2000 U.S. Open at Pebble Beach, Tiger Woods met his father for a game of golf at Big Canyon Golf Club in Newport Beach, California. Earl Woods had not been traveling to many tournaments, leading to speculation that he was not doing well. In a quiet moment, Earl asked his son, 'Do you want me to be around more?' Tiger looked at his father, and realized the time had come to declare his independence.

'I'll be all right, Pop,' he said, and Earl Woods knew the day had come.

'He was saying, "I've grown up," said Earl. He was declaring his freedom. It meant I had done my job.'

The kid had become a man, growing mentally and physically before our eyes, exceeding not only our expectations but also his own. This was no longer the 155-pound whippet who burst on the scene in the mid-nineties to win three U.S. Amateur titles and a Masters before his 20th birthday. This was a full-grown 25-year-old who had grasped hold of his destiny with an interlocking grip.

He can bench press 300 and cause the ground to shake. He can stick that look on you, put it right in your face – and don't expect him to back down. Not with his game. Not with that desire he has to win. Michael Jordan was the same way. Nicest guy in the world off the court. A cold-blooded killer in the game. He'd get inside your head, step on your throat, and hear the bones crunch.

Michael was one of Tiger's role models. He carefully observed the demeanor, and applied it to what his father taught him about competition.

Watch Tiger. You'll get a lesson in how you're supposed to compete. Watch him go into a trance and lock onto a tournament. You will never see a more focused athlete. 'On Saturday [at the U.S. Open] I was waiting on the first tee for the round to begin,' remembers Dr Trey Holland, the United States Golf Association President. 'Tiger comes up the steps that lead to the tee, and he's laughing and joking with his caddie, very loose, very relaxed; then he gets on the tee, puts his right hand on the head cover of his driver and starts staring down the fairway. The smile is gone. The eyes widen. Just staring, for a full two minutes. I'd never seen that kind of concentration. People are yelling, "C'mon, Tiger! You can do it!" I don't think he heard a word of it.'

They used to say the same thing about Nicklaus, back when he was the man. They said that Jack managed his game better than anybody, that he had the best mind in the game. Tiger is Jack in a better body, with his father's Green Beret discipline and his mother's power of Zen.

'When you've got Tiger on your ass, the way we did at the [2000] Players Championship, it's the worst kind of pressure,' said Freddie Burns, who caddies for Hal Sutton. 'It's like somebody putting 300 pounds on you and all you can lift is 285.'

Then, just like Nicklaus, watch him when the event is over. He'll be standing there by the 18th green with his cap off, his hand out, and what are you supposed to do? He's the perfect gentlemen. Golf's ultimate warrior can morph into Bobby Jones. He brought an athlete's mentality to golf, but kept it genteel. It is an interesting mix.

Tiger Woods has more than just transcended the game. By sweeping both Opens, the PGA Championship and the Masters, he has thrown the sport of golf on his back and taken it into pop culture. Golf is cool because of Tiger Woods. Golf has even become socially acceptable.

Behind the 18th green at Valhalla, his agent, Mark Steinberg, said above the crowd noise, 'Tigermania was rampant when he won [the Masters] in 1997, but that was a one-time thing. Now, he is world-icon status.' Woods had just won the PGA Championship for his third straight major of the 2000 season. Steinberg knew what it meant. 'I used to put the word arguably in front of it,' he said. 'I'm his agent, and I work with him closer than anybody in this world, businesswise, and I travel with him around the world. There is no argument to this. There is no bigger entertainer in the world than Tiger Woods. There is nobody even close. I'm talking about actors, entertainers, singers. There is no greater entertainer in the world today than Tiger. Jordan never got this big.'

From the playgrounds in Harlem to the grill room at Bel-Air Country Club, everybody wanted to know what this kid was really like. Now he was being called the world's best athlete. A golfer, the world's best athlete, better than the Olympians who were going to Sydney, better than Vince Carter, who could fly better than any man, better than Randy Moss, the best wide receiver in the NFL. Yet, people really didn't know. They really didn't know what he was like away from the course. Tiger wanted it that way.

We caught some rare glimpses of the human side. We saw he likes to pop up in Vegas, at Stanford football games, up and down the coast in Southern California, and occasionally in Orlando where he finds shelter at Isleworth County Club.

When he's off the public stage, Tiger likes to slip in and slip out of the picture. Two days after he won the U.S. Open, he was caddying for college teammates Jerry Chang in a U.S. Amateur qualifying round in Las Vegas. Pair of shorts. Sunglasses. No hat. The week after the won the British Open, Tiger got in his SUV and drove down the Florida Turnpike with his girlfriend to Singer Island, Florida, where they took scuba-diving lessons and headed on over to the Bahamas. It was real low-key. No cameras. No reporters. No problems.

Being the richest and most powerful athlete and/or entertainer in the world has its down side. It could be hell to be Tiger Woods. You've always got people wanting a piece of you. You're like a movie star, a politician, a lightning rod for attention. You've also got people wanting to kill you, if for no other reason than you're a man of color playing the game that still symbolizes racism, the good old game of golf.

But being the richest and most powerful athlete and/or entertainer in the world also has its up side. You can host your own series of concerts (TigerJam), and hang out with sports celebrities and actors like 'M' (Michael Jordan), Junior (Ken Griffey, Jr.), A-Rod (Alex Rodriguez) and Sammy (Samuel L. Jackson). Then there's always Marko (Mark O'Meara), Butchie (Butch Harmon), and Stevie (caddy Steve Williams). You get right down to it, that's a pretty good support group.

What's Tiger got more of than anybody? It's not money or talent. It's pride and will. No matter what he does, he wants to do the best at it. Fishing? Wants to kick O'Meara's butt. News conferences? Wants to do them like a pro. Corporate outings? Gets into them. Commercial shoots? Has there ever been a better, more spontaneous ad, than the Nike commercial from the summer of 1999. Tiger Woods Foundation Clinics? His name is on them.

He'll get on the phone and call Bob Wood, the president of Nike Golf. He'll talk investment strategy with the executives at American Express. He'll make young girls giggle and grown men cry. Tiger has turned golf into a game for the people, or at least he's trying. What's so cool is the way he's doing it. He's toned down his act, 'brought it down a level,' says college teammate Notah Begay, and the result is almost Hoganlike. He's dressing in grays and blacks. His fist pumps no longer look like he just scored a touchdown. And the way he loses is textbook. Watch the way he takes his cap off on the 18th green, shakes his opponent's hand, his opponent's caddy's hand, and his own caddy's hand. Listen to what he says about his opponents. It's total class.

Has success spoiled Tiger Woods? Stupid question. If you can judge a man by how he plays a round of golf, how he acts in tough situations and relaxed environments, then no, success has not spoiled him. In fact, based on what you hear in locker rooms and press rooms around the PGA Tour, Tiger Woods gets more style points for the way he's reacting to his fame than he does for actually attaining it.

He's trying to be a role model, trying to be a leader, trying to be a diplomat, and he's winning athletic contests under more pressure, more media attention, and more fan intensity than any athlete in the history of any sport.

I don't know if Earl Woods was right when he said his son would be bigger than Gandhi and Mother Teresa, but it's hard to argue with the impact he's had on the world. Maybe Earl didn't raise the Messiah or the Chosen One, but this Eldrick Woods is once in a lifetime, one of a kind.

We can't wait to see what he does next. We know it will be better than what he did before.

# PART I

## The Tiger Effect

*Tiger has a contribution to make in this world. I'm not sure what it is yet. The signal still has not come.*

– EARL WOODS

# One

# IMPACT PLAYER

Robert Walker, the golf photographer, was walking past a laundry on the lower west side of Manhattan in the winter of 1997. It was one of those raw February weekend-afternoons in the city, but there was an unmistakable warmth emanating from the small black and white television set. Gathered around, Walker saw black people, Asian people and Hispanic people, all of them transfixed on the image they were seeing on the TV screen. This was not basketball or football they were watching. This was the new fascination. This was Tiger Woods.

Walker only wished he had his camera. The scene reminded him of a track NBC filmed to air before its World Series telecasts, a series of vignettes of people from all over the country, gathered around their TV sets in garages and bars, living rooms and country farms, listening to the call of the game. It was almost as if that setting depicted a twenty-first-century picture of the new national past time.

Tiger was in the midst of a final-round 64 that would come one stroke short of stealing the Pebble Beach Pro-Am title from Mark O'Meara, his Orlando neighbor and big brother. It was the day Woods hit a thunderstruck second shot over the sea wall and on to the 18th green, a thundering second shot that was as emphatic as a Michael Jordan slam-dunk. A new hero was being born, and in two more months, he would complete the first phase of his dynasty by winning the Masters by 12 strokes.

'For some reason I recall the TV being black and white,' says Walker. 'Maybe it wasn't black and white, but it seemed to be black and white because it is a black and white kind of image – a have and have not kind of thing. I found it very compelling that you had this game which is constantly referred to as a "rich man's game" being paid attention to by this poor segment of society.'

Alrick Washington, an upwardly mobile American with disposable income, became hooked on the game of golf by watching Tiger Woods win the 1997 Masters. Washington grew up in the underside of Oklahoma City. His parents divorced when he was four. He remembers his mother raising him and his sister in an apartment along with three other families. There were 13 people in this house, four mothers and nine kids just trying to survive. Sometimes the power company would turn the electricity off. Sometimes there wasn't enough food to feed them all. And when his mother, Beatrice, could no longer support him, she shipped him off to his grandmother, Clovee. Growing up in this environment made Alrick want more. Much, much more.

He played quarterback on the football team, guard on the basketball team, and shortstop on the baseball team, but at 5'4", and barely 140 pounds little Alrick Washington wasn't going to play pro sports. He ended up at Southwestern Oklahoma State, where he earned degrees in math and computer science, and played college baseball.

Golf was never on his radar screen. 'If it wasn't the Cowboys and Tony Dorsett,' he remembers, 'I'd be flipping the channel.' But in April of 1997, something changed. Football season was over, and he was working the clicker when he saw this 20-year-old black kid in total command of himself and the situation at Augusta National Golf Club, the deepest-rooted old-school club in the South. The experience motivated him into buying a set of clubs at a garage sale.

Alrick went from computer programmer to consultant in the electronic-data field. Billing by the hour, he put away enough money to buy a house for himself in a guard-gated community in Arlington Heights, Texas, and for his momma, too.

In his back yard, Alrick Washington has a six-hole putting green with a sand trap and a chipping station. If he's not working, you can usually find him there with his three sons, Todd, Rayshod and Garland.

'Like 90 percent of the blacks playing recreational golf, it was Tiger who influenced me to play,' he says. 'When I saw him win the Masters in 1997, I thought, 'Man, I'm going to try this golf thing.'

The golf thing has proved addictive. He reads *Golf World* cover to cover and is always watching the Golf Channel with his son. When Tiger comes on screen, little Garland always says, 'There's my boy!' The kid's already swinging dad's clubs, and he'd rather watch the morning replay of Viewers' Forum than cartoons.

The Washington Boys are doing better than daddy did, in that apartment with the four single mothers and eight other kids in Oklahoma City. Little Garland's got wallpaper in his room with a golf background, a set of U.S. Kids Clubs in his room with the bag stand retracted, pictures of Woods, Jack Nicklaus and Ben Hogan on his wall, and the same type of love for the game as his father.

'If you could see this kid, it's scary,' says Alrick.

The old man isn't too bad, either. Four years after taking up the game, he's down to a 4 handicap and playing the Hogan forged irons. Business is so good that he can afford to visit the Jim McLean Golf School at the Doral Resort and Spa in Miami. Through golf, he is meeting people that he never thought he'd meet before. Like the day at Doral when Greg Norman flew in on his helicopter, and McLean introduced him.

He is not Tiger Woods. He is Alrick Washington. He represents the changing face of golf in this country.

Veteran caddy Cayce Kerr was working for Fuzzy Zoeller at the Masters in 1998, the year after Tiger's historic victory and Zoeller's politically incorrect take on what the champion's dinner would be with Woods selecting the menu. As fate would have it, Woods and Zoeller were paired together in the second round, along with another golfer who wasn't exactly in Tiger's inner circle, Scotland's Colin Montgomerie.

'It's the first time the Masters has gone to threesomes,' says Kerr. 'Needless to say, things are pretty tight. The press is on them. The fans are on them. There's a lot of tension in the air. We get to the 6th hole, and the pin is on the left, just on eight paces where they always put the pin on Friday. All the guys knocked it stiff, and walking off the tee there was one guy in the group who stepped up and said, "Let's all walk off the green with 2s." That man was Tiger Woods. Everybody had 3-footers that they had to grind over, and guess what everybody walked off the green with? That's right, all 2s. I try not to do anything emotional out there, but when Tiger Woods walked off that green he gave me a high five. And I've got to tell you, that guy has been my hero ever since.'

Michael Wilbon, sports columnist for the *Washington Post*, was in his office on Fifth Street in downtown D.C., on February 7, 2000. Tiger had won a Masters and a PGA Championship, had worked his way through a 'slump,' a swing change, a metamorphosis in his public persona, and was coming off a record-setting year in which he won 10 times worldwide, earned over $6 million, and nearly $40 million more in off-course endorsements. It's the Monday that Tiger has come from seven strokes back with seven holes to play to trample rookie Matt Gogel and win the Pebble Beach National Pro-Am. Wilbon has the genesis of a something working on his computer screen, but there's a breaking story and Wilbon is getting ready to craft a new piece. The phone rings, and Wilbon immediately recognizes the voice. He's got his column. It's a slam dunk.

'I've got goose bumps,' says Michael Jordan. 'Can you believe that? I'll tell you what else – I'm ticked off that I missed it. I'm ticked off because I was supposed to be there, front and center, watching it first hand, right there by his side when he was doing it. But I knew if I was there [as Woods's amateur partner] you guys would have killed me in the paper for not being on my new job.'

Jordan, a total golf junkie, a man who isn't warmed up until it's the third 18, has just taken over as president of the Washington Wizards. It is a job that's definitely cut into his golf schedule. Michael was scheduled to be to be Tiger's partner in the Pebble Beach Pro-Am, but WDed at the last minute, leaving Tiger to play with his college teammate, Jerry Chang. Jordan, the man Woods emulated, was in awe. Total awe.

'You see the way he creates negative thoughts in his opponents' minds?' Jordan said. 'What he's got is confidence that borders on being cocky . . . Intimidation can be so successful. Tiger has that. And once it gathers, it takes so much to break it. I think that in an individual sport, it can have a greater impact than a team sport. I still had to rely on teammates, on four other guys at any one given time. With Tiger it's just him against the course. In some respects, he's in more control than I was.'

John North, a service manager at Arrigo Dodge in West Palm Beach, Florida, is not a golf fan. He's a Dale Earnhardt man, not a David Duval man, and nothing against Tiger Woods, but Richard Petty was and will always be king. Still, there was something about Tiger's performance in the U.S. Open that hooked him, that got him fired up the way Darrell Waltrip gets him fired up.

'I have to admit, I couldn't stop watching it,' he says. 'I know there was no drama, but I had a sense that I was watching history. You couldn't pull me away from it. At one point my wife came in the room and said, "Since when did you start watching golf? The only sport you watch on TV is stock-car racing." '

Tommy Roy, the executive producer for NBC Sports, left Pebble Beach on Sunday night and flew to Los Angeles for Game 6 of the NBA Finals. He knew he had just been at the controls for something special, something he'd never probably see again. But the full impact of it wasn't really clear until he arrived at the Staples Center on Monday night. It was there in a totally different environment that Roy was surrounded by basketball people who had never before considered themselves golf people. These were people that Tommy had seen around NBA arenas for years. And what they had to tell Tommy was that like John North the stock-car fan, they couldn't get up from the TV set on that Sunday. They sat there and watched the entire telecast, all six and a half hours of it. And when it was over, they had been converted, just as John North had been converted on the other side of the country in West Palm Beach.

'I'm speaking as the son of a golf pro,' said Roy. 'Golf didn't used to be cool. It was all about playing football, baseball and basketball. Golf was not cool and this kid has made golf cool, no doubt about it.'

Paul Spengler, general chairman of the 100th U.S. Open, and senior vice president of golf development for the Pebble Beach Company, was telling this story outside the press tent at the British Open: 'There's a husband and a wife who were attending the U.S. Open on Thursday. The man's in a handicap golf cart given out by the United States Golf Association. The woman's obviously a big Tiger Woods fan. The man's riding on the cart path by the sixth green, and in the crush of the crowd, he gets tipped over. There's a big commotion. The man requires medical attention. The paramedics arrive and the woman apologizes . . .

' "As soon as Tiger finishes the round," she tells him, "I'll meet you at the hospital." '

Peter Kessler, the Golf Channel host, walked 50 holes with Tiger at Pebble Beach during the 100th U.S. Open. When it was over the scene was too historically overwhelming. In the end, he broke down and cried.

'I was just keenly aware of what I was witnessing,' he said. 'I never saw Bobby Jones, and I never saw [Ben] Hogan, but I did see Jack in his prime, and I saw Arnie win his last tour event in Palm Springs at the Bob Hope. I saw Gary, Jack, Lee, Tom, Seve, Greg, Nick and Nick. It was my sense after following Tiger 50 in the U.S. Open, that this was the best that anybody had ever played golf, and I got to see it. I felt so lucky and honored, and because I had an appreciation for what it meant historically, I started to cry. His mom hugged me and comforted me like I was two years old and then Joanna started crying because I was crying, then Kultida started crying because Joanna was crying, and then Tiger emerges from the scoring tent. Tiger looks at both of them and then looks at me and they say, "It's Peter's fault, he was crying first," as we were sharing my handkerchief. Tiger hugged the girls, and hugged me, and laughed at me, and went out to get his U.S. Open trophy.'

Mark O'Meara, the winner of the Open Championship and the Masters in 1998, is one of Tiger's closest friends. Before the Millennium Open at St. Andrews, they went on their annual fishing trip to Ireland. To hear O'Meara tell it, Tiger was as into catching the biggest fish as he was the Claret Jug.

'Well, he cannot throw the fly rod as good as I can,' said O'Meara. 'I kicked his butt on the river once again. We fished the Sunday of the Western Open in the black water for Atlantic Salmon. I caught a 19-pound, 2-ounce Atlantic salmon. He flew in from the Western, saw the pictures, so we took him Wednesday morning after the two-day outing we did for J.P. McManus at TK.

'I wanted him to catch a fish, but he couldn't get anything to bite, so he went in for breakfast. I went in the river, threw in my fly rod, worked it, worked it, wham, caught a 7-pound Atlantic salmon. It was my first one ever with a fly rod. I went over with my fishing guide, netted it. I was so excited. Here comes Tiger back after breakfast. He sees the fish and says, "I've got to have one." I'm in the river, trying to coach him, saying, "C'mon, man, that's a good drift, that's a good drift" He said, "I like this. I'm getting better. I'm really getting better."

'Every player needs an out, so fishing has become his out. And he wants to be great at that. He's so strong, he tries to shoot it, and the loop just tails so when it hits the water it's getting all mangled up. The fish is on the other side of the river, so you have to be really precise with your casting. You know what, the last two nights he started to get it. He's saying now when he's in the shower, he's thinking about that casting.'

Former vice president Dan Quayle made the pilgrimage to the Millennium Open at St. Andrews and was one of a record 130,000 spectators who witnessed Tiger Woods complete the career Grand Slam. In college, Quayle alternated as a No. 1 or No. 2 man on the DePaw University golf team, so he understood the game on the competitive level. He was struck more than anything by the regal nature in which Tiger Woods went about his business in a efficient manner, taking no practice swings, standing over the ball for what seemed like no time at all, before sending these lasers out over the Old Course. More than anything, he felt the aura of domination that Woods cast over that sacred holy ground.

'You can't pick it up on television,' remarked Quayle. 'But he's so majestic, so confident. It's just so apparent in his walk, the way he carries himself. If he was hitting a shot, many times players on a parallel hole would stop to watch him. I thought, isn't this interesting? They're there watching this fellow. They know where he is, not just on the leader board but on the golf course too.'

Tom Fazio, the golf-course architect, and the man put in charge of 'Tiger Proofing' Augusta National, was on a Colorado vacation with his wife at Beaver Creek the day Tiger completed the career Grand Slam. She wanted to go hiking but he wanted to watch Tiger make history at St. Andrews. Eventually, they reached a compromise: Tom would go to the gym with his wife at the resort, walk on a treadmill, look at the mountains and they'd enjoy the Open during a workout. Like the millions who watched in the United States that Sunday morning, the Fazios couldn't pull themselves away from the telecast.

'This goes on for two hours and she's worn out,' says Fazio one day a month later. 'She wants to go. No, I tell her, I can't leave, it's not over yet. So I pick up smallest barbell, start exercising with it. Two days later I can't move my arm. I've got tennis elbow. I've got tennis elbow from watching Tiger win the British Open.'

Fazio laughs. He is in the kitchen of his home in Ashville, North Carolina, making breakfast for his family. He's talking about the impact Tiger has had not only on golf but also in his community. 'I've got six children and they've all gone to public school,' Fazio says. 'So I see a lot of different kids. And what I see in the young people today is that they're almost being non-prejudicial in all phases. It's different than the era we grew up in. In Tiger Woods's case, it's one more piece that helps that situation. He transcends all races.'

Barry Van Gerbig, president of Seminole Golf Club, watched Tiger Woods win the U.S. and British Opens from his summer home in the Hamptons. Van Gerbig grew up hanging around Seminole with Ben Hogan, and knew Jack Nicklaus back in the days when Nicklaus was doing what Tiger Woods is doing today. Admittedly, Van Gerbig may have been a little tough on Tiger when he first came out, but so were most of the game's traditionalists. They thought Tiger was a little over the top on his celebratory acts, that he basically needed to study Hogan and Nicklaus a little closer to see how to act as a professional.

Nowadays, what Van Gerbig sees in Woods is something incredibly different. He sees a stoicism, a toned-down Hogan-esque sort of demeanor that defines the manner of a true champion. They see a Nicklausean tactician who knows not only how to win, but lose, with honor and dignity. 'Tiger is over-whelming the game, and he's overwhelming the golf community, and he's doing it in a way that has tremendous grace,' says Van Gerbig. 'I'm mesmerized by it.'

Van Gerbig used to be of the school that consider Butch Harmon the reason for this transformation, but the more he sees

Tiger, the more he realizes that what Tiger has can't be taught, that it's not what some of his critics labeled a painted-on image. This was the real deal here, a once-in-a-lifetime experience, a young man who just needed some time to grow.

'You can't teach class,' says Van Gerbig. 'You can prompt and you can tutor, but somewhere deep in this young man's soul he's got class. I am totally impressed with this guy.'

Brian Gaffney, an assistant club professional at Admirals Cove Golf Club in Jupiter, Florida, was practicing at Valhalla Golf Club in Louisville the week before the PGA. Gaffney qualified by the tournament through a top-25 finish in the PGA Club Pro Championship. Little did he know that it would get him a practice round with Tiger Woods.

'The golf course was open just to players, and as I was teeing off on the back nine, somebody said, "Hey, did you know that Tiger Woods is here?" ' said Gaffney. 'I thought, hey that's pretty cool. I'm on the same golf course as Tiger Woods.

'I get to about the 12th hole and first some maintenance workers and then some PGA officials come up to me and ask: "Did you ask to play with Tiger?" I'm thinking, "Oh sure. The last thing Tiger Woods wants to do is play a practice round and watch somebody else slap it around." Later on, somebody else tells me, "You've got to; he really loves to play with other guys." So now I'm thinking I should do it.

'I go over to the first tee, to the putting green there, and waited for him to come by. I was more nervous then than I was the entire week of the PGA. I thought he'd be ten minutes. It seemed like an hour. Finally he drives up in a cart, just him and his caddy. I walked over, and he could tell I was going to ask a question, so he stopped. I said, "Hi, I'm Brian Gaffney, a club pro. Would it be OK to play a few holes?" He looked at me, paused for a second, smiled, and said, "Sure, let's go." I ran back to the putting green to get my balls and met them on the first tee. Out of respect I said, "Look, I'm only going to play one ball. You don't have to worry about me holding up." His caddy says, "Good, we play one ball and we play fast."

'The first hole or two I'm so nervous, but Tiger made me feel so comfortable. He asked me how I got in the tournament and I told him by finishing eighth in the National Club Pro tournament. He stared at me a second and said, "You know, that's good playing, good going." I couldn't figure out what to say to him. What am I supposed to say, "How are you playing?" We get to the third hole and I hit an iron in there about ten feet. He says, "Good shot, that's solid," and he proceeds to hit it four feet. I went over to him on the fourth tee and said, "Thanks, Tiger, for allowing me to do this, this is a real treat for me." He just says, "Now let's have some fun." I tell you what, he was the nicest guy in the world.'

George Burger, general chairman for the 2000 Presidents Cup, and 7-handicap at Robert Trent Jones Golf Club in Manassas, Virginia, is having dinner two nights after Tiger won the PGA Championship, at the Sheraton Suites Hotel in Cuyahoga Falls, Ohio. Burger is in town for the NEC Championships, a $5 million tournament that Woods won at Firestone Golf Club in 1999, to begin his six-tournament PGA Tour win streak. The NECs bring together Ryder Cup and Presidents Cup participants, and Burger is a friend of PGA Tour commissioner Tim Finchem, who worked in Washington politics before he switched careers and was fast-tracked to his present position as czar of professional golf.

Schooled at Georgetown, Burger's day job is to serve as a consultant to government figures, so he knows how images are constructed, and how they play to the public. He wonders how the International Management Group is going to manage this phenomenon, if they'll have Tiger go to the Oscars or the MTV Awards, if he'll eventually take on a greater cause than the Tiger Woods Foundation, if he would throw himself behind an NAACP or a National Black College Fund.

Can you imagine, Burger asks, what a day's worth of Tiger's phone time could mean to a worthy cause, and then the subject gets around to the prophesizing of Earl Woods, who long ago felt he was training the Chosen One who would do things for the world far beyond the limitations of golf.

It makes Burger think about the shot Tiger skipped off the cart path, under the trees, up the ramp of the 17th green at Valhalla, to save par on the 71st hole of the PGA. Maybe the kid can't walk on water, but he has mystical powers, the greatest smile in the world, an intelligence that the Washington operative sees as borderline genius, and an open passage to what seems like the world's heart.

'The guy's become bigger than life,' he says. How big? What's his potential? Burger doesn't hesitate. 'Could be as big as Martin Luther King,' he says.

David Fay, executive director of the United States Golf Association, was in his office at USGA Headquarters in Far Hills, New Jersey after Tiger Woods finished out his summer with victories at the NEC Invitational and Canadian Open. It was an election year, and that got people to thinking, provoked their consciousness, made them think . . . what if? What if Tiger Woods ran for President? Would he not be a good candidate, maybe better than the choices? Stanford educated. Understanding of the corporate world. Able to make the tough decisions. A good delegate of responsibilities. If anything, he was overqualified for the office.

'He's clearly a special human being, and he's got talents that go far behind doing tricks with a golf ball,' said Fay. 'It's a matter of how he wants to harness his energies or focus his energies. Can he make a difference in the global arena, in the human arena? I think he can.'

It was as if Fay were writing an essay on a subject that had been well thought-out long before Tiger Woods completed the Grand Slam at St. Andrews. He had been on to this kid long before America discovered him. He had studied world leaders like this as a political-science major at Colgate.

'When I look at Tiger Woods, I think of Arthur Ashe,' said Fay. 'I don't know what he's going to do with his life after golf, if he's made that decision – but he certainly has the ability to have an impact on the world. By virtue of his athletic ability he's been given a platform. But he's such a bright person and a caring person, that he can take what he's done on the athletic field and do something with it; perhaps more so than any other athlete. I don't think there are any limits to what he can do. He can't send a rocket up to space, or solve a mathematical formula. But talking about a world leader who can motivate people? Sure he can be.

'Could he run for President if he wanted to? He's eleven years away from that. He can impact the lives of others in that Arthur Ashe type of way. He can start that now and he is starting that now. When I look at Tiger Woods, I think of Jackie Robinson and Arthur Ashe, and he could go even beyond that. Hopefully the world is a more tolerant place than when Jackie burst on scene and when Arthur did. There's still a lot of discrimination and bigotry, but if anybody can deal with it, it would be Tiger.'

Professional golfer Rocco Mediate had just finished tied for 15th in the 65th Masters. Yet he had to stick around and watch the finish. As Tiger Woods made his way up the 18th hole at Augusta National, Mediate and his wife, Linda, had positioned themselves just outside the scoring hut, behind the green. There, he had a front seat for history.

'That last putt was absolutely electrifying,' Mediate said in front of the clubhouse an hour later. 'It was simply the most intense thing I've ever seen in my life. When he made that putt and the arm went up, your hair stood up on end. It was friggin' ridiculous. Anybody else you throw in there, they can't breathe. What was cool about it was he was walking around, looking at his putt, fixing the sleeve on his shirt. What if he gimps it by like this, or hits a spike mark? I'd be dying. But he's walking around fixing his shirt, looking around; he's enjoying the moment. He's enjoying the most intense moment in golf history.'

The idea of a golfer winning four straight major championships in this era was unheard of. Some, like Jack Nicklaus and Arnold Palmer, refused to call it a Grand Slam. Some, like Masters chairman Hootie Johnson, called it, 'the greatest achievement in modern-day golf.' The Irishman Darren Clarke said that, if Woods won four-in-a-row, he could call it whatever he wanted to call it. Woods had mentioned that having all four on his coffee table at the same time certainly constituted some sort of Slam in his mind.

'All the arguments,' said Mediate, 'Jack and Arnie bitching about him not getting a double dip. Kiss off. He won four-in-a-row. Just 'cause you couldn't do it, doesn't mean he can't. They have to leave this kid alone. I don't care what it's defined as. The Grand Slam is defined as four in a year. We all know that. Tiger knows that. But when you win four-in-a-row, that's something else. So don't give me this crap about not getting a double dip. I don't want to hear that. Hey, if you win four-in-a-row, it's the most amazing accomplishment in golf history. Who cares when you do it? What if he wins the next three? What does that mean?

I guess it's only one and two thirds.'

Some golfers, like Phil Mickelson and Hal Sutton, have refused to acknowledge Woods's superiority. Not Mediate. He knows that on any given week he can beat Woods. But on weeks like the four major championships, beginning with the 2000 U.S. Open, and ending with the 2001 Masters, no man alive is capable of stepping up to him. Four straight in this day and age? Are you kidding?

'The only one who will ever do that again is him,' said Mediate. 'That's the only one who will ever do it again. No one is ever going to do that. No one who's even thought of, who is an inkling in their father's eye, who's going to do that . . . nobody. All these big young studs who are coming up from all over the world, he's going to do this . . .' Mediate stamped his foot on the blacktop. 'Step on their neck,' he said. 'For the next ten to twelve years, it ain't happening.'

Butch Harmon, the swing coach, had just left the Tiger Woods news conference that was still in progress at Augusta National. He was totally drained, and heading to the parking lot, when two writer friends asked him to put this in perspective.

'The talk of what it is, is totally immaterial,' said the 60-year-old son of the former Masters champion. 'What it is, is fantastic. It's something that no one who's walked on this planet has never done before. That's the way you have to look at it. That's the best part. It doesn't matter what it's called. It is what it is. You can call it whatever you want.'

'Did you think we'd ever see this?' he was asked.

'I wasn't sure I'd see it so early. I always had a feeling this kid was destined for greatness. I think his timetable is a little quicker than what I thought, but not quicker than what he thought, because he's always had the confidence in himself.'

'What about in a world without Tiger, before he came to you at Lochinvar Golf Club in 1993. Was winning four straight majors possible?'

'There never was anyone who had this ability. He doesn't have a weakness. His biggest strength you can't see. It's his mind, his heart, his guts, his determination, his desire to beat you, to succeed, his love of the moment, his ability to control his nervous system, his emotion, and his heart rate. We've never had a player like this.'

'You know this kid as well as anybody. He's thinking about winning the next three, isn't he?'

Underneath that Titleist cap, behind those sunglasses, there was a twinkle in Butch Harmon's tear-stained eyes.

'You bet he is. He never had any other thought in his mind at all.'

# Two

# Millennium Man

Tom Strong was there for what he calls 'The Launch.' As tournament director for the Greater Milwaukee Open, he received a call in March of that year from IMG in Cleveland. On the other end of the line was Hughes Norton, the highest-profile agent in the golf business. Norton wanted to know if Strong would consider giving Woods a sponsor's exemption for the GMO. Strong knew that the U.S. Amateur would be held the week prior to his tournament, that Tiger Woods was going for his unprecedented third straight Amateur title, and that the chances of Tiger Woods turning pro the following week were strong. Strong told Norton that he would get back to him, knowing what the answer would be.

'It didn't take me long to say, sure,' said Strong. 'We'd do it in a heartbeat. It was huge for us. It lent credibility to the tournament. There were some players who didn't quite understand it. There was a lot of controversy going on, but I saw a very nice young man who conducted himself very well.'

The date was August 27, 1996, and golf as we know it would never be the same. It was on that day that the Tiger Woods Era started, and while the total impact wasn't felt until the millennium year, Tom Strong knew that very first week at Brown Deer Park Golf Club that this was the start of something truly unique. 'Every tournament director who had him in that fall swing felt the same way,' said Strong. 'Tiger impacted ticket sales, corporate

17

sales, TV ratings. He impacts everything there is about a golf tournament.'

First and foremost, that includes the very heart of what Tiger Woods is all about, the competition. Three years and 364 days later, Strong was sitting in his office at Firestone CC in Akron, Ohio. He is now the tournament director for the NEC Invitational, one of four World Golf Championship events that boast elite fields and $5 million purses. On the television screen over his head, Tiger Woods was working on a 9-stroke lead with 3 holes to play in the third round of Strong's tournament. He was doing this one week after winning his third major championship of the year, offering no letup to what is being called the greatest golf season in history. To Jim Nantz in the CBS tower behind the 18th green, this was an encore performance. To Woods, it was just another week on the job.

'Look at what we're watching now,' said Strong. 'Tiger shoots 61 yesterday. Phil Mickelson shoots 65 and loses four shots to him. It's unbelievable.'

In reality, it was quite believable. Woods closed out the weekend with rounds of 67-67 to win by 11 strokes, finishing the tournament in the dark by flaring a 168-yard 8-iron shot to 2 feet. With cigarette lighters glowing, it felt more like a rock concert than a golf tournament. Woods tapped in, strobe lights flashed, and golf had another Tiger Woods moment.

Nantz came out of the tower that night wiped out. 'My reservoir of words to describe it is bone dry,' he said. 'What do you say, he's remarkable, he's unbelievable, he's incredible. None of them are appropriate. We are the visual medium, so you'd like the picture to speak for itself, but there are times when you have to put a caption to it, and you just think, okay let me go back to this special dictionary that I was reserving for one or two occasions in my entire career. The over-the-top adjective list. Those pages have already been ripped out and used and served their purposes. In many ways I'm thankful this is our last golf event. I'm waiting for football to begin. I don't have anything else to say.'

In Trumbull, Connecticut, the editors of *Golf World* were preparing a cover for the September 1 issue of their magazine. Eight photographs were selected of Tiger raising the trophy at his eight victories that year. The headline was simple: the best season ever In the media center that Sunday at 9 p.m., Tiger was asked to rank it. There were really only two other candidates: Ben Hogan's year in 1953, when he won five of six tournaments, including the Masters, the U.S. Open and the British Open. Or Byron Nelson's year in 1945, when he won 11 straight and 18 overall including the PGA Championship. Woods discounted Bobby Jones's grand slam, because it included the British and U.S. Amateurs. As a student of the game, Woods leaned toward Lord Byron.

'Nelson won 18 tournaments in one year,' said Woods. 'That's not a bad year.'

Woods knew Nelson from playing his tournament at the TPC at Las Colinas in Irving, Texas. It was one of his favorite stops on the PGA Tour, because of its connection to Nelson, and because the Four Seasons – Las Colinas had one of the best workout facilities in the world. Woods was now a fanatic on training; he was going to the gym on a daily basis to keep the physical and mental edge he had on everybody.

Nelson never lifted weights and neither did Hogan. The only man to pump iron in the 1940s and 1950s was Frank Stranahan, and Stranny was such an eccentric that he never got the credit for being a pioneer. Woods visited the weight room at Stanford, but he really got into getting stronger when swing instructor Butch Harmon showed him a picture of Hogan at impact. Harmon knew Hogan through his connection at Seminole Golf Club, where his father was the head professional. He passed on stories of Hogan to Tiger, and they studied his swing together. Although Hogan wasn't buffed, and was only 5'8" and barely 150 pounds, he was wiry. Through the ball, he was a model for Woods to emulate.

'Well, I understand why he had to hit a lot of golf balls, with that move he had to make off the ball,' said Woods. 'One, the shafts were pretty weak. So obviously, that's why he lagged it so much. And the real weak grip and the lag coming down, he tried to prevent hitting the ball left. He cleared it an awful lot. He cleared and tried to hole on and bow it so it doesn't go left. But you can see with that action, the timing that is required; that's why he hit so many golf balls.'

The Woods swing, reconstructed by Harmon, was still not where Butch and Tiger wanted it on a week-to-week basis. Like all golfers, Tiger's posture would go bad from time to time, and when it did, he sucked the club too far inside, which caused him to fire his legs and get the club 'stuck' behind him. When he wasn't 'arcing his plane,' as he described in news conferences, he would get in trouble.

For the most part, though, Tiger could deal with his misses. The 18 months he took to rebuild his golf swing created a window whereby Woods had to rely on his short game to survive. Now he was the total package. Through training and maturity, he had grown to almost 6'2", and just over 180 pounds. His golf swing, while still prone to bad passes, had a repeatability to it, and the dreaded distance control problem, caused by 'flipping' at the ball, was now history. Put that with the best wedge game and pressure putting stroke in the game, and you could see why Tiger had not only the greatest season a golfer ever had, but the greatest four-year cycle in golf history.

And there is no one who benefited more from the timing of the Tiger Woods era than PGA Tour Commissioner Tim Finchem, who orchestrated a landmark television contract just after Tiger won the 1997 Masters and who was getting ready to renegotiate another as Tiger made his march through history. 'Four years ago, I said then the most interesting question about Tiger is how he challenges the big records,' said Finchem, sitting in a corporate hospitality suite at Firestone. 'In our sport, the big records are multi-year, multi-decade achievements. I still think that comparing what Tiger's done against Nicklaus, Nelson, Hogan and Snead will be the most interesting part of his career. That's already beginning to play out, perhaps sooner than we imagined.'

Tiger Woods was now more than just a 24-year-old kid winning major championships. Tiger Woods was now the summer's hot action movie, this big budget film where the plot kept getting thicker. First he was Arnold Schwarzenegger in *The Terminator* winning the U.S. and British Opens by 23 cumulative strokes. Then he was Tom Cruise in *Mission Impossible* the hero who found himself jumping from the jaws of danger and into the arms of an adoring audience just when it was time for the kids to go back to school. This was memorable stuff being carried out by the most dynamic entertainer in the world; the type of adventure and drama that had you either marveling at the way he blew up his opponents, or hanging on the edge of your seat because you really didn't know how it was going to turn out. That was the final scene, at the PGA Championship, where Tiger found himself down to his last putt, and the target shrinking 6 slippery feet away. We came away asking, when's the sequel?

It started with a six-tournament win streak in January that was the closest anyone has ever come to threatening Nelson's 11-straight, and reached its climax in mid-August, with Tiger dashing across the set in Louisville, Kentucky. Bullets were flying, helicopters shooting, death was just a trap door away. In this scene, the guy trying to kill him was a baby-faced assassin, an unassuming man named Bob May, and Bob May's got him hanging onto a nail, legs dangling over a cliff. Tiger's downhill par putt had a 6-inch left-to-right break in it. It would be Tiger's 272nd stroke in the 82nd PGA Championship, and the most important one in his career.

When he made the putt, punched his fist toward the ground, and turned to the gallery encircling the 18th green, Tiger bore a striking resemblance to Louisville's most famous athlete, the incomparable Muhammad Ali. You just knew at that point that Bob May was doomed, that Tiger was not going to lose.

That victory at Valhalla concluded what was arguably the greatest season not only in golf, but in all of sports. With victories in the U.S. Open, the British Open and the PGA Championship, Tiger had won three major championships in nine weeks. And if that wasn't enough, the next day he was back on the range at Isleworth Golf Club in Orlando, doing what Tiger does to keep being Tiger. To the surprise of no one in his camp, he was hitting balls.

'That's just him,' said Harmon. 'That's his desire.'

Nobody in golf works harder than Tiger Woods. The Saturday night before the final round at the PGA, he was the last player on the range and putting green. He didn't want to leave until it was right. And while 18-under-par was enough for Tiger to take May into a playoff and survive, it still wasn't up to his standards.

So he was out at Isleworth, beating balls, because the last two drives he hit in the playoff at Valhalla were hardly stellar – one 50 yards right and one 50 yards left. It was the same old story: Woods rotates his body at such whirlwind speed that his arms get 'stuck' and the ball is likely to go anywhere.

Most people would be ready to take the year off. Tiger was already working on next week. No one has ever won four straight professional majors. He would go to the Masters in seven months knowing that many people would not consider it a Grand Slam if he won at Augusta in 2001, but that wouldn't prevent him from making it an argument.

It is this maniacal drive for greatness every time he punches the clock that in part makes him so insanely popular. As Tom Watson put it after Tiger won the PGA, 'Someday I'll tell my grandkids I played in the same tournament with Tiger Woods.

We are witnessing a phenomenon here that the game may never, ever see again.' We were also witnessing an athlete who was now doing it the right way, who befriended his idol Michael Jordan, and learned from him, how to play his role. 'How could you not at least set your sights on being like him,' Woods would say. 'All he's accomplished, the way he's done it. He's the ultimate. Why not try to be like him one day.'

In the Millennium Year, 2000, Woods's Q Ratings were so high that he became a pop culture icon. Wherever you went, people were talking Tiger. You heard his name in airports, in restaurants, in hotel lobbies. You heard it on sports radio. You saw it on the cover of *Time and The New Yorker*. You watched him because you want to see what's next. Was he going to win by 15 this time, or would some no-name come out of the minor leagues and take him extra innings? Would he power the ball nine miles, or would he hit that low boring punch cut, the 'stinger' that knuckles out there about 245, center cut? Where's the trophy, and how's he going to find it?

He did this with a tremendous sense of his position on golf's time line. Ten years after Shoal Creek, Eldrick 'Tiger' Woods played golf at such a high level that he transcended not only the game, but all the social and color barriers that for generations had stereotyped the sport as an uncool white-man's game. That made him different from Jordan. 'Never had to deal with that,' Michael said. It was a subject they had discussed, intimately at times. 'The other thing, as Michael calls it,' said Woods.

Part black, part Asian, part American Indian, Tiger was a United Nations. He took golf and made it appealing to everyone. He not only raised the bar, he tore down walls. Black-white, red-yellow, Hispanic-Norwegian, Catholic-Hindu, Jewish-Muslim, man-woman, boy-girl, rich-poor, Blue Blood – Redneck, Old School patriarch – Generation Y computer geek: It did not matter. It was his summer, his moment in history, and you were there with him, glued to that TV set, pressed up against the gallery ropes all as one, looking to see this amazing talent in full bloom. You were captivated by Tiger, amazed by Tiger, even inspired by Tiger. You saw incredible elasticity, will, heart, strength and coordination. You saw not only what he was able to do to a golf ball, but to his sport.

Tiger Woods took golf and put it on the front page of the *New York Times*. He became the most in-demand figure in the world. Montel called. He said no. Oprah called. He said no. Barbara Walters called. He said no. *60 Minutes* called. He said no. *Vanity Fair* called, wanting to send Annie Liebowitz over for a photo shoot. He said no. Don't want to get overexposed – how could he not get overexposed?

Tiger was on the wish list of every sports talk-show host from Miami to Seattle. It seemed at times that every time we turned on the TV he was there: playing golf through Manhattan for American Express, making a golf ball dance off his sand wedge for Nike, teaching his own golf school for Buick, eating a bowl of Wheaties for General Foods. There wasn't a moment that we weren't all dialed into him, downloading his score off the internet, checking out what he did on a daily basis. His score was the only number that mattered. If he didn't play, it wasn't a tournament. If he did play, there was a sense that everybody else was competing in the B Flight.

'He is the chosen one,' said Mark Calcavecchia after Tiger won the British Open, and he was not mimicking Tiger's father Earl, who proclaimed that his son would one day become bigger than the prophet Muhammad and Mahatma Gandhi.

There was a Jordanesque quality about him, a combination of his captivating athletic ability and an intoxicating smile. After outdueling Tiger at the Players Championship, Hal Sutton tried to make the point that nobody was bigger than the game, not even Tiger Woods. But Hal Sutton was wrong. The game didn't outdraw the NCAA Final Four and the NBA All-Star Game. Tiger Woods did.

It wasn't only the shots he hit. It was the reaction to the shots he hit. It wasn't only the tournaments he won. It was the way he won them. Twenty-two times he held the third-round lead of a golf tournament. Twenty times he won. In one stretch he played 24 tournaments, won 14 times, finished second in four others and proved, like Nicklaus, to be a gracious loser on the rare occasions when he was defeated. He did this against a group of golfers that were bigger, stronger and arguably more talented than any group of golfers Jack Nicklaus himself ever competed against.

And he was making it look easy. That was the scary part about it. He was making it look so easy that it threatened the future of the game. For years, there has been a cry for the next dominant golfer to come along, and when he arrived, Tiger Woods was too dominant. He won three of his first four major championships by 12, 15 and 8 strokes. He won the Grand Slam at age 24, making him the youngest winner ever.

'Nicklaus won the most majors and I would never deny that he's the greatest player who ever lived,' said Gary Player. 'But nobody's ever dominated like Tiger Woods.'

He dominated with such style and grace, that when he did let go a stream of four-letter words during the Saturday morning telecast of the U.S. Open, the offense was quickly pardoned and forgiven. The free pass showed just how powerful and respected he had become.

In the old days (and with Tiger the old days are only two minutes ago), such a breach of etiquette during children's cartoon hour would have hung him to golf's cross. What this proved, beyond doubt, was Tiger's immense popularity. By skating on this, it actually enhanced his legend as the most powerful figure in the game. Perhaps, as Earl Woods kept telling us, Tiger was the next Messiah.

'Tiger has a contribution to make to this world,' said Earl. 'I'm not sure what it is yet, but the stage is set. The signal still has to come.'

Signal? To Earl, this was preordained. His son would ultimately have a cosmic purpose in this world, other than just winning golf tournaments. There were still hearts to win over. Until Earl signed off on it, this was still a work in progress.

Nicklaus won 18 professional majors. Woods would not reach his pinnacle until he had scaled beyond that mountain, until he became the largest sculpture in golf's pantheon. His quest would not be over until he became the greatest golfer who ever lived, and to do that, he would have to keep on grinding, keep on winning, keep on doing it in the midst of the wildest crush of humanity that sports has ever seen.

Six straight wins? No problem. Tiger went for his seventh with a high school buddy carrying his golf bag. Death threats? It's just a way of life. Innocuous questions at news conferences? Tiger answers them thoughtfully. The British tabloid media? Tiger handles them diplomatically. Cameras going off in the middle of his backswing? Tiger has learned to put up with it. Some jerk at the Ryder Cup yelling, 'Tiger, you suck!'? Tiger can handle it.

'Most guys, it'd bother them or piss them off,' says Tom Lehman. 'But with Tiger it's just water off a duck's back. It didn't even faze him.'

Jordan never had to deal with what Tiger Woods has to deal with to do his job. Neither did Pele, Ali, or Gretzky: They were never forced to walk through the maw of a golf gallery, never asked to sign the volume of autographs, never held under year-round media scrutiny, never asked to do the things that Tiger was asked to do from ages 20 to 24. That's what makes him so special, that he was able to achieve what he was able to achieve with all that pressure, and do it in a way that was completely different from the way in which he burst on the professional golf scene just four years ago.

'One of the things that's phenomenal to me is how he handles everyday life,' says his agent, Mark Steinberg. 'It's amazing how patient he is in dealing with that. There's not many things in his life that are easy for him, and I don't want that to come out the wrong way, because he's got all this fame and money. (But) it takes more time for him to do things than other athletes and to answer your question, yes, it is amazing when you see it up close.'

Nobody saw it more than Steinberg. He was the day-to-day guy, but Tiger had surrounded himself with good people. His inner circle was tight, and they were whispering the right stuff into the kid's ears. 'I'm trying to deal with the other stuff,' Tiger said during his Western Open win in 1999. 'I'm learning. I've talked with MJ about it. He tells me I have it tougher than he did because the fans can't reach out and touch you in the NBA.'

What Tiger did was the equivalent of Jordan learning to dunk the basketball again. In 1997, he won the Masters by 12 strokes, won three other tournaments in the United States, and made over $2 million on the PGA Tour. Yet he realized then that the game he brought to the golf course every day wasn't good enough to sustain a career destined for greatness, that to chase the legend of Nicklaus and to have longevity, to win on tight golf courses, to survive in U.S. Opens and PGA Championships, he would have to reinvent himself.

In the time between his victory at Augusta and the beginning of his indomitable run, Tiger Woods made changes to his game, his camp and his image that were all designed by none other than Tiger himself. It seemed like the only thing he didn't change was Butch Harmon, his swing coach.

Harmon's job was not only to hone Tiger's swing, but to polish Tiger's act. As a kid who grew up in the clubhouses at Seminole and Winged Foot, Butchie (as Harmon is sometimes known) schooled Tiger in some of the finer points of decorum. 'He was criticized early in career for saying he won without his A game, but he was being very honest, his standards [are] very high,' says Harmon. 'The truth is that when Tiger's on his A game, no one can beat him. He just didn't need to say it. He's come of age now.'

With Harmon assuming more of a leadership role, Tiger's father, the former Green Beret, had seemingly gone underground, taking a step back not only in the public eye but in the decision processes that would mold his son's career. Earl said it was always part of his plan to do it this way, but there were those who wondered if perhaps he was told to tone down his presence, that he was hurting Tiger by constantly preaching about his son being the Messiah.

This was no longer about Earl, and about the remarkable parenting job the crusty old soldier did with his prodigy. This was about Tiger. It was his show. And while Earl was there as a counsel, it was increasingly clear that Tiger was not only hitting the shots, but calling them as well.

He fired his caddy, fired his manager, reworked his golf swing, changed balls, put on 20 pounds with a top-secret weight-lifting program, quit being so bitter around the golfing press, decided that it was better to low-key it than to do a sack dance, and took on a much more dignified, professional demeanor on and off the golf course. He may have cussed like a sailor during the U.S. Open at Pebble Beach, but that didn't make him evil. If anything, it made him more human, more easy to understand.

What wasn't human was the 203-yard 7-iron he hit from the cabbage on the 6th hole at Pebble Beach, up the hill, into the wind, out of Open rough, to 12 feet. Only Tiger could hit that shot. Only Tiger could have made the putt on the 70th hole to keep his run of holes at Pebble without a bogey alive. Only Tiger could have saved par from the hay on the Road Hole during that opening round at St. Andrews. Only Tiger could have won three out of four majors.

'Cut him open, and I'll tell you what you'll find,' says Rocco Mediate. 'A bunch of wires and levers, and a big-assed heart.'

There was no par-four too long, no putt he couldn't make, no shot he failed to pull off when he really needed it. Yet the brilliance was not so much in the magical will, or the shot making, or the incredible distance. It was in the U.S. Open he played without a three-putt on those *Poa annua* greens at Pebble. It was in the 72 holes he navigated at St. Andrews without hitting one of those 112 bunkers. One hundred years from now, they'll be talking about that as if it were fiction. Yet it is true, so incredibly true that it defies belief. No three putts in an Open. No bunkers at St. Andrews. No challengers within miles.

'He's better than the other players by a greater margin than I was,' Nicklaus said. 'He can get on a run and win three of four of these things in a row, and all of a sudden that majors record isn't that far away.'

The hype has not gone to his head. The money hasn't turned him into a couch potato. If anything, the praise and riches have made him hungrier. Week after week, tournament after tournament, he arrives ready to play, ready to find something that he can win with, able to carve out pars with an L-wedge, a putter, and a total lack of fear. Like Nicklaus, he plays with his head now, avoiding the catastrophes, letting his opponents beat himself. It has become a work of art to watch him at work, letting the tournament unfold as he patiently waits to make his move.

'I told him, to be a great player, you have to learn how to win all ways,' said Harmon. 'Nicklaus, Palmer, Trevino, Player, Watson, all had ability to play the game when they were not totally there. Jack especially. Jack Nicklaus was so smart, that course management saved him. He'd win by out-fighting you, by out-scrapping you, by out-thinking you, by making the putts he needed to make. That to me is a test of a great player.'

Like Lee Trevino, like Arnold Palmer he simply loves the pure experience of hitting golf shots – almost as much as he loves hitting golf shots when they mean something. At the British Open, it was a 5-iron that he had to hit with a high draw into the 16th green on Sunday, moving the ball 2 – 3 yards right-to-left to a target no larger than a window pane. It was like Beethoven composing the right refrain at the end of the Eighth Symphony. 'Not only does he have all the golf shots, he's not afraid to try them under any circumstances,' says Trevino. 'Most professionals, when they are coming down the stretch and trying to win a golf tournament, hit the shot they rely on the most, which is their favorite shot. Tiger won't do that. Tiger will hit the shot he has to hit, or hit the shot that's called for, regardless of whether the pin is back, front, left or right or whichever way the wind blows.'

He has not done what Ernie Els, Lee Janzen, Mark O'Meara, Davis Love III, Justin Leonard and (until this year) Phil Mickelson have done. He has not gone off on sabbatical, taken a two-year leave of absence, become distracted by a baby or a woman or a hobby or the money. He has kept taking his reps, not just trying to win every time he shows up but believing he can win every time he shows up, and putting in the work that very few can match.

'Everybody worked out harder this past offseason, practiced harder, and became more determined,' says Janzen, the two-time U.S. Open champion. 'And he's still at a level no one can match.'

This is more than just natural ability. This is about a desire to get better, an ability to never make the same mistake twice, a swing that is technically flawless, a body that keeps getting stronger, an instinct to know when history is calling, a fire that's always burning, an aptitude that is borderline genius, and a thirst for greatness that is seemingly unquenchable.

'He has raised the bar to a level that only he can jump,' said Tom Watson. 'He is something supernatural.'

# Three

# THE SELLING OF TIGER WOODS

It is 8 a.m. on the morning after he won the NEC Invitational, and Tiger Woods is bent-over with the flu. He is here in a parking lot at Firestone CC, where less than 12 hours earlier he celebrated his four-year anniversary of turning professional by winning the 23rd tournament of his career. Now he's back on the job, sucking it up when he should be in bed, fulfilling a corporate responsibility for American Express.

There is a clinic scheduled for 2, 500 people at the Raymond Firestone Public Course, and Woods doesn't want to disappoint them. Amex is one of the headliners in his portfolio, and they've just aired the latest in a very appealing line of Tiger Woods television commercials. In the ad, Tiger plays his way through Manhattan, hits shots in Central Park down the corridors of Wall Street, and Park Avenue and sinks a putt on the Brooklyn Bridge. According to *Golf World*'s Ron Sirak, Amex has paid Tiger an estimated $26. 5 million for five years, a contract that includes days like this one at Firestone, and exhibitions at the other World Golf Championship events at Kapalua, Hawaii and Valderrama, Spain.

Driving across the North course at Firestone, Woods sees the hill by the driving range packed with Amex cardholders. Walking onto the tee, he connects with swing coach Butch Harmon, who will fill the role of master of ceremonies. 'Butch,' he says, 'you've got to help me out here today.'

The Amex deal involves an intricate integration of Tiger (who epitomizes the Amex 'Do More' theme), the WGC, Amex (the corporate sponsor of the season-ending event in Spain), and the Internet. Those who attended the clinic had used their Amex cards to purchase tickets to the NEC Invitational. Others who didn't participate in the promotion could log on to a special Web site and view the exhibition live, or download it along with a Tiger screensaver and exclusive interviews. Just this campaign alone has brought together three agencies (Ogilvy-Mather, Momentum and Digitas) to put it all together in coordination with Tiger's manager, Mark Steinberg.

To get this kind of across-the-board synergy in the communications and business worlds, Steinberg renegotiated Tiger's Internet rights back from Nike, allowing IMG to get more new media exposure and expand the value of the Woods account. It was a shrewd overall deal not only for Woods and IMG but for Amex in its competition with MasterCard. According to Sirak, 'It's no coincidence that the only week of the PGA Tour season that Woods is out of the country is the MasterCard Colonial. Why does he pick the German SAP Open? Not only does Tiger weaken the field at the Colonial, but by playing in Germany the same week, he attracts media attention somewhere else. It's also safe to say the one World Golf Championship event he will never skip is the Amex tournament. He can skip the Match Play but never the Amex as long as they're his sponsor. Plus it's a win-win for Tiger. He gets a $1 million guarantee for playing in Germany. He wins there the first year (1999). He goes over this year, finishes third, but debuts the new Nike ball and everybody's writing about that instead of the Colonial.'

Amex has a think tank of executives that meets once a week to strategize ways to maximize its relationship with the world's most famous athlete and entertainer. At the NEC Invitational a co-promotion was put together with Buick whereby cardholders would meet at a designated parking lot and get free admission to the tournament – and the clinic – by test driving a new Buick to the course.

It may sound incestuous, but as one advertising industry executive said, 'Tiger is an industry all by himself.' Besides Nike, Amex and Buick, his blue-chip portfolio now included long-term contracts with Rolex, EA Sports, Wheaties, TLC Laser Eye Centers and *Golf Digest* and was estimated to be worth $45 million in 1999, including appearance fees for overseas tournaments.

'We're not interested in contractual relationships,' said Steinberg. 'We're interested in business partnerships.'

The most Michael Jordan ever made in a year was $45 million. Woods passed that mark in 2000, and is only beginning to reach his potential as a golfer and a corporate spokesman. *ESPN Magazine* estimates that Tiger will make $6 billion before he's through, with 75 percent of that coming through endorsement income. Burns Sports, a firm that brings companies and athletes together, conducted a survey of 1, 500 U.S. advertising agency and corporate marketing executives. Woods was easily voted the 'most appealing athlete product endorser.' As a mixed-race person, Woods also had tremendous international appeal, and was as big in parts of Asia as he was in America.

'Tiger and Michael bring a lot of the same things to the table,' Bob Williams, president of Burns Sports, told the *Detroit News* 'Tiger has a 10,000-watt smile and can be charismatic when he wants, yet serious and determined when he's on the course.'

Like Jordan, Woods was also unthreatening to the white corporate world, and that's why companies like Amex threw their arms around him and the Tiger Woods Foundation. Tiger embraced diversity; as a 'Cablinasian,' he was what one advertising executive described as the future of the world. The key for Steinberg was knowing when to say no, so that he wouldn't burn out Woods. That was clearly the case after a grueling PGA and then the NEC.

'Why we linked up with Tiger is that we saw from the beginning a person who was well received by both young and old, who cuts across so many demographics both here and around the world,' says Jon Hayes, Vice President of Global Media Advertising for American Express. 'Tiger is the combination of focus, hard work, determination and earned success. We felt he represents the ideals and values of American Express.'

At the Firestone exhibition, Woods was the consummate professional. Tiger has a reputation for giving everything he's got, whether it's a round of golf, a commercial shoot, a news conference, or a corporate clinic. Harmon did most of the talking while Tiger went through his repertoire of shots, finishing with his now-famous routine of dribbling a ball off his wedge, popping it in the air, and sending it out into the driving range with a baseball swing. When the exhibition ended, he boarded his private jet for a flight to Palm Springs, California, where he played in a made-for-TV prime-time match against Spain's Sergio Garcia called 'The Battle at Bighorn.'

The Battle at Bighorn was important to Woods not from a competitive standpoint, but because it appealed to a nighttime audience that generally doesn't watch the weekend telecasts of golf. It is good for Woods to be shown in his Nike clothes, but it's even better for his image to be displayed during the commercial minutes that feed the ABC telecast.

'The scope is wider now,' says Steinberg. 'We don't look at it as it's Tiger vs. Sergio so much as it's Monday night golf. I think there's cachet to that. I think it's something that's real. I think it's something that people want to see. Presumably it's going to get a double-digit rating. If it gets anywhere near that, then this is something that people want to see. I think that's broadening the fan base. Do we do it next year? I have no idea. We'll get through this year, see how it goes, see what the reaction is. Maybe Tiger doesn't want to do that next year.'

In 1999, Woods played David Duval in what was billed as the Showdown at Sherwood, and the media perception was negative. The spin was that this was a contrived attempt by IMG to create a rivalry. Steinberg feels like everybody missed the point. 'Golf is viewed as sport,' he says. 'We want to have golf be entertainment. That's what basketball is. The NBA All-Star game is simply entertainment. The Showdown at Sherwood and the Battle at Bighorn are golf's mid-season All-Star games.'

Tiger lost 1 down to Garcia and made $400,000 instead of $1. 2 million, but the ratings were huge (almost a point higher [8. 6] than three pre-season *Monday Night Football* games featuring Dennis Miller in the booth), which made the program a commercial success. During the Battle at Bighorn, Buick debuted a new television ad that Tiger filmed in Toronto after the British Open. It was so important for Buick to shoot this commercial and have it ready for the Battle at Bighorn that the auto maker asked Tiger to cross the picket lines during a Screen Actors Guild (SAG) strike. The commercial shows Woods using his golf clubs to compete in fencing, the javelin throw, archery and table tennis; Buick is the official car of the 2000 Summer Olympics.

Woods is not only the greatest and most famous athlete in the world. He also has the best commercials. Some of them border on brilliant, and none was more important to Tiger's career than the now-famous Nike spot filmed on a hot summer day at Orange County National Golf Club just before the 1999 U.S. Open. The reaction was a true measure of Tiger's ability to move the needle. 'Him doing what he does every single day of his life turned into talk around the world,' said Steinberg.

Kel Devlin, Nike Golf's director of sports marketing, spotted Tiger killing time during a lunch hour. Devlin convinced the production company that they might check it out. Tiger liked the idea, and on his fourth take, produced a priceless and timeless video. Forty-nine times he tap danced a golf ball, presumably a Titleist, off the face of his 60-degree sand wedge. He went in between his legs, behind his back, and at one point caught the ball and made it stop on his grooves. Getting a cue from directors, he popped the ball up one final time, and with perfect balance and rhythm, took a baseball swing and ripped a nice draw about 120 yards out into the driving range.

Tiger high-fived the crew, knowing he had just created a masterpiece. 'It went wonderfully, it was funny, entertaining, lighthearted,' said Woods. 'Players liked it, the public liked it, everybody liked it – except one of my sponsors.' That sponsor was Titleist, which began legal action against Nike because the commercial implied that the ball Tiger used in the commercial was not the Professional he was contracted to play.

The popularity of that spot triggered a chain reaction that led to Tiger leaving Titleist and Steinberg renegotiating the original Nike contract done by Hughes Norton in 1996. As Dave Kindred wrote in a January 2000 *Golf Digest* column, 'The resulting 30 seconds of film bedazzled all eyes. The national buzz burned images of the Nike brand into the pop culture psyche. *Golf World* reported that, coincidentally or not, Nike soon doubled Tiger's pay to maybe $80 million in the next five years.' According to Sirak's sources, Nike would pay between $17 – $18 million a year guaranteed, plus a percentage of the company's profits. The numbers would have been higher had Steinberg not received back the Internet rights, but there was a huge upside there. It was a scenario where everybody walked away happy except for Titleist, which lost the No. 1 player in the world. Titleist's defense was that they could not break their budget to pay to Woods the $7 – $8 million it would have taken to keep him, plus there would have been the issue of brand confusion. Tiger would continue using the Titleist prototype blade irons, but his golf bag billboard would be stamped Buick, a deal Steinberg orchestrated in late 1999.

Aired for the first time during the 1999 U.S. Open at Pinehurst, the Nike commercial captured the spontaneity and brilliance of Tiger at a time when the Behavior Police were criticizing Woods the loudest. Titleist's position not withstanding, that commercial did more for Tiger's mass appeal than all the words that had been written. On *Viewer's Forum* the popular Golf Channel call-in show, host Peter Kessler found himself fielding more questions about the Nike ad and less about Tiger's club slamming and cursing. 'I think it was a big turning point in his perceived image,' said Kessler. 'He'd been going through a few years under this incredibly strong spotlight as a really young guy, trying to figure out how to make his world work for him.'

While the Nike commercial just happened by accident it was Steinberg's concept to 'humanize' Tiger and bring him to the masses with campaigns that would show a lighter side of his client. Steinberg wanted to shift the emphasis away from Woods, the money machine who was now challenging Jordan as the world's most marketable athlete. It was a reverse spin from the original Nike commercials, where Tiger was in your face ('I am Tiger Woods') and confrontational (telling everybody in that first 1996 Nike ad, 'there are courses I can't play because of the color of my skin').

The new Tiger was self-effacing, and the new ads used ironic twists on some old hot-button topics. For example, when Tiger first turned pro and said he won 'without his A game,' it incensed just about everybody in the locker room. When he taped a Buick commercial three years later, one of the scenes depicted him giving lessons at a golf school, where he held up a cardboard sign and said 'All together now. I didn't have my A game today.' It was subtle enough that real golf fans picked up on the humor, yet innocent enough that it worked even for those who didn't pick up on the joke.

Most of the commercials had little or no dialogue. The Wheaties ad, which aired during non-golf shows, had Tiger eating his cereal while a voice said, 'It takes a lot to win major championships.' Tiger looked into the camera and said quite simply, 'A lot.' When the camera panned away, it showed thousands of boxes of Wheaties and Tiger sitting there smiling.

'Better eat your Wheaties,' he said.

Even the five-year $30 million deal Steinberg orchestrated with Buick had more than just financial benefits. There was mass market appeal in Tiger signing a contract with a mainstream car maker whose average owner was 67 years old. With Tiger behind the wheel, Buick hoped to show that its cars, especially the Rendezvous SUV coming off the assembly line in 2002, had some staying power. 'He's such a great kid, such a great person,' said Steinberg. 'He's warm, funny, entertaining. He tries to have fun day-to-day, but I don't think anybody knows that. I thought it would be a good thing for people to understand more about Tiger's personal life. I don't mean what he does every day, but just feel as though as they know him a little more.'

Kessler's theory was that Woods realized his responsibilities in the months before the Nike commercial was shot. A message had been sent, in conversations with his father, Jordan, his inner circle, and Arnold Palmer, that convinced Woods he better work on his public perception. Tiger had become more than just an athlete. He had crossed over into the realm of icon.

'He was bringing people into the game, and because of that he had a responsibility to be classier and better than everybody else. He was playing better than everybody else in a game where half the shots we hit make us unhappy, and where traditionally where you play with your buddies on a Saturday morning you'll hear language considered horrible, but it's part of the game. That's the reason somebody chose a four-letter word for the game. All those other four-letter words were already taken. Tiger realized he had a responsibility to behave better than anybody else for a number of reasons.'

A noted golf historian, Kessler thought that the comparison shouldn't be made between Woods and Nicklaus, or Woods and Palmer, but between Woods and Bobby Jones, who also had to control temper problems and who was more popular in his time than any other American athlete.

'When Arnie and Jack were at their most popular, they weren't bringing in all kinds of people into the game. They were sort of pleasing people playing the game, upper class, white people. The elite. They pleased businessmen, businesses, and more corporate types. Tiger brought kids to the game, people who didn't even know what golf was before. People were talking about it on talk shows including Larry King, who doesn't know that 8 isn't a bogey. It was a whole new class structure, and at some point he realized the need to set a behavior code to demonstrate to all these people who were unfamiliar with the game, what golf was, how it was played and how to act playing it.'

The new Nike commercial was a symbol for all that, and it sent a message that was a polar opposite to the first attempt made by Phil Knight to sell Tiger's image to the world. It crystallized the concept that Tiger had reinvented himself.

'By that point, he had softened most of the hard edges,' said Kessler. 'When he did that commercial, what people saw was somebody as handsome as a model, somebody who could have been on the cover of *GQ* somebody fit enough to compete in the Olympics, somebody who seemed comfortable in their own skin, who was happy to share his gift and who made it clear that he knew it was a gift that he was sharing – even though he recognized that gift without work ethic equals nothing, and in this case, like a great actor, melding all his talent, work ethic, and acting skills for one 30-second moment of perfection.

'That solidified it.'

# Four

# SOLID FOUNDATION

On July 30, one week after he flew home from St. Andrews with the Claret Jug given to the British Open champion, Tiger Woods was on his plane again, heading to New Orleans. It was the type of trip that he would make four times in 2000, but this one was a little different: When his Citation 10 touched down at an executive airport, there was a Buick waiting for him (he requested a Buick) and a police escort to the Hilton Hotel, where he was given the key to a 2,000-square-foot suite that had previously housed Presidents Reagan, Carter and Ford. If he craved a late-night snack, one of the city's prized chefs was on call. If he wanted to go fishing, a guide would be waiting in the lobby.

It was decadent and ironic, considering the injustice Tiger had once experienced as a black child growing up in Southern California. Now that he was the world-famous Tiger Woods, and not little Eldrick Woods, there weren't enough favors people could do. There wasn't a club in the world that wouldn't have him, or a city that wouldn't throw the red carpet at his feet. The same kid who was thrown off a course when he was a kid because he was dark skinned, the same teenager who was called the N-word at his own club, was now welcome everywhere – and with open arms.

'Anything he wants while he's here, we are ready, willing and able to take care of his needs,' Nancy Broadhurst, co-chair of the organizing committee to oversee Tiger's visit, told the

*Times-Picayune* before his arrival. 'Like any good host, you want to make him feel special.'

The reason for this trip in the middle of his recovery time, after St. Andrews and before the PGA Championship, was not to fulfill a corporate obligation. The reason for this trip was the Tiger Woods Foundation, a nonprofit organization that was founded in 1997 so that children wouldn't have to grow up feeling the same sting of racism that Woods felt as a child. Through the foundation, Woods hoped to impart a change in this country, creating an environment where the kids he would be meeting at the City Park Bayou Oaks Golf Course in New Orleans wouldn't go through the same indignity.

Woods explained these feelings at the start of the 2000 season, during a news conference before the Mercedes Championships at the Kapalua Resort on Maui. 'America is the melting pot of the world,' he said then. 'We have all the different ethnic races, religious choices. I just want to make golf look like that. If that's one thing I can have, that's one thing I really want to have happen. I know how it feels to be denied, not to play this game. It doesn't feel very good. I don't want these kids to have that opportunity to feel that kind of pain. I want them to go out there, and if they want to play the game, they should be able to. But if they don't, that's their choice. We as adults who play the game of golf should always provide them the opportunity to play the game. From there, it's up to them.'

Woods grew up in a middle class neighborhood in Cypress, California. His father worked at McDonnell Douglass, negotiating contracts for materials in the rocket program. His mother was Thai, and their mixed marriage created a stir. While she was pregnant with Tiger the Woods's house was pelted by limes and BB-gunfire. As the only black child in his kindergarten class, Woods was tied to a tree by the older children in what he believes was a racially motivated act of cruelty. While that first Nike commercial may have been over-the-top, there was a sad truth to it.

'I was always treated as an outsider,' Woods said. 'We were the first and only black family for many years, and we had many problems. I've been denied many things because of the color of my skin, whether it was at school, socially or in golf. That's just the way it was. It doesn't make it right. I just learned to grow with it and grow through it.'

There was an attempt to ban him from the Navy Golf Course in Long Beach, California, where his father had playing privileges as a former member of the U.S. Army. At the 1990 PGA Junior Championship at PGA National in Palm Beach Gardens, Florida, a 14-year-old Woods said, 'They don't like me at my home course. They try to shut me out. I think it's my skin color. My dad outranks them all, and he happens to have a son who plays golf. The pro let me play when I was four, but all the members got mad because I was beating them.'

Tiger was still having trouble at the Navy course as late as 1994, the same year he won the first of an unprecedented three consecutive U.S. Amateur tournaments. As Woods remembers, he was hitting balls on the range when a group of Army men began deliberately firing balls into a neighboring house. Because he was black, Woods was accused of taking part in the prank. 'This guy phoned in the pro, and said, "This little nigger was hitting balls in my house," ' recalled Woods several years later. 'The pro comes screaming out there accusing me of doing this. I said, "Hey, I'm not that bad a player. I'm firing it in the opposite direction. How am I going to hit it behind me? Open your eyes, bud." '

Woods went home and told his father, who wasn't surprised. In many respects, America wasn't much different in the'90s than it was when Earl was growing up in Manhattan, Kansas, trying to break the color barrier at Kansas State. Earl Woods was the first African American to play college baseball in what was then the Big Seven conference. Like any other black man at that time, he had to use separate restaurants and public bathrooms from the rest of the K-State team. It was the same for him later on in the service, and the fact that he rose to lieutenant colonel in the Green Berets was a testimony to his perseverance.

'People think it has changed,' Tiger said. 'It really hasn't.'

In 1996, Tiger and Earl began staging clinics for inner-city children in what would be the genesis for the Tiger Woods Foundation. In a Golf Channel interview that aired on December 16, Woods sat on the set of *Golf Talk Live* with host Peter Kessler. Tiger, with his Nike beret on backwards, talked about his plan to break down walls and grow the game. Kessler asked Woods about the *Sports Illustrated* Sportsman of the Year story, in which his father said that some day, Tiger would have more influence on the world than Gandhi and Mother Teresa.

'Not every dad says that, but I know where my dad is coming from,' said Tiger. 'Deep down in his heart he truly believes I can change a lot of things for the positive. As time progresses, I'm going to do my darnedest to do that, try and basically give kids in the inner city the chance to play the beautiful game, not only that, a lot of kids in the city have been put down and told you can't do this, you can't perform, you can't go to this school, you can't, you can't. It's just a main theme. One of my goals, we're working on a program now, [is] to write up a psychological program of how we can go into the inner city and build these kids' self esteems up, as well as giving them an opportunity to play golf.'

New Orleans, the host city for his third Tiger Woods Foundation clinic and fundraiser of the year, had an ulterior motive that it was trying to disguise with the Cajun cooking and the fishing trips for reds and specks. The Big Easy was throwing its red carpet out for Tiger in hopes he would return in the spring to play the Compaq Classic. By committing to a week at English Turn, Woods could mean $1 million in ticket, concession and merchandise sales, not to mention the impact on the local economy. Sensing the public perception, Broadhurst stressed it wasn't how much red carpet could be rolled out for Tiger. 'It was about how our city can open more doors for inner-city parents and children in our community, and how we, in our city, try to make New Orleans a better place to live,' she said. 'If we lose sight of that, then we might lose out on getting him back.'

Whether it's New Orleans, Oklahoma City, Denver or Norfolk, these stops are pretty much scripted. Two days before the clinic, the foundation hosts a series of workshops for parents and students ranging from the history of minority golf to a talk by the father himself, Earl Woods. 'What's the most important thing they get out of it?' asks Earl. 'Tiger's positive attitude and his will to win. He preaches like I preached to him – "I earned everything I have. No one gives you anything." That's the new element he's introducing to the inner cities.

'Because of Tiger, kids are willing to earn their way out, rather than wanting someone to give them a way out.'

On the night before the clinic, there is always a fund-raising dinner featuring a charity auction. The New Orleans dinner, at Kabby's Sports Edition Bar & Grille, was attended by 380 people who paid $1, 500 to $10,000 per table, depending on the level of sponsorship. Woods worked the room and sat next to Archie Manning and his wife, Olivia. The Classic Foundation, which runs the Compaq Classic, earned the designation of silver sponsor by donating $25,000. Tournament Director Rick George wasn't expecting any quid pro quo, but hoped to get 60 seconds with Tiger just to let him know how grateful the city was to have him. 'If there was a secret button to hit,' he said, 'I'd have hit it by now.'

The four-course meal included turtle soup, Louisiana field greens with a sugarcane vinaigrette dressing, and a double entrée of grilled fillet topped with Woodland mushrooms and blackened crawfish cakes. The dessert was a cookie shaped into a putting green, with a chocolate golf ball and a chocolate title bearing the Tiger Woods Foundation logo.

During his speech, Woods talked about the junior golf tournament he played at English Turn in the early'90s, and called New Orleans a 'wonderful city.' There was excitement in the audience when Woods said, 'Hopefully one day I'll come back and play in the tournament here.' Responding to the whoops, hollers and whistles, Woods just smiled.

'I thought I said "hopefully," ' Woods said. 'I recall I didn't do very well. I'd like to take on the golf course again.'

The clinics are usually scheduled for an urban park and last for 60 minutes. Representatives from the Tiger Woods Foundation come in a week early and pick 125 participants from inner-city golf programs. Of that 125, the best 25 golfers get one-on-one instruction from Woods. Lightning cut short the lessons and moved the outing to Municipal Auditorium, where Woods conducted his exhibition from atop a covered ice-hockey rink. All of the children were outfitted in black shorts and white shirts from Nike and visors from Titleist.

Jarrett Carr, 16, was one of the few who received instruction before the thunderstorm. Tiger gave him a simple lesson – shoulders back, left arm straight – and the ball flew further. 'I never thought I'd get a chance to meet him,' Carr said. 'It's something I'm going to cherish for the rest of my life.'

When Tiger first started doing these clinics, Earl would stand in front of his son while he took full swings and hit lob wedge shots over his head. As Earl has gotten older, Tiger concludes his exhibition with the wedge routine he made famous in his Nike commercial. This one ended with Tiger attempting to hit the hockey goal with a sand wedge. Although he missed that target, he connected during a question and answer session, where he talked about the importance of doing homework and the speech impediment he overcame as a child. He told the story about the one junior tournament he quit, and the vow he made to never quit again.

'People have no idea how many hours I put into this game,' Woods said. 'My dad always told me, "There are no short cuts." These kids may not play golf. They may not be what I am in a golfing sense. But they could be what I am in a business field or a medical field.'

Forty-two cities bid to host Tiger Woods Foundation junior clinics in 2000. Oklahoma City, which hosted Woods in late May, put up $25,000 in public money as part of its package. Norfolk, the last stop of the year, was the twentieth foundation clinic that Tiger put on since turning pro.

As Tiger knows, the change will not occur overnight. He is committed to this project knowing that it may be another generation before all the walls are torn down. 'It's not going to happen right away, but as long as we keep making change in a positive direction, then change is good,' he said. 'People are going to try to speed up the process. I'm going to try to speed up the process, but we can only do so much. It's all based on knowledge. Until people understand cultures, perspectives on how they view other races, then we're going to be in the dark.'

Tom Woodard, director of golf for the City of Denver, shares the same perspective. In the early'80s, Woodard was among a group of black golfers – including Calvin Peete, Jim Thorpe, Adrian Stills. Ron Terry, Lee Carter, Alfred Martin and Bobby Stroble – who had their PGA Tour cards. Until Tiger came along 15 years later, there was a gap when no African-American golfer made a mark on professional golf.

The Tiger Effect is now a wave that's just beginning to build far offshore. But people like Woodard, who has 375 children in his program, can see it coming. 'The impact Tiger has is going to be farther down the road, I would say 10 years because a lot of the young kids – 12, 13, 14 – are starting to play because of him,' Woodard said. 'I will say that having grown up in Denver, being familiar with the public golf courses in Denver, I am seeing more juniors of color, I'm talking about 16 and under, on the golf courses, than I have in a good 15 – 20 years.'

Woodard's 12-year-old son is one of those kids. He's a total golfaholic who thinks he's going to be the next Tiger Woods. Woodard tries to tell him that the game of golf isn't as easy as Tiger makes it look.

'The thing I don't think these kids realize is that somebody like Tiger comes along once in a lifetime. Not just as a golfer, but as an athlete who can have an impact on their sport. Like a Wayne Gretzky. I talk to my son about it. He thinks it's easy to do, easy to accomplish what Tiger has accomplished. So it's getting all these kids involved in the game, but I don't think they realize how special he is.'

What makes Woods so special is that he realizes his responsibility to give something back, that he didn't become so embittered that he became a racist himself. He took from Earl an ugly history of America in the '50s and '60s, and lived through some of the bigotry himself 20 and 30 years later. He then became a hero who walked the walk, who put in the time, the energy, and the attention, to impact a change.

There is more work to do, but Tiger Woods doesn't mind work. Making golf look more like America may be his greatest challenge, but he has never backed down from a challenge. Maybe Earl Woods was right after all. Maybe there is a greater calling for his son than just winning golf tournaments.

'My father always told me, you have to care and share in life,' Tiger has said. 'If you care about something, you'll share. I care a lot about golf, and I care about kids. I'm going to share whatever I can with them. I'll share them my heart. That's about all I can offer to them.'

# PART II

## Flashback

*Watching him do that had the same aura as watching Nelson Mandela come out of jail. It was moving to me because I knew what it was doing to people all across the country.*

—*African-American activist*
DICK GREGORY

# Five

# WALKING THE WALK

In order to understand where Tiger is today, we have to go back more than four years to the summer of 1996, to a time when golf was much different than it was at the end of the millennium. We were still in search of the next dominant player, but on our radar screens was this kid that kept popping up from time to time at PGA Tour events, and every time he did, there was a buzz. It seems like a lifetime ago that Sandy Lyle stood outside the clubhouse at Riviera and said, 'Tiger Woods. Is that a golf course?' We could now ask the question of Sandy Lyle, 'Is that something bad you get in bunker?'

Woods had already given signs of being able to peak for the majors by winning three straight U.S. Junior titles and two straight U.S. Amateurs. There was growing speculation that Woods would turn pro right after his third straight U.S. Amateur. Earl Woods was already on the IMG payroll, hired in a scheme devised by superagent Hughes Norton to be a 'talent scout' at AJGA events. Phil Knight and Wally Uihlein were hanging around, talking money and long-term commitments. *Golf World* picked up on the story, and ran a picture of Woods on its August 2 cover under the headline: 'Will he or won't he?' Tiger was sitting next to a fountain outside Versailles, looking contemplative.

Behind the scenes, the decision had already been made. That July he had played a practice round at Royal Lytham during the British Open with Davis Love III and Brad Faxon, two of

47

Titleist's most loyal product endorsers, and Wally Uihlein, Titleist's president and CEO. Woods had his epiphany in the second round of the tournament. Playing the last 13 holes in seven under, he had shot 66 to make the cut by two strokes. 'I'm finally learning how to play within myself,' he said at the time. 'I'm finally learning what this means. For the first time in my life, I was able to swing easy at every shot. I'm learning how to control my body speed and my distances, learning not to explode through the ball all the time. At this level, it's all about discipline, how to control yourself, and I'd have to say that the way things went today, I'm making some progress.'

Tiger also showed progress in dealing with the crush of media. When asked about his poor record in major championships to that point, he joked that if Jack Nicklaus could count his two U.S. Amateur victories, so could he. In fact, he might as well tack on the three Junior Amateurs as well. 'I've got five majors,' he said.

The 66 tied the British Open amateur scoring record set by America's Frank Stranahan at Royal Troon in 1950 and guaranteed Woods the coveted Silver Medal for low amateur. But Woods wasn't at Lytham for the Silver Medal. He wanted to capture the Claret Jug, and he was not pleased on Saturday to shoot only 70 on another perfect day. Earl, however, saw the transformation. His son was playing badly and shooting 70 in a major. 'I'm pleased with Tiger's development because that's what it's all about – gaining experience and exposure to the pro game at the highest level,' he said. 'At age 20, this is his sixth major, and he's made four cuts. All this experience will come back and pay dividends later. I'm not concerned about him going out and winning. I realize he's in over his head but he has the talent and the desire and when you combine those with age, you have a volatile situation – he can catch on fire.'

Another 70 on Sunday moved Woods up into a tie for 22nd, his best finish in a major championship and a professional tournament. His 72-hole total of three-under 271 tied the championship record set by Ian Pyman in 1993 at Royal St. George's for the lowest aggregate by an amateur. A bogey at the last hole cost Woods the record, but he was distracted by the noisy fans who had been drinking in the beer pavilion, and was unable to get comfortable after resetting over his second shot.

'I was looking for the Claret Jug,' he said. 'But, on the week,

I'd have to say it was a whole lot of fun. It's been important to me to see my game improve in big tournaments such as this. I'm pleased with how much better I'm hitting the ball and my decision making.

'Finally, those are starting to show up in my scores.'

Michael Bonallack, secretary of the Royal and Ancient Golf Club of St. Andrews, and a past British Amateur champion, could see the progress Woods had made since the 1995 Open at St. Andrews. Bonallack gave Woods his highest praise, saying he was as good as Nicklaus was at a comparable age.

'I'd have to say he struggled with links golf last year, especially landing his iron shots softly and on the hard ground and getting the right feel for pitch-and-run shots,' Bonallack said. 'This year, he has showed a much more complete game. He's added a new dimension. I think we're looking at a future champion for many years to come.'

Nicklaus, who shot 66 the same day Woods shot 66, faded on the weekend with scores of 77 and 72 but was pleased to see Tiger play so well. 'Obviously he has a marvelous future in front of him,' Nicklaus said. 'He's getting such great experience at such an age, competing in important tournaments like this, and he's making the most of them. He's going to be around for a long, long time – f his body holds up. That's always a concern with a lot of players because of how much they play and how many balls they hit. A lot of guys can't handle it, the physical and mental side. But from what he's shown me, it looks like he can. I see lots of brightness in his future.'

Tiger knew leaving Royal Lytham that afternoon that it was probably his last professional tournament as an amateur. His canned quote to reporters was still, 'I will know when the time is right. As soon as I get there, I will tell you.' But with Nike and Callaway talking the numbers they were taking, the college degree – even one from Stanford – could wait.

On *The Tonight Show with Jay Leno* Tiger said he would turn professional if something 'viable' came along that outweighed Stanford and amateur golf. By viable, Tiger meant megabucks deals with Nike and Titleist. The contracts hadn't been signed because that would impinge on Woods's amateur status with the USGA. But in Orlando, IMG was already hunting for a townhouse at Isleworth that eventually would be Tiger's tax-free haven. The corporate wheels were in motion.

There was one final sign. Tiger went to the Western Amateur at Benton Harbor, Mich, and was eliminated in the first round by Terry Noe, the 1994 U.S. Junior champion. He was flat, and that told Woods his motivations would be taxed playing amateur golf. It was like that AJGA event in Castle Rock, Colorado. 'He told me that he was leaning toward turning pro,' Earl said. 'The reasons he gave were his British Open performance, and his recent collegiate success. Every horizon had been covered. He is mature physically and mentally, and he's ready to move. I told him we would talk again, but it accelerated the preparation I had been doing just in case.'

One week later at the PGA Championship, spectators at Valhalla Golf Club in Louisville were observed looking at a pairings sheet and wondering why Tiger Woods's name wasn't on it. It was a good question, considering he played in the other majors, and also because of the money that awaited. Tiger wasn't a professional yet. Only pros played in the PGA.

Tiger turning pro was now a hot rumor inside golf's inner circles. In the locker room at Valhalla, Joe Moses of Nike's Golf Division, was ducking the other tour reps and agents who heard it was a done deal and that Earl and Phil Knight had agreed to terms. It was also that week that the Woods family told a handful of the writers they trusted that Tiger would turn pro after the Amateur – but the writers were asked to sit on the story. If they wrote it, they were betraying the trust of the Woods family forever. If they didn't write it, they risked getting beat on the story. The Amateur was still two weeks away. Tiger was home in Cypress, honing his game, still not 100 percent on his decision.

Before he left for the Amateur, Tiger told coach Wally Goodwin that he'd be back at Stanford for another season. At the Sunday night Amateur dinner at the Portland Marriott, Fred Ridley, chairman of the World Amateur Championship selection committee, approached Tiger and said, 'I'd like to make an announcement that we're going to have you at the Philippines. If there's a problem, I don't need to make the announcement.'

'Go right ahead,' Woods said.

Greg Norman, Fred Couples and Ernie Els, who were at Firestone CC in Akron, Ohio, playing the NEC World Series of Golf, already knew that Tiger was turning pro. He had consulted with them, and they all told him that with his talent and market power, he didn't need a college degree. That's what agents and accountants are for. 'He made the right choice,' Els said at Firestone. 'He can't accomplish anything more in amateur golf. He's won everything. He's done everything. If he stays amateur, his level is not going to go up. Out here, he's learning quicker. Give him two years, and he'll be as good as anybody.'

Pumpkin Ridge Golf Club in Cornelius, Oregon, is located approximately 15 miles from Nike's world headquarters in Beaverton. It was just another piece of convenient fate in the Tiger Woods story that the site of his last U.S. Amateur triumph, and the corporation that would soon pay him at least $40 million, were in the same county. Phil Knight, Nike's cofounder and CEO, was in the gallery for five of Woods's six matches. One day he tried going incognito by wearing sunglasses and the shirt issued to tournament volunteers, but Knight's presence was just another harbinger that the Nike-Woods relationship had been verbally consummated. Wally Uihlein, Ely Callaway and Hughes Norton were also among the spectators at Pumpkin Ridge, but it was Knight who had the biggest presence.

'What Michael Jordan did for basketball, [Woods] absolutely can do for golf,' Knight said. 'The world has not seen anything like what he's going to do for the sport. It's almost art. I wasn't alive to see Monet paint, but I am alive to see Tiger play golf, and that's pretty great.'

The hype and speculation swirling at Pumpkin Ridge was intoxicating. Tiger stayed focused, moving through qualifying and the first five rounds of match play unscathed. He shot 69 and 67 for medallist honors. The Witch Hollow course at Pumpkin Ridge had five par-5s. Tiger could reach four of them with irons. He wasted J. D. Manning 3 and 2, played the last nine holes against Jerry Courville to win 4 and 2, then stiff-armed 17-year-old Charles Howell 3 and 1. Team Tiger was on schedule. Sports psychologist Jay Brunza was off the bag (retiring his 36 – 3 match play record), replaced by Bryon Bell, Tiger's best friend from Western High.

There was no hard feelings between Jay and Tiger. After the Manning match, they visited Waverly CC, site of Woods's third Junior Amateur title. Tiger thought Brunza could help better from outside the ropes, and Bell did a better job with club selection. 'I trust Tiger's judgment about what he needs to win,' Brunza said.

Tiger kept moving through the quarters and semis, dispatching

D. A. Points, 3 and 2, and Stanford teammate Joel Kribel, the Pacific Northwest and Western Amateur champion, 3 and 1. At the Western, where he joined Ben Crenshaw, Curtis Strange, Rick Fehr, Scott Verplank and Phil Mickelson among the tournament's two-time champions, Kribel took pride in finally going 1 up on Woods, who won at Point O'Woods in 1994. 'I've got something I can give him grief about,' Kribel said. 'Before this, it seems like I was in a total eclipse behind him. Maybe I'm breaking through and people will see me a little bit.'

The giant Tiger shadow moved back over Kribel on the back nine at Pumpkin Ridge. Kribel was 2 up after four holes, shot 32 on the front, but Woods hardened. He got up and down from a bunker, 50 yards out at the 11th, and made two birdies and an eagle coming in. Woods, now 41 – 3 in USGA competitions, pointed to his head. 'All I have to do is stay strong up here,' he said.

In the final Woods would face Steve Scott, a University of Florida sophomore-to-be who had lost to Buddy Marucci in the 1995 U.S. Amateur semi finals. Scott barely qualified, shooting 79 and 66, but moved through his bracket and defeated Florida teammate Robert Floyd for the right to face Woods. 'If I should happen to be the one to upset him and keep him from winning three in a row, that would be pretty big,' Scott said. Their match would turn into a classic, with 15,000 people overrunning Pumpkin Ridge to witness it. 'All these people,' Tiger's mom Kultida Woods said. 'They are here to see my Tiger.'

Maybe they were, but they ended up seeing a lot of Steve Scott. The Gator had his teeth in Tiger for most of the match. Three up after five holes, Scott shot 68 and was 5 up at the lunchbreak. He seemed relaxed and poised, spending the intermission in the merchandise tent with his girlfriend/caddy, Kristi Hommel. Woods cursed himself, then sat down with Team Tiger to assess the damage.

'For some reason, I just didn't have it,' Woods said. 'I can't explain it. I might have been tired. It might have been the situation I was in. I was searching for it. I just couldn't find it.'

Harmon spotted a flaw in Woods's posture. Brunza helped him find his focus. He came out in the afternoon a different person and won the 21st, and 22nd and 23rd holes to close the gap. At the 27th hole, Woods outdrove Scott by 113 yards, made birdie, and was 1 down with the back nine to play. 'That gave me a big boost going into the back nine,' Woods said. But this Scott kid was tenacious. He holed a flop wedge from an impossible lie one hole later, and celebrated by jumping in the air and pumping his fist. Scott shouldn't have done that. That was like tugging on Superman's cape.

Tiger put it right back in Scott's face. He ripped a 357-yard drive at the 553-yard 11th, reaching the green with a 5-iron and draining a 45-footer with a 3-foot break for eagle. 'I was feeling a little heated,' Tiger said. 'I took it out on the golf ball and happened to catch it perfectly flush.'

Now it was the Gator's turn. He went 2 up again when Tiger missed a 4-footer for birdie at the 32nd hole. This is when Scott sensed he might have delivered the knockout punch. He saw Tiger's head drop. 'That's when I thought I'd win the match,' he said. 'He was looking frustrated. I thought that would rattle him a little bit, but it didn't.'

The closest Woods had been to elimination before this was at Waverly, where Ryan Armour had him dormie with two to play in the 1993 Junior Amateur. Going back there with Brunza on Thursday night had been an inspiration. He kept telling himself, 'I've been here before,' and with that to draw on, Tiger Woods did what only Tiger Woods, Joe Montana, John Elway and Michael Jordan have the ability to do.

First he birdied the 34th hole from 5 feet. One down with two holes to play. Momentum on his side. A 7-iron into the 35th hole. Another birdie coming up. But Tiger hit a bad shot, blocked in a 7-iron 30 right of the cup. Scott was in good shape. The match could be over right here. He had one option. Waverly. Tiger had to pretend he was Nicklaus. He had to will the ball in the hole. 'It was just one of those putts that I felt no matter what speed I hit it, it was going in,' Woods said. His eyes got wide as the ball was tracking to the cup. He had that mask on his face, that wild-eyed look only the great ones get, and he started striding across the green, picking up momentum for that celebration dance of his, where he throws that one big uppercut and then a couple of jabs at the air, as the ball disappears in the hole. Tiger Woods had found that fifth gear once again, leaving Steve Scott standing there with nothing to say but, 'Unbelievable.'

Woods had hit 28 of the last 29 greens, shot 65 in his closing 18, and sent the match into overtime. Scott's 70 should have been good enough to win, but not against Tiger. In sudden death, he had an 18-footer for birdie on the first hole to putt Woods away. When he missed, short and right, it seemed inevitable. Tiger was already thinking ahead to the cut 6-iron he'd hit at the 194-yard 11th, the 38th hole of the match. He smoked it over the flag, 5 1 2 feet away, and Scott was feeling the heat. He missed the green, boldly tried to hole his chip, and lipped out a 6 footer coming back for par. Tiger missed his birdie putt, but tapped in from 18 inches for par and the match. Both hands went above his head, almost in disbelief. It was the first time he led all day. It was the sixth time in six USGA finals that he had been taken to the final hole and beyond. 'Given the circumstances,' he said, 'this has to be the best I ever played.'

He was too numb to know the significance of winning three straight U.S. Amateurs. Tiger did know that in three days, there would be a news conference in Milwaukee, but when the writers asked that Sunday night at Pumpkin Ridge, he told them he still wasn't sure. Then he drove to the house where he was staying near Pumpkin Ridge and told his parents, 'Yep, it's time to go.'

# Six

# VESTED INTEREST

There had been issues involving the amateur status of Tiger Woods from the day Earl Woods started receiving checks from the International Management Group. How could the United States Golf Association turn its back on what appeared to be an obvious breach of the rules? Or if not the rules, then the spirit of the rules?

The USGA was sensitive to that, of what it looked like for the greatest amateur golfer since Bobby Jones to have a relationship with IMG. So when August 20, 1996, rolled around, and Tiger took the podium at the Greater Milwaukee Open to announce he was turning professional, there was hardly any surprise, and a great sense of relief. It was all much cleaner this way.

David Fay, the U.S. Golf Association's executive director, had been working with Earl Woods since Tiger won the 1991 U.S. Juniors at Bay Hill, making sure there was never a breach of the amateur guidelines. At the urging of Mark McCormack, they met at Gold House, the USGA's headquarters in Far Hills, New Jersey, the week of the Buick Classic at Westchester in 1994. Tony Zirpoli Jr., the USGA's director for regional affairs, amateur status and public golf, also served as a consultant but was not present at that meeting. 'When it was clear that Tiger was going to be a prominent player, we made an offer to him and his father, much like we made to Phil Mickelson,' Fay said. 'The code can be tricky. We told them, "We're here if you have any questions." We wanted to make it quite clear that Earl had a grasp on the interpretation of amateur status.'

One of the issues that came up through the course of their discussions was a minority golf clinic set up by John Merchant at Brooklawn CC near Bridgeport, Connecticut, the week of the 1995 U.S. Open. A major corporation was willing to fly Woods from Southampton across the Long Island Sound for the outing, but that would have been a violation of USGA regulations. Tiger could accept auto transportation, which included the tolls, but he could not fly in the helicopter.

Merchant, an attorney based in Southport, Connecticut, the legal advisor to Team Tiger, and the first African American to serve on the USGA's executive committee, practically memorized the rules and decisions pertaining to amateur status. 'Under oath, I would say we observed every regulation,' he said.

The big issue, of course, was Earl's employment as an IMG consultant. It looked sleazy, but as long as there was no quid pro quo, the Earl Woods – IMG relationship was perfectly within the boundaries of the amateur status code. Just as long as he didn't designate himself as an agent, it was also within the guidelines for Earl to negotiate with Nike and Titleist. The USGA was not, as reported, looking to bust Earl and Tiger Woods.

'If you ask me, Earl always had his son's best interests at heart, and he received good counsel from a number of quarters, including the USGA,' Fay said. 'We made it clear to him we don't take away amateur status on words. It's actions. Actions by the player himself that would be constituted as legally binding.'

It just looked too suspicious when, three days after winning the Amateur at Pumpkin Ridge, Hughes Norton worked the room while Tiger was standing at a podium in Milwaukee, making his announcement. Norton was making sure key people had the right numbers, telling reporters that not in the history of sports has an athlete been as financially secure from day one. Obviously those deals hadn't been done in 72 hours.

Hughes Norton was clearly one of the big winners in this. Up to the last minute, Leader Enterprises of Orlando was hoping to sign the Woods account and had representatives in the clubhouse at Brown Deer, trying to convince Tida that IMG would have a bad influence on her son's career. Tommy Limbaugh, a former college football coach and recruiter, was working it hard for Leader. Limbaugh claimed the only reason Leader had a presence in Milwaukee was because Earl promised him at Pumpkin Ridge that IMG did not have Tiger's management contract locked up. Limbaugh interpreted that to mean it was still a ballgame. 'They kept trying and trying and trying, but you know what? Ripping IMG worked against them,' Norton said. 'Tida told me that no one pitched their own plusses. That was all they could sell.'

An argument could be made to give Norton golf's comeback of the year award, because after Greg Norman and Nick Price left IMG two years before, Norton had been moved behind Alastair Johnston as head of Mark McCormack's golf division. But Norton had been working on Earl and Tiger Woods for seven years, and all those hours of nurturing the relationship had paid off in the most lucrative motherlode in the history of golf.

'I'm a voracious reader, and I had read a lot about Tiger,' Norton said. 'I'd like to tell you it was brilliance on my part, that I knew he'd win six consecutive USGA championships. The fact is, I was just doing my homework.'

So was Wally Uihlein at Titleist, who began laying groundwork with the Woods family and John Merchant by supporting and underwriting the National Minority Golf Foundation long before it was politically correct. It may seem like Uihlein was flying under radar, but, as he states, 'We would not be doing our job if we didn't get to know these people, and we don't have to make an apology for knowing them for years.' Tiger had been using a Taylor Made driver, but at the U.S. Open, switched to a Cobra model similar to the one Greg Norman was using that featured a bore-through shaft. With as much clubhead speed as Norman and Woods generate, the reduced torque created a more stable feel at impact. Cobra, which is owned by Titleist's parent company, American Brands, gave Woods the option of actually using equipment from two different companies. The other plus with Titleist was that Uihlein would allow Woods to use forged clubs, and not the perimeter-weighted cavity-backed irons that other equipment companies were forcing players to use. Tiger could stay with his Mizuno blades until he was comfortable with a set of irons that Titleist could make for him.

'You do the right things that are in the book,' Uihlein said. 'At the same time, you're walking the walk.'

When Tiger walked to the podium that day in the media tent at Brown Deer Golf Club, and began with the seemingly innocent words, 'I guess, hello, world,' it began a new era. He was no longer the amateur golfer who hit scruffy two-piece balls out of plastic milk crates at the Stanford golf course range. Eldrick 'Tiger' Woods, an African-Asian-American who had been programmed for this day since he was born, was now a packaged product, a corporation, and an icon. The Stanford cap and the Lochinvar shirt were gone, replaced by the ever present swoosh. This was the commercial payoff, a place in Nike's pantheon next to Jordan, Deion Sanders and Andre Agassi. The problem was that 'Hello World' happened to be the theme and title for the Nike advertising campaign launched the following day with a $350,000 three-page layout in *The Wall Street Journal* and in television commercials that aired on ESPN and CBS. The age of Tiger Woods's innocence had ended, but he was still a kid at heart.

Tiger had flown in on the Nike corporate jet, which was part of the deal, and he talked about finally trading in his father's old 1988 Toyota Supra for some new wheels. He was amazed that the Milwaukee tournament had given him a courtesy car, and with all the clothes and bags Nike had delivered to his hotel room. Technically, this was his first week on the job, but he hadn't seen any money yet. The night before at dinner, when the check was passed in his direction, the only thing Tiger could produce were some $25 gift certificates. 'I'm still broke,' he said. 'I guess I'll still be eating at McDonald's for a while longer.'

Other than that opening line, Tiger said all the right things. He was articulate, charming, sincere, prepared. He had matured from that opening news conference at Augusta National in 1995. The Stanford experience had served him well.

Tiger on the decision: 'My timing is just right because let's go back to the '60s. I don't think I would have been able to play in these tournaments. Or I wouldn't have even been given the opportunity to play a golf course because of the racial segregations at the time. But now the doors are opening. Not all the doors. I'm not saying all the doors. But doors are opening and now we have an opportunity to get more diversity in such a great game. Tennis has come along. Every sport was like that. That's the way it was then. That's not the way it's going to be.'

Tiger on the pressure: 'One of the beauties is that I'm not even worried about that. It's nice to get a whole lot of money. The great thing is that I get to do something I've always dreamt of doing, ever since I was a little kid watching Nicklaus on TV or watching Watson play well or all those great players play. I'm out here now with them, playing.'

Tiger on the value of a Stanford education: 'I talked to my parents about that. They told me whether you get your degree tomorrow or fifteen years from now, it doesn't matter. They never gave me a time limit on it. As long as I get my degree. That's all that matters, and I made that promise to them and to myself and I will do that.'

Tiger on his strengths and weaknesses: 'I think my strongest point is my mind. I think I proved that in the U.S. Amateur, my ability just to hang in there. The weakest attribute is I just don't have the experience out here. I don't know where to stay, what restaurants to eat in, so I'm going to have to stick to McDonald's. Something greasy.'

Tiger on the money: 'It wasn't about money. It was about happiness. Whether the time was right and how happy am I? And that was the deciding factor. I know my golf game was good enough. Was the time right? Am I ready and the answers all pointed to yes.'

Tiger on his personification of a role model: 'I've been very blessed to have the opportunity to become a role model. Not too many people in this world have that opportunity. And if I have the status that hopefully I will obtain, it's amazing how much money I could get to help the youth in the inner city and get them playing if they choose to play golf. But I think the most important thing is to have the opportunity, and hopefully with my status that I'm hopeful to attain that this will happen. God, I sure hope it does.'

Sitting on the dais next to Tiger at Brown Deer, decked out in Nike from head to toe, Earl Woods waited for the news conference to end. At one point, Tiger reached around to squeeze his hand, thanking him and Kultida for the job they did as parents. 'They have raised me well and I truly believe have taught me to accept full responsibility for all aspects of my life,' Tiger said.

It was a wonderful moment, not contrived at all, and it would have benefited Tiger if Earl headed straight to the car. Instead, he hung around and made himself available to the quote-hungry press. All they had to do was wind Earl up and make sure their tape recorders were running.

First Earl was asked to compare Tiger to Arthur Ashe and Muhammad Ali.

'There is no comprehension by anyone on the impact this kid is going to have, not only on the game of golf, but on the world itself,' Earl said.

Then he was asked about Tiger's ability as an athlete.

'He would probably be a 400-meter runner and he'd be kicking Michael Jackson's ass. If you think his swing is pretty, you ought to see him run.'

Earl meant Michael Johnson, the 200-and 400-meter Olympic gold medal winner.

Finally, Earl was asked about Tiger's killer instinct.

'You don't want to tangle with Tiger on a golf course,' Earl said. 'He's what I visualize in the Old West as a black gunslinger. He'll cut your heart out in a heartbeat and think nothing of it.'

The guy was a quote machine, but the last thing Tiger needed was his father's hype. There was already enough jealousy in the locker room. Robert Gamez had popped off about all the ink Tiger was getting. Scott Verplank said, 'Those amateur championships aren't going to scare anyone.' As Steve Stricker noted, 'Here's a guy who hasn't even gotten his tour card yet, and he's making $60 million.' Earl hadn't done his son any favors.

'There will be some guys who will be jealous of him, for sure, the same way they're jealous of Greg Norman and his big airplane and big boat,' said Davis Love III. 'I've already heard some guys say "I hope I get him in the Shark Shootout or the Diners Club Matches," stuff like that. They'll be gunning for him, and that's good. That will make him tougher, and he'll prove to them how good he is.'

Tiger certainly wasn't intimidated, either. The crowd on the first hole Thursday stretched from tee to green, and was sometimes six deep. He took the worn Tiger headcover off his driver – the one Tida made for him, with 'Love From Mom' stitched in Thai – and bombed a drive 336 yards down the center of the fairway. People either gasped or laughed. As Larry Dorman wrote in *The New York Times* '. . . these people were seeing Tiger Woods for the first time and realizing they would be seeing him for a very long time.'

There were so many people that it was impossible for Tida to see her son play his first professional round of golf. 'I think the only way to watch my Tiger now is on TV,' she said. Walking with a media armband inside the gallery ropes, Jeff Rude of *Golfweek* counted 16 Nike logos. 'He wears swooshes like Deion Sanders wears jewelry,' Rude wrote. GMO Executive Director Tom Strong estimated the first-day crowd at 20,000. 'It's kind of hard to tell, though,' he says, 'because everybody is following one guy.'

Tiger birdied three of the first five holes he played, shot 67, and still trailed by five strokes over Nolan Henke. What he learned that day is that no matter who it is, somebody is going to shoot a low number on the PGA Tour. On that Thursday at Brown Deer, it was Henke. On Friday, it was Steve Lowery (64). One day soon, it would be him.

'I thought I got off to a really good start,' Woods said. 'It was an ideal start, really. Perfect. Shooting 67, that's a good number and I'm right in the tournament.'

It was then that Tiger learned the difference between amateur and professional golf. At Brown Deer he followed up the 67 with a 69. Those scores would have taken medallist honors at Pumpkin Ridge. At the GMO, he was eight shots off the lead.

'It's weird,' Woods said. 'I'm going along making pars and then look up and it's like, "Geez." But then again, you've got to expect it. These guys can go really low.' It all caught up with him Saturday, and he shot 73, returned to his hotel room, and crashed.

Bruce Lietzke, the 22-year veteran, played with Woods that day and had nothing but high praise for Tiger's decorum and professionalism. 'There wasn't a lot to see today, because he was off his game, but he handled himself wonderfully,' Lietzke said. 'He didn't let his temper get out of control. We need good guys at the top. If he does become the next ambassador of golf, I think it will be in good hands with him.'

A closing 68 on Sunday included a hole-in-one, but even with three rounds in the 60s, Tiger Woods had finished tied for 60th. This clearly was not amateur golf anymore. This was the big leagues, and as Love and Harmon both advised, he'll be the hunted, not the hunter.

The future of golf had just entered the present tense. From August 29 through September 1, 1996, Tiger Woods played his first tournament as a pro, recorded his first birdie as a pro, made his first hole-in-one as a pro, and deposited his first check as a pro. More important than all that, though, was that he acted like a pro.

'All the amateur titles Tiger has won won't mean anything, and he'll have to prove himself in a hard environment where there is no mercy,' Harmon said. 'He's got the intelligence and the tools to succeed very quickly. My only worry is that he's losing two of the best years of his life to do something that is very demanding for a young person. Considering everything, he's made the right decision, but he's doing to have to grow up faster than I'd like him to.'

# Seven

# HOT BUTTON

Butch Harmon was right. Tiger Woods had to grow up in a hurry, both as a golfer, and as a public figure. He had to deal not only with getting his tour card, but the implications of a Nike television commercial that debuted on ESPN during its coverage of the GMO and was aired on Fox during its Sunday coverage of the NFL and on ABC during Monday Night Football Game. The content and the tone of that Nike commercial was definitely the buzz when Tiger arrived at Glen Abbey on Tuesday to practice for the opening round of the Canadian Open.

As an amateur, Woods had downplayed the race issue. He had never so boldly made the statement that the Nike Commercial made, and coming on the heels of his smiling 'Hello, World' entrance in Milwaukee, it seemed slightly over the top and, at the very least, poorly timed.

Set to a New Age symphony soundtrack, and run over highlights of Tiger winning his three U.S. Amateurs, the words that seemed so out of character for Tiger were words that Nike obviously knew would raise brand awareness. Tiger had signed off on them, but nobody had ever heard him say:

There are still courses in the U.S. I am not allowed to play because of the color of my skin.
Hello World.

I've heard I'm not ready for you.
Are you ready for me?

On Tuesday night, *Nightline* devoted its entire show to the Tiger Woods phenomenon, focusing on the race issue and opening with the Nike commercial. At Milwaukee, Woods told the media that he had approved the copy, because it provoked thought and raised a social issue that needed raising. 'It's a message that has been long awaited because it's true,' he said. 'Being a person who is nonwhite, I've had to experience that. The Nike campaign is just telling the truth.'

Maybe it was, but what bothered many was not the message, but the tone in which it was delivered. Woods not only had never played the race card, but at the 1995 U.S. Open, he went as far as clarifying to reporters through a statement that to call him 'black' or 'African-American' would be incorrect. Handed out in the media center at Shinnecock Hills, it read:

'The purpose of this statement is to explain my heritage for the benefit of members of the media who may be seeing me play for the first time. It is the final and only comment I will make regarding the issue.

'My parents have taught me to always be proud of my ethnic background. Please rest assured that is, and will be, the case, past, present and future. The various media have portrayed me as African-American, sometimes Asian. In fact, I am both . . .

'On my father's side, I am African-American; on my mother's side, I am Thai. Truthfully, I feel very fortunate, and equally proud, to be both African-American and Asian!

'The critical and fundamental point is that ethnic background and/or composition should not make a difference. It does not make a difference to me. The bottom line is that I am an American . . . and proud of it!'

During a news conference at Glen Abbey, Woods explained that he issued that statement out of respect to his mother. 'By saying I'm black only is an insult to my mom,' Woods said. 'If you understand the Asian cultures in general, by denying that is a big insult. I love my mom to death, and I don't want to see her hurt in that way.' Woods also confirmed that he received requests from the African-American community to clarify his heritage.

The weighty questions raised in the Nike ad were obviously playing off the fact that Woods was black, not a young man of mixed culture. Larry Dorman pointed out the hypocrisies in columns he wrote for *The New York Times* and *Golf World* 'The ads make you think, all right,' Dorman wrote. 'About exactly how far removed the advertising world is from the real world.' Financial affairs expert James K. Glassman followed two weeks later in a column that ran in *The Washington Post.* Glassman called the ad campaign by Nike 'discordant, dishonest and even vile.' He wrote: 'The ad is telling blacks and other minorities that racism is so virulent in this country that, no matter how good you are, you will be despised and rejected by white (people). You have to stand up to them (in Nikes, of course) . . . The only problem is that, in the case of Mr. Woods, it's based on a lie.'

Glassman called Nike, requesting a list of the courses that Woods could not play. He got a call back from James Small, the company's public relation's director, who admitted that 'Tiger Woods can play on any golf course he wants.'

The man who wrote the ad, Jim Riswold, creative director for the Wieden & Kennedy advertising agency in Portland, stuck by his words. The ad was obviously successful, because people were talking about it. 'It's created as hailstorm,' Riswold said in an interview with Jeff Rude of *Golfweek.* 'I can barely sit down, my butt hurts so much. A lot of the criticism comes from the golf community. It's close-knit. They don't like to be surprised. They like to know what's coming. Still, I don't understand why I'm accused of hurting golf.'

On the putting green at Glen Abbey, Jim Thorpe said he thought Riswold missed a wonderful opportunity to send a positive message about Tiger Woods and his family. 'Nike could have made a beautiful commercial if they had used his photos and used the wording like, "With hard work and education and unity among the family, I made it and you can do it too," ' Thorpe said. 'And then Nike comes up with their line . . . I personally don't think Tiger's ever been turned away from a golf course because of the color of his skin. Maybe years ago guys were. But I personally don't think a young man of his status, with the best amateur record since Bobby Jones, and probably as well known as Bobby Jones, I don't think any club in this country has ever turned him away from playing a round of golf. I personally feel if we let it die, it will all blow over. His job is to just play golf and prove to the world he can compete against the best players in the world, not to make racist statements. The [Charlie] Siffords, the [Lee] Elders, the [Calvin] Peetes, the Thorpes, the [Jim] Dents, we kind of smoothed that over. Just go play golf. I think the only pressure that will be is on his game.'

Until Woods came along, Thorpe was the only African American playing the PGA Tour. During the Tuesday pro-am at Glen Abbey, he was coming down the 10th fairway, and just saw Tiger coming off the second tee. They had a brief conversation, Thorpe telling Woods not to worry about some of the jealousy he was hearing in the locker room, but he didn't really have the time to get into the Nike ad.

'This isn't anything like Jackie Robinson,' Thorpe said. 'That road's been paved, plus he doesn't have to worry about making money, where we had to do the Mondays and stuff. Tiger's got it made. Every time Charlie Sifford won a tournament, they changed the rule at the Masters so he couldn't play. With Lee Elder and Charlie, you'd hear the N-word, but I didn't have to go through it. They pretty much paved the way, and every time I see these guys I thank them. I tell them I appreciate it. He [Elder] told me, "James, I really appreciate that. Sometimes the efforts we made, people don't give a damn."

'The PGA Tour has been wonderful, not just for me but a lot of guys. We made a lot of money, met a lot of people, been a lot of places. You know what? My advice to Tiger would be, Just go do it. Forget about the other stuff. We've got political leaders that can take care of the races. It's like coming here. I'd be a damn fool to come to Glen Abbey Golf and Country Club and walk into their membership office and ask if they have any ethnic members. I've got to be stupid. All I have to know is we're playing for that one point two [million]. If they don't have any members, I don't give a damn. As long as we're playing for that money. That's what we have to look at. From the No. 1 player in the world to the guy who finishes rock bottom, if you can play, they're going to pay you. If you're colorful, they're going to pay you more. It's just like I told Calvin Peete one time, "Peete, you're a wonderful player, you won 12 tournaments in four years. It's not that you're a bad guy. You're just quiet." When it comes to doing corporate stuff, of course they're going to take the Tom Kites and the Peter Jacobsens over you. It's just that simple. It's not because you're black.

'Tiger should just go out there and be Tiger. He's a household name, a drawing card, one of the biggest drawing cards ever. I'd love to see him work closer with the inner-city programs, get involved with a lot of minority programs and see if we can get more Tiger Woodses out there. There's no reason there should be this big a gap between Tiger Woods and me. He's a wonderful young man. God bless him.'

Stuck in the middle of this hailstorm was Tiger Woods. Ranked 344th on the money list, coming off back-to-back weeks where he won the Amateur, turned pro, played in his first pro tournament, and had flown from California to Oregon to Wisconsin and now Canada, the Nike ad had created a distraction. He had made $2, 544 in Milwaukee. He needed about $250,000 more to gain exempt status on the PGA tour for the 1998 season.

At IMG's offices in Cleveland, Hughes Norton and Bev Norwood turned down interview requests from *Good Morning America, Today, CBS Morning News, Later With Tom Snyder, ESPN Up Close, Outside the Lines, Fox's After Breakfast, Xtra, Nickelodeon, Access Hollywood, Live with Regis and Kathie Lee*, Roy Firestone, Oprah Winfrey, David Letterman, Jay Leno and Larry King, and guest appearances on *Martin* and *Cosby* At Glen Abbey, Tiger posed for a *Golf Digest* cover and tried to keep his mind centered. The goal here was a tour card. He fought his driver and 3-wood early in the week, shot 70 and 70, rested on Saturday while the remnants of Hurricane Fran wiped out the third round, then came back on Sunday to shoot the day's low round (68) in bad conditions to tie for 11th place.

As was the case in Milwaukee, he attracted a larger gallery during the final round than the last group that included tournament winner Dudley Hart. 'It's nice to look in the gallery and see so many kids,' he said. 'They can relate to me. I'm not far from being a teenager myself. When people yell, "You're the man," I always say, "Not legally." '

The check for $37, 500 moved Tiger up to 204th place on the money list, and he headed south across the U.S. border to Quad City, having converted another group of people.

So far, Tiger was two-for-two at the box office, and either one-for-one or oh-for-one as a corporate pitchman. 'He already has a following that is big, or bigger, than J. D. (John Daly),' said David Duval. 'He's kind of a cult hero.'

67

## Eight

# GETTING THE GRIP

They seemed less concerned in Quad Cities about the courses Tiger Woods didn't play as opposed to the one he was about to play: Oakwood Country Club. A story in the *Quad City Times* said the Woods commitment was the biggest thing to hit this corner of the world since grilled pork fillets. And in Davenport and Bettendorf, Iowa, not to mention Rock Island and Moline, Illinois, grilled pork fillets are huge.

'We're all grinning so hard our faces hurt,' said tournament chairman Todd Nicholson. An extra 15,000 walk-up tickets were printed, but it was not enough to handle the demand. Oakwood never saw crowds like the ones Tiger brought to town. Bob DeGeorge drove 300 miles and brought a three-step stepladder all the way from Brookfield, Missouri. 'We sold over 31,000 pork chip sandwiches, and that's more than we had people last year when the weather was bad,' said tournament director Kym Houghham. 'Normally we're at 65,000 people. We had over 100,000 tickets with Tiger. At times we couldn't get tickets out to the gate fast enough, and the volunteers had to use Magic Markers on the backs of people's hands. As prepared as we were, we weren't prepared enough.'

The state fair atmosphere was just what Tiger needed after the media circus in Toronto. Tiger was also getting beaten up by a few players who were jealous of the attention he was getting, and that seemed to subside in the Quad Cities. 'Tigermania is healthy for golf,' said defending champion D. A. Weibring. 'I don't think there's a resentment over Tiger. It's a fascination.'

At Milwaukee, Bruce Lietzke had said the only resentment toward Tiger was coming from 'the typical few bozos who get in trouble on proam day.' In Canada, however, one player asked Steve Jones if the PGA really asked him to sit out the Grand Slam of Golf so Tiger could take his place. And John Cook, after reading Earl's 'black gunslinger' quote in the *Los Angeles Times* warned that this wasn't going to be quite the same as amateur golf.

'This is not college anymore,' Cook said. 'There's one hundred and fifty guys who will look him straight in the eye and say, "Let's go." When he learns that and he earns the respect of his peers, he will be fine.

'Tiger's a good kid. He respects the players. I don't think the people around him respect what this is, why he's here and why he just earned all that money.

'That's the only thing that I worry about is people around him think that he can just kind of sidestep everything and go out and win fifteen majors. That's not going to happen.'

John Feinstein, author of *A Good Walk Spoiled* and a former tennis writer and columnist for *The Washington Post* said the same thing in a story he wrote for Newsweek and in an interview with Forrest Sawyer on *Nightline* He called Woods a 'tennis parent' and drew the comparison to Stefano Capriati, the overbearing father of Jennifer Capriati. 'Like Stefano, Earl hasn't had a full-time job since 1988, "sacrificing" to be at his son's side. Earl Woods says he won't travel full time with Tiger. That would be a bonus.'

Earl and Tiger took great offense to this characterization of their relationship. Tiger called it 'slanderous,' but again, Earl didn't do Tiger or himself a great service by being so visible at Quad City, and by telling local columnist Tom Johnston. 'Before this tourney ends, he will hit one shot that people will be talking about for thirty years.' Players read those quotes and started saying, 'The kid's all right, but the old man's bad news.'

Quad City was held the same week as the President's Cup, the international competition between the 12 best players from the United States and the 12 best players from Australasia and Africa, so the field wasn't that strong. Odds on Tiger to win were 20-1 at the Imperial Palace Race & Sports Book in Las Vegas, which looked like a great bet Saturday night after Tiger went 64 and 67 in the second and third rounds to open a one-stroke lead over Ed Fiori. Leaving the Presidents Cup the next morning were Dorman of *The New York Times*, Diaz of *Sports Illustrated*, Ron Sirak of AP, Jeff Babineau of the *Orlando Sentinel* and Phil Rogers of the *Dallas Morning-News*. The press tent on Sunday at Robert Trent Jones Golf Club was deserted as all the top writers flew from Dulles to Moline Airport for what was anticipated to be Tiger's first professional victory. That 20-1 bet looked like pretty good money.

'He hits wedge to ever par 4 and he reaches ever par 5 n two,' Fiori said. 'How do you beat a guy like that?'

The answer is: You don't. You let Tiger beat himself. It doesn't happen often, but it did on Sunday at Quad City. Through three holes, Tiger had opened a three-stroke lead. At the fourth hole, a 460-yard par 4, Tiger wanted to hit his patented power cut, a shot where he takes the hands out of his swing and hits it hard, left-to-right. Instead of the power cut, Tiger hit the dreaded 'double cross,' a left-to-left hook that splashed in a pond. At that point, Tiger probably should have taken his drop, chipped out, and attempted to make an up-and-down bogey from the fairway. Instead, he elected to hit a 6-iron 200 yards through an opening in the trees. The heroic shot turned out to be a bad play, as his ball hit a oak limb and took a hard detour into the swamp. From there, it was pretty easy to make a snowman, a quadruple bogey 8. Three holes later, trying to make something happen, Tiger took driver at the 344-yard seventh, hit wedge onto the green 8 feet, and proceeded to four-jack for a double bogey. It was like the end of the first round at Oakland Hills, all over again.

But instead of quitting, Tiger sucked it up and finished strong. He played the last six holes in two under to finish tied for fifth, four shots back of Fiori, who won for the first time since the 1992 Bob Hope. 'Walking up the 14th fairway, he said to me, 'If I birdie out, I can still win,'' said his then caddy, Mike 'Fluff' Cowan. 'That probably impressed me as much as anything.'

Afterward, Tiger admitted he saw progress. 'It's hard to say right now what I learned,' he said. 'I'll know better in a couple of days. I will tell you one thing: I will learn a lot from this.'

That night, Woods went out to dinner with Earl, Butch, Norton and Bryon Bell, who was now a premed student at UC San Diego, at their hotel in Moline. They decided that Tiger was mentally fatigued, otherwise he would have punched out on the fourth hole and made no worse than double bogey, and that he never would have four-putted from eight feet at the seventh. By the time dessert came around, they were laughing about how bad Tiger had taken the gas. With the tie for fifth, Tiger earned $42, 150 and moved up to 166th in the money standings. He was trending in the right direction. He was one swing away.

'The one thing he's going to learn from this is how hard it is to win a tour event,' Harmon said. 'The way things were going, I don't think he thought it was too hard. Even though I wish he had won the tournament, in the long run, this may be better for him. He'll come away from this realizing that it's not easy to win out here, no matter who you are.'

Nine

# POOR JUDGMENT

There was more to tournament golf than just the act of hitting golf shots and shooting scores. There are unwritten rules that must be abided by, situations that should be handled in certain ways. The protocol was established long before Tiger Woods turned pro in Milwaukee, and will be part of the game's framework long after he retires. He may have been a special case, but respect goes both ways, and what Tiger took away from the 1996 Buick Challenge was a greater appreciation for how the system works.

Emotionally, physically, he was spent. Including the U.S. Amateur, he had played in five straight tournaments. There were two events remaining on his schedule after the Buick – Las Vegas and Texas. The problem was he had accepted his seven allotted sponsors exemptions. He simply needed a week off.

Woods began to realize that after he flew back to Orlando from Quad City. Since August 19, he had played twenty-three rounds of competitive golf in thirty-three days. This didn't include practice rounds, or time on the range.

At the B.C. Open, played the week after Quad City, Woods was asked the hypothetical question: What would you do if you secured your tour card? Would you honor your commitments and play out the string? His response sounded thought-out. 'They've been nice enough to grant me an exemption and I feel a need to honor them,' he said. 'And if I couldn't do it this year, I would talk to the tournament director about coming back next year.'

Like all the tournament directors in that fall swing of 1996, Bob Burns anticipated Tiger Woods's arrival. He personally drove to the airport in Pine Mountain, Georgia, to meet Tiger's plane. Everything, according to Berry, seemed fine. Tiger did a news conference and played a nine-hole practice round with Davis Love III and Peter Jacobsen. He talked to Davis about making the Ryder Cup team. But Mike Cowan, who was carrying Tiger's bag at the time, could sense a problem. 'He looked beat,' Cowan said. 'He was just kind of putting one foot ahead of the other, but I didn't think it wasn't anything a good night's sleep couldn't cure.'

That night, Woods went back to the house he was renting at Callaway Gardens and decided to withdraw. Earlier in the day, he had told Berry that he would be in the pro-am on Wednesday, and at the Fred Haskins Award Dinner Thursday night, where he would be honored as college golf's Player of the Year.

'He looked me straight in the eye and said, "I'll be there," ' Berry said. But late Tuesday night Berry got a call from Norton, and at 6: 15 the following morning he and Mark Russell of the PGA Tour staff huddled in the Buick Challenge tournament office to come up with a plan. They called Norton and offered to let Tiger·skip the pro-am, get some rest, and tee it up Thursday. Norton called back at 6: 30. Tiger was already at the airport. The plane was fueled and ready to taxi down the runway.

That day, Norton issued a statement on Tiger's behalf. Claiming he was mentally exhausted and that it would be a 'disservice to myself and those who came to watch me play,' Woods elected to skip not only the tournament, but the dinner. 'The past five weeks have been the most challenging in my life – and at the same time the most physically and mentally draining,' Woods said. 'Withdrawing from a tournament at the last minute is not something that I am accustomed to doing. I have expressed my apologies and my regrets to the officials of the Buick Challenge.'

First of all, Woods did not personally do that. He let Norton do the dirty work. Secondly, Norton should have stood up to Woods, advised him to rest and maybe skip the tournament, but at least show up for the dinner. His father had committed Tiger to it four months earlier. More than 200 dignitaries had traveled to Callaway Gardens at the tournament's expense. A video was produced. Including flowers, decorations and the special meals, it cost Buick $30,000 to put the event on.

Norton didn't see what the big deal was all about. 'It's tough for the tournament here, but [withdrawing] was not something [Tiger wanted] to do,' he said. 'There wasn't any other choice. He's going to take three days to try and recharge his batteries and relax . . . I'm amazed that it took this long. I thought he might hit the wall before now. I think most people would have withdrawn from B.C.'

The reaction was what it should have been be – pointed and strong against Tiger. He had violated protocol and broke an unwritten rule. It made him appear like he was bigger than the game. 'I feel badly for him. But he's stepped off the anonymity sidewalk; he's in the parade now,' Jacobsen said. 'He's going to be scrutinized, and he'll probably take some heat for this. One thing, you can't compare him to Nicklaus and Palmer anymore because they never did this.'

Tom Kite: 'I can't ever remember being tired when I was 20.'

Davis Love: 'Everybody has been telling him how great he is. I guess he's starting to believe it.'

Curtis Strange, a former Haskins winner: 'This tournament was one of seven to help Tiger when he needed help to get his card, and how quickly he forgot. But I bet the Buick people won't forget.'

Tiger was back in Orlando when these quotes ran in *USA Today* Larry Guest, columnist in the *Orlando Sentinel* and a noted critic of IMG, crafted a 'Dear Tiger' column, advising Tiger to be careful in his dealings with Norton. 'You'll recover from this deep rough,' Guest wrote, 'and hopefully learn from this PR gaffe, which doesn't totally surprise me given that your hired advice is International Management Group – an outfit notorious for raising high-handedness to an art form . . .

'The next time a sticky situation arises – and there will be more of them, for sure – address it head-on. NEVER, NEVER, NEVER again leave your IMG rep Hughes Norton and a cold, impersonal prepared statement to plead your case, as happened this week. Your own pleasing smile and natural charm will be far more effective in defusing volatile situations and disarming critics.

'Face the music. Be accessible. Openly apologize if the case warrants. This is definitely one of those cases. Say you're sorry. Say you'll try to make it up to Columbus and the Haskins Award sponsors. Cop a plea that you're young and learning. The world will give you the benefit of the doubt and drape an arm around your shoulder.'

The problem was that Earl and Butch weren't out on the road with Tiger. They both said that if they were at Callaway Gardens, Tiger would have been at that dinner. That didn't do the Haskins Commissioner or Bob Berry much good. He received a short unsigned apology note from Tiger, but it was dictated and not personally written, and it came from IMG's office in Cleveland. There were no promises made to return for the 1997 Buick Challenge, as Tiger said there would be at the B.C. Open. There were no offers to reschedule the dinner.

But Tiger must have read Guest's column, which appeared Friday, September 27. He personally called Berry on Sunday to apologize. 'We were right in the middle of the rain delay, and I gave him all the time he wanted, but he didn't have a whole lot to say,' Berry said. 'He said, "Maybe I'll see you next year," and left it at that. It's history as far as I'm concerned. I don't have any hard feelings. He's got to learn, I guess. Maybe when he matures . . .'

Over the weekend, Tiger went fishing with Mark O'Meara on one of the lakes in the Butler Chain near Isleworth. Sunday they played golf, even though Tiger claimed that he didn't touch a club during his time off. At one point in the conversation, Tiger must have thought he had a sympathetic ear.

'The media's been hard on me,' he said.

O'Meara told it to the kid straight. He told him he should have gone to the dinner. He also told him, 'The media made you what you are.'

# Ten

# LEAVING LAS VEGAS

Although he would take severe heat for it, the week off was a
blessing. In his last tournament before the Haskins Dinner –
Buick Challenge WD, Tiger Woods had finished third in the
rain-shortened B.C. Open. The $58,000 check moved him up to
128th on the money list, which secured his playing privileges for
the 1997 season. A finish in the top 150 made him a tour member,
and guaranteed him unlimited sponsors exemptions. Every sponsor in the world would want him. He was Tiger Woods. He was
locked in.

But Woods wanted more. 'I've just got to keep going,' he said.
And where he went after a week off was Las Vegas, the distraction capital of the world. He would be staying at the MGM
Grand, in a penthouse suite that featured a television in every
room, an expansive view of the Vegas Strip, and its own private
elevator. It wasn't quite the Best Western in Binghamton, New
York, where he stayed for the B.C. Open, but it would have to do.

The digs were arranged for Tiger through Butch Harmon and
a friendship Harmon had with Frank Tutera, a senior vice
president at the MGM. Tutera had been a PGA Tour rules
official in his previous life, and it would be his job to keep Tiger
under wraps. Three weeks before the trip to Vegas, Tiger had
gotten into a little trouble at Quad Cities. According to an
Associated Press report, Woods had produced a fake I. D. card
and had been playing blackjack for 42 minutes at the Lady Luck

River Boat Casino in Bettendorf. The *Des Moines Register* ran the story on the front page of its sports section on October 13 with the headline: 'Underage Tiger Woods Gambled on Iowa Visit.' He had also been denied access at a nightclub, and when it was mentioned that 'This was Tiger Woods' and he should be granted VIP status, the bouncer reportedly said: 'I don't care if it's the Lion King,'

Harmon and Tutera would not let that happen while Tiger was under their watch in Las Vegas. They knew that Tiger had become a lightning rod. 'I'd had to have the press covering all my screwups when I was twenty years old,' said Harmon. 'He just happens to be in a fishbowl, and everything he does is news.'

Tuesday at the TPC – Summerlin, Tiger conducted his weekly news conference. By now he knew the questions. He had his programmed answers. The only thing new would be the Buick Challenge and the Fred Haskins dinner. He'd address it once, and move on.

It hurt Woods that three of the guys who took shots at him – Love, Jacobsen and Strange – were supposedly his friends. Love was a Titleist man. Jacobsen and Strange were both part of the IMG family, and Jacobsen was Mr. Nike. Tiger was prepared for the question, saying he had received messages from the players who criticized him and turning it around on Steve Hershey, the *USA Today* golf writer who wrote the story. 'The guy who wrote it may have had an agenda,' Woods said. 'Those guys actually had been very nice to me. Davis has been great, Peter's been great, and those guys have told me that that's not exactly what they said, so it's just one of those things.'

The tournament started Wednesday, a day earlier than most PGA Tour events, and ran for 90 holes through Sunday. Tiger was paired in the opening round with Nevada governor Bob Miller at the Las Vegas Hilton course. He shot one-under 70, and was tied for 83rd. Miller and Woods talked about Stanford, since the governor's son was attending the university. The story of the day was Funk, who also played the Hilton course and shot 63, one stroke off the lead. Funk woke Wednesday morning and read quotes in the *Las Vegas Sun* from Tiger's news conference. Asked about the B.C. Open, Woods had innocuously said he wished the final round hadn't been rained out, because he thought he had a chance to win. To illustrate just how hypersensitive some of the middle-level players were about Tiger, Funk took it as an insult.

'I think I was walking away with that one and nobody was going to catch me,' Funk said. 'I sure wasn't going to let him catch me. He failed to mention he was six shots down with about 10 holes to go if we had kept going. I got a little fired up about that. All the articles have been going, "Tiger, Tiger, Tiger," kind of forgetting everybody else is playing good golf, too.'

Tiger jumped back into the picture on Thursday, shooting 63 at Summerlin in a round that could have been in the 50s. He started with three straight birdies, but went par-bogey on the back-nine par 5s that he could easily reach in two shots. The upside was his putter was working. On Tuesday night, Harmon spotted Scotty Cameron of Titleist and grabbed one of the limited edition Scottydale models that were earmarked for Japan. Butch just wanted Tiger to have a different look, something to get a little confidence going. He also had Tiger work on putting a little more hinge in his backstroke. Tiger had been getting the blade shut, and pulling a lot of short putts.

But all everybody was talking about was the Buick Challenge, the Fred Haskins Dinner and Tiger. Paul 'Zinger' Azinger shot low (64) that day, and was brought in the press tent at Summerlin. Zinger's always had a good perspective, and he was stopped on his way out by Mark Purdy, the sports columnist for the *San Jose Mercury News* and Bob Burns, golf writer for the *Sacramento Bee*. He stuck around for 15 minutes, which is something Woods has to learn to do. (Tiger's got to hang out, develop relationships like the ones Azinger has, and he'll get better treatment in the press. If Norton were wise, he'd advise Tiger of that.)

'The good news,' Zinger was saying, 'is he doesn't ever have to worry about money as long as he lives. The bad news is there are two potential bad-news scenarios. And one I don't think will ever happen but he could burn out and say, "Hey, why am I doing this? I don't need the money." I don't foresee that happening. The other bad news is there's resentment. There's resentment from players and people in general. The unfortunate thing is the numbers came out at all. Nobody knows how much Callaway paid me. Nobody knows how much Titleist pays me. Nobody knows how much Guess Watch paid me. How much Tropicana paid me. But because of Hughes Norton, everybody knows, everybody knows. There are people who resent that. It's just human nature.'

'Do you?' Azinger was asked.

'I don't resent it. I think it's great. Now if I play good, it drives my market value up. I love it. Honest to God I don't begrudge anybody anything. It's not for me to determine Tiger Woods's market value. I don't know what Tiger Woods's market value is. Hughes Norton knows what it is. He pulled it off. IMG pulled it off. Those are great numbers. I wished I was gettin' them, but I didn't win three straight U.S. Amateurs and turn pro at the age of 20. I just think that he might have been better served had those numbers not been disclosed.'

'Have you talked to him?'

'I haven't talked to him. Everybody really likes Tiger out here. He's an incredibly likeable kid. The withdraw thing [in Georgia] there were a couple of articles I read that suggested, "Hey man, you've got a tremendous smile and a great personality, and if you have to do it, you do it. Don't let somebody write a withdrawal letter, an excuse for you. I think Larry Guest wrote one of the stories, and the other one was Furman Bisher (in the *Atlanta Constitution-Journal*).'

'Is what he did that big a deal, where his agent says there isn't a player who hasn't done the same thing?'

'Well, at the same time there isn't a pro who can get $40 million from Nike either. He was going to be the main draw, plus there was the dinner. There were a lot of things that opened him up for some criticism. Hey man, I withdrew from the Canadian Open a couple of weeks ago and nobody said a word. No great loss. I withdrew on Monday morning. I was at home. I just never went.'

'Is there a difference between withdrawing Monday morning and Tuesday night in protocol?'

'Generally nobody notices. If John Daly would have done it, it would have been a big flap. If Tiger Woods does it, it's a flap. If Fred Couples does it, I don't think there's a flap, maybe I'm wrong. I don't think there's any doubt that Tiger Woods is the No. 1 draw right now on this tour, and the fact that it happened opened him up to criticism, and the way it was handled. Again, I think Hughes should have been a better counselor and advisor to Tiger Woods. He's only 20, man.'

'Stuff you had to learn like that at 20?'

'Hey man, I never had to pay income taxes the first four years I tried to turn pro. I lived in a motor home for three years. Nobody knew who I was. I got big gradually, and I wasn't that big. I was never a giant draw . . . nobody has been on this level since John Daly was and still is. He was a giant in this game. He'd walk down the fairway and you could tell it was his group because there would be masses of people following him. Now they're following Tiger Woods. I think what ought to be written is a story about how for so long there were no superstars out here, and where was golf going? Now, Greg Norman's here, Fred Couples is here, John Daly is here, Tiger Woods is here.'

Burns read a quote off his notebook from Payne Stewart's news conference, where Stewart said that he wasn't jealous because Tiger Woods had put golf on the front pages of the sports sections during the baseball playoffs and football season.

'That's a great line,' Azinger said. 'I think for the most part everybody likes Tiger Woods. He's just a nice, likeable guy. The guys not even legal for crying out loud. He can't even gamble in the casino. He's got to have people around him.'

'Do you think if he turned around and went to the dinner last week, this would have a totally different spin?'

'Definitely . . . That's all he had to do. In hindsight I think he probably wished he withdrew from the pro-am and played in the tournament, but obviously he needed to play here, this is the big-money tournament. I think he just realized once he got his card that he just didn't need to play there and it was a perfect place for a week off. Unfortunately he showed up and the dinner was planned and all that happened. It was one of those things where somebody should have said, "Hey look. If you withdraw Tiger, it's going to be a big deal. Think about it." It's one of those things where maybe the agent should have said, "I'm not going to withdraw for you. I'm not going to write the letter to the tournament." If Tiger handled it himself, maybe it would have gone over better. But the fact it didn't happen that way opened him up to criticism. Eventually people are going to forget about it, but it's a good story right now. He's twenty years old, and he's going to be out here for another thirty years before he goes to the Senior Tour. This is absolutely nothing. The kid withdrew from a tournament. It should have been handled differently, but it's not a big deal. I wouldn't blame Tiger Woods. I would blame his agent. That's what I'd do.'

Friday at the Desert Inn, Woods again started hot. Five under through six holes, with an eagle and three birdies, the putts stopped falling and he cooled off. In a 27-hole stretch beginning

Thursday at Summerlin, he had gone 15-under par, but instead of taking it deeper, Tiger backed off. At the 15th, a par 5, he hit a long iron approach to the green from an awkward stance, and reinjured the groin pull that dogged him at the Amateur. From there, Tiger literally limped in, three-putting the 15th for par, missing a little birdie putt at the 16th, making bogey at the 17th, and saving par at the 18th with a gutsy iron shot from a fairway sand trap. He blew off all interviews after the round to get treatment. There was speculation that he might WD.

Tiger kept everybody hanging until he came back out Saturday and shot 67. Seeing Woods gimp up the 18th fairway, Rude said, 'Look at him. Venturi. Congressional. Sixty four.' A closing par and Woods was at 268, four shots off the lead, tied for seventh place. From the gridlock at 83rd on Wednesday, he had climbed 76 places on the leaderboard. He had six more places to go. A big line formed at the autograph tent. Woods took a glance and turned away. He had to get treatment in the locker room. The MGM stretch limo was waiting outside the clubhouse. Yeah, this beat Quad City and B.C.

Sunday was the stuff that makes for legends. Tiger turned in 32, made birdies at 11, 13, and 14, drove it over the 15th green (317 yards away) with a 3-wood, made par, then hit driver-6-iron into the 560-yard 16th to shoot 64. It was a high voltage madhouse. Behind the 17th tee, Greg Suttles of Las Vegas screamed out, 'LETS GO MR WOODS SHOW EM WHAT YOU GOT! ITS ALL YUUUUUU' Mr. Suttles was one of the many African-American men and women who traipsed around Summerlin to check this Woods kid out. 'Ask Robert Gamez, "What does he think of my man now?"' Suttles said.

Big Al Ramsey was head of the security force escorting Woods around the course. 'He's way cool, man,' Ramsey said. 'I was at his news conference and the media tried to bait him, get him to react to what some of those old pros were sayin' back east. He told' em, "Man, I know those guys. They don't mean it."'

Standing in the 18th fairway, describing the shot for ESPN, Frank Beard whispered in his hand-held microphone, 'The pin's back left. The water's left. But nothing seems to bother him. He doesn't know what water and sand is. He certainly doesn't know what fear is.'

Tiger Woods hit 2-iron, 9-iron into the 18th green on a 444-yard par-4, two-putted for par, and went to the practice tee anticipating a playoff. Love, Mark Calcavecchia and Kelly Gibson were behind him with a chance to tie. Tiger came off the 18th green and Butch was there to tell him, 'This isn't over yet,' but Woods knew that already. ESPN asked for an interview. He declined. Beard, the on-course commentator, tried again on the practice range. Woods politely said no. 'He said he absolutely would not do it,' Beard said. 'He's a cocky bastard.'

Tiger hit balls. He had a 3-wood, because he knew it was the club he'd use in the playoff – f there was a playoff. 'The Girl From Ipanema' was playing in the Hard Rock tent. The blimp's motors could be heard overhead. The sound of Tiger's shots, one every 45 seconds, interrupted the background music.

'Can we get a report on what's happening out there?' said Fluff.

'If there's a playoff, do you know what hole it starts on?' said Butch.

Michael Carey, operations coordinator, listened to his walkie-talkie. 'Davis just birdied 16 to tie.'

Frank Cavanaugh of the PGA Tour's field staff drove up in a golf cart. The sudden death playoff would be holes 18, 17 and 18 again, if needed. 'All right,' he said, 'we'll see you on 18.'

It was 3: 54 p.m.

'Calcavecchia and Gibson had to finish by now,' said Fluff.

'I didn't hear any roars,' said Butch.

Lee Patterson, the tour's media official, came out from the press tent.

'Where's Davis?' said Tiger.

'It looks like about 8 feet,' said Patterson.

'Hell of a shot,' said Butch.

'It's a hell of a shot with that water there,' said Tiger.

Thirty seconds pass.

'Do you know if he made it yet?' Tiger said.

Mike Shea's voice can be heard on Patterson's walkie-talkie.

'Rolling . . . rolling . . . rolling . . .' Pause

'Nooooooo.'

Pause

'It looked like it broke right.'

Tiger: 'It does.'

He just had that putt.

'I tell you what,' says Fluff, 'that's one putt I'll never misread again.'

Four p.m.

'The swing feels good,' says Tiger.

Fluff is cupping a cigarette.

'The Girl from Ipanema' is playing. The blimp is circling.

'What shot do you think I should play?' Tiger says to Butch.

He hits a cut. He hits a draw.

'Beautiful,' says Butch.

'Any updates?' says Fluff.

'Yeah,' says Carey. 'They went off the air.'

At 7 p.m. Eastern (4 p.m. Pacific, where the tournament was) ESPN cut to its NFL Primetime show. They would come back for live updates. Love hit his drive at 18 left center of the fairway.

Would this be where Tiger Woods won his first tournament, hitting balls on the range at Summerlin, 'The Girl From Ipanema' playing, Fluff puffing and Butchie trying to act cool, calm and collected?

Mike Shea is on the walkie-talkie again, describing Love's second shot into 18:

'Coming in long and right . . . He's got a 30 footer.'

Tiger pulled a banana out of his bag. Potassium for energy. It is now 4: 10 p.m. He heads to the putting green, and can hear the moans as Love misses.

He is very cool. He is smiling. The P. A. system crackles: 'Test. Test. Has everybody had a good time so far?' There's a big roar. He heads to a golf cart, and rides out to the 18th tee.

It is 4: 20, and real quiet. Tiger is waiting for Davis.

'Great playing, Tiger.'

'You, too, stud.'

'I haven't seen you all week. I've seen Butch, but not you.'

'I've been here.'

Love and Woods both use Titleist Professionals, 90 compression. From their short practice round at Callaway Gardens, Love remembered that Tiger used No. 4s. He had No. 3s.

Mike Shea had them draw lots from his hat. Davis won. He had honors.

'Any time you're ready,' said Shea.

'Play well,' said Love.

'All right,' said Woods. 'Good luck.'

His hand seemed to be shaking, just a little.

Davis had his wooden driver. He roped a low cut. 'Good shot,' said his brother Mark, who was carrying his bag. 'Good one.'

4: 24 p.m., Tiger takes 3-wood, rips it right next to Davis's ball.

Walking down the fairway, somebody outside the gallery ropes yells, 'JUST LIKE THE AMATEURS TIGER! YOU OWN THIS!'

It is 4: 30 in Las Vegas, 7: 30 at ESPN's studios in Bristol, Connecticut, They've cut into the highlights show for Tiger. That's how big this was. Bigger than the NFL. Bigger than Berman.

Tiger did own it. He owned the playoff and he owned Love. It seemed like he owned everything there was to own that day. He was Mr. Woods. The Man. The cheers went up when Love missed his par putt. 'tii gerr . . . tii gerr' Inside the mind of that 20-year-old, mixed with the excitement, was the sense that this would happen. He was not surprised. He would wait a couple of weeks, and tell people that he expected to win one of these seven tournaments.

Back in Cypress, he knew Earl was sitting in front of the TV, with Joey and Penny, probably crying. He did the news conference and the trip to the volunteer tent. Outside the clubhouse, Tida was holding court. 'I hope this win will tell a lot of people that he is the real one,' she said. 'Every time the curtain is up, he's right there. Encore every time.'

The stretch limo was waiting. He had done enough signing and hand shaking. He compressed his body into the back seat, and rode back into Las Vegas. He rode the private elevator up to the MGM penthouse and looked out over the city. Earl was right again. Something like this had to happen in Las Vegas. As Larry Dorman wrote in the *Times* this is the city where there are no sure things, no can't miss propositions. He had chosen, as Dorman wrote, 'the perfect time and place to lay waste to conventional wisdom. He is a sure thing. He is a can't miss.'

Tiger Woods showered and changed clothes, then rode that private elevator down to dinner at a private room Tutera had reserved. Tida was there, so were Butch and Jay and Bryon Bell and Jerry Chang. Everybody made a little speech and they drank Dom Perignon to toast the winner of the 1996 Las Vegas Invitational, the richest college drop-out in America: Tiger Woods.

He ordered a big, fat, juicy pepper steak, this kid who earlier in the week had to borrow $20 from his mother so he could go to McDonald's. The waiters brought out the covered, sterling silver dishes. Tiger was famished. At the count of three, the waiters pulled the lids off the plates. Sitting in front of Tiger were two McDonald's cheeseburgers.

## Eleven

# TIGGER IN THE MAGIC KINGDOM

A the win in Las Vegas, and a third-place finish at the Texas Open, Woods had a new goal. With one more victory, he could qualify for the season-ending Tour Championship, a $3 million event with a $540,000 payoff for first place. He moved to 40th on the money list after Las Vegas, and 34th after Texas. Best of all, he was heading home to Orlando, for a week at Isleworth, and the Disney World/Oldsmobile Classic. The Magic were in town. Maybe it didn't feel like home yet, but it was home.

There was also a better vibe working as a result of a new Nike commercial that debuted in late October. Instead of going in your face, Woods was now portrayed in home movies, saying as a child, 'I want to win all the big tournaments, the major ones, and I hope to play well when I'm older and beat all the pros.'

At Nike headquarters, the company line was the 'Hello World' commercial wasn't pulled because of the backlash to it, or because David Fay, the USGA executive director, had pointed out that the shirt Woods wore in that ad was from Lochinvar, the all-men's club in Houston. 'I think they're both great for their own different reasons,' Woods said.

This didn't come up in Tuesday's news conference at Walt Disney World, but once again the race issue did because every week it was a new tournament, a new group of writers and a new set of TV people. 'Golf has been such an elitist sport, and – I hate to say it – a white-dominated sport for so long that people have been afraid of bringing this issue up,' Woods said. 'They thought the Shoal Creek incident solved everything. That's wrong. Unfortunately minorities are not allowed to play certain clubs, or are allowed to be members. So people of certain religious beliefs are not allowed to join clubs, as well as females. I'm not usually that blunt, but it's something that needed to be said.'

By now he had it on auto-pilot, but since this was a hometown gig, Tiger showed up 20 minutes early and spent nearly 40 minutes holding forth. Then, when it was over, it was over. There was no hanging around with the writers, no one-on-ones with radio or TV. That's just the way he works it. Everybody gets the same quotes. Only a chosen few get privileged time.

The format of the National Car Rental Classic at Walt Disney World, like Vegas, is a pro-am. For some reason, playing with a bunch of chops doesn't seem to bother Tiger. While they're slashing, he does his own thing. They meet on the green, Tiger maybe reads a putt, and then the amateur gets out of the way. He knows what to say, how to say it, and when to concentrate. It's an amazing ability. Butch thinks it's part of his Buddhist upbringing. Part of a discipline. It also helped to work with a sports psychologist since age 13.

At Disney, Tiger was without Butch. The coach had to go home and take care of the members at Lochinvar, but they communicated on the phone. Earl was with him, but didn't hang around the golf tournament much. He spent most of the time back at the Isleworth villa, resting. He wasn't feeling well.

Tiger kept both of them feeling young, especially Butch, who's 53 and a Vietnam vet. He calls his coach 'old man,' and teases him constantly about his age and his putting stroke – 'It's so ugly, but you make everything!' Butch gets his shots in, however. The Monday after Vegas, they went shopping at a mall in San Antonio. Butch wanted Tiger to get some new clothes – 'You can't wear Nike 24 hours a day' – and to spend some of the $297,000 he won at Summerlin. When it came time to pay the bill, Tiger handed the salesperson a credit card. It didn't go through the computer. No problem. Tiger whipped out another card. That didn't go through the computer, either.

'Well, you activated them, didn't you?' Harmon said.

'What's that?' said Tiger.

Shaking his head, Harmon reached for his wallet.

'That just shows he's a kid,' he said.

Butch may have developed into Tiger's best friend. But when he's out on the road, playing tour golf, there's nobody around Tiger's age that he can relate to. His two pals, Bryon from high school and Jerry from Stanford, are both in med school. He likes to listen to Montell Jordan, the new young king of the hip-hop scene. There's not many guys in pro golf who listen to Montell Jordan other than Don Wallace, a former Southwest Louisiana quarterback who works as general manager of the PGA Tour's Scoreboard/Tournament Operations Department. Don and Tiger like to joke about getting mistaken for each other, since they're about the only black faces around other than McDaniel, when he's covering the tour for *Golf World* and the caddies. At Stanford, there were a lot of people hip to Montell Jordan. You say that name out on the PGA Tour, and most people will probably think you're taking about Montel Williams, the talk-show host.

At least when he was home, he could hang around with his new neighbor, Ken Griffey Jr., and eventually he would get to know Penny Hardaway, since he lives at Isleworth, too. But early on, there was no denying the cultural and the age gap that existed for Tiger Woods.

'What I miss is going to a buddy's house or a dorm at 11 at night and just hanging out,' Tiger said. 'Those are the good times, when you shoot the bull and you find out a lot about yourself. That part I do miss.'

The Disney people were just ecstatic about having Tiger in their field. Tournament Director Michael McPhillips had been in communication with Hughes Norton ever since Tiger turned pro. At one point, he sent a set of Tigger head covers to IMG, just in case Tiger needed a spare, and one day, McPhillips called Norton from his car phone, saying he was driving around Orlando with six strawberry milk shakes from McDonalds, and was there a neutral drop point near Tiger's home.

'You're doing your homework,' Norton said.

At the Southern Open, Tiger said he wasn't going to play Disney, which triggered the hosts of one Orlando all-sports station to rip him pretty good. The essence of it was: First Shaquille O'Neal leaves and now this kid moves in. We don't need either one of them.

But McPhillips was always hopeful. He had established back-gate security gate clearance for Woods, which would cut 15 minutes off his drive time from Isleworth. He had a newspaper ad prepared, just in case, with a Tiger's head and a GUESS WHO'S COMING headline. When Tiger finally did commit on the Friday of San Antonio, McPhillips was going into a staff meeting by the swimming pool at Shadows on the Green. Trying their best to put on disappointed faces, McPhillips and Disney Golf Director Steve Wilson made it seem like Tiger wasn't playing. 'Of course you know Michael made a promise,' Wilson said, and with that, McPhillips took off his Foot-Joys and jumped into the swimming pool. 'Disney is a place where dreams come true,' McPhillips said. 'And fortunately mine did.'

A whole new operational plan had to be set in motion. Buses were added to the tram transportation. The number of Port-o-Lets was doubled. Bleachers were put up behind the Magnolia range. More pairing sheets were printed. A detail of four marshals, two security guards, and two undercover officers were assembled. A welcoming committee met Tiger's plane at Orlando Airport on Sunday night with a courtesy car. And McPhillips had special maps drawn up, showing the courses and also where all the McDonald's were located between Disney and Isleworth.

The Tiger story kept getting bigger, and the press room reflected it. Normally Disney gets a sparse media turnout, but this looked like a Doral press room, with Larry Dorman there from *The New York Times* Dave Sheinin of the *Miami Herald* John Feinstein of *Golf Magazine* and Rick Reilly of *Sports Illustrated* joining the usual suspects who normally cover Disney. Reilly flew in from Mark Mulvoy's retirement roast in New York, possibly to write a cover story. Tiger had yet to make an SI cover. His three Amateur victories came on the week of the *NFL Preview issue*. If he won, he'd be on the front of 3.5 million magazines. He did make the covers of *Golf* and *Golf Digest*, the two largest golf publications in the United States. And once again, the big winner on the TV side was the Golf Channel, which had also broadcast Quad City, B.C. and Texas.

Tiger had his usual slow start on Thursday, shooting 69 on the Palm Course. It was a round that started with a bang, as the first fairway was lined four-and five-people deep from tee to green, a sight Wilson thought he'd never see at Disney. 'Tiger hit that first drive so far, I said, "He's probably going to have to take a drop in [the] Chip 'n' Dale [parking lot]," ' Wilson said. 'The ball went forever.' The round seemed to last that long, too, and Tiger double bogeyed the last hole to shoot 69. That put him in a tie for 59th place, which was 24 spots better than Vegas but still back in the pack.

Friday's round at Lake Buena Vista changed that in a hurry. Tiger lit it up with a 63 that put him two shots off the lead. It can happen in a hurry with Tiger, and once again, it did. Tiger said he wasn't that sharp, but he made a couple of snakes and seemed a little disappointed coming off the course. The reason was the bogey he made at the 105-yard seventh hole, his 16th. 'I had too much speed at the bottom (of the swing),' he said. 'And it was downwind, too. I just hit a bad shot.'

There were so many people at LBV that alternate parking had to be opened at Planet Hollywood. Tiger spent five minutes in the autograph tent, headed home, and went to the Magic game that night with Griffey. 'It's pretty phenomenal,' Fluff Cowan said. 'Not many people even realize what a strain playing this many weeks in a row is on a guy, and that's coming off a U.S. Amateur victory. The U.S. Amateur is like playing two golf tournaments in one week. He's been on an incredible stretch, and he's still pretty sharp. His disposition has been pretty good. His disposition is a large part of what allows him to do the things he does.'

Woods played that day with Steve Szabo, a psychiatrist from Tampa, who described Tiger as having 'an innate goodness about him,' and 'a young man any family would take pride in.'

Szabo's son, Doug, was caddying. 'Between nine and 10, at the turn, he said, "Can you imagine I'm 20 years old. I wake up every day and get to do the thing I like to do most. This is my work now," ' Doug Szabo said. 'I think it's a very telling thing. He still likes coming out knowing everybody expects a lot of him.'

A 69 on Saturday put Woods in a four-way tie for fifth, one shot out of the lead. He three-putted the 18th to lose a piece of the lead, but didn't seem frosted about it. It was a day of almosts, and he was fighting the onset of the flu. One thing that made him feel good was the size and makeup of the gallery. 'I think it's great, because look at all the kids out there right now, out there following,' he said. 'That's our future, and the game's future. They're out there walking with a person they can relate to, me being so young. They can relate to me as a person rather than say a Jack Nicklaus. The age difference is what draws a lot of kids, and I think it's beautiful. It's also nice seeing . . . how can I phrase this nicely? . . . I guess more minorities in the gallery.

That's also where the future is heading. That's where the game will go, and where I think it will go.'

And no, he did not miss Stanford. It was the 19th of October. Midterms. Tiger is more a guy for finals. As in final rounds.

Sunday he came out wearing red, and red on a golf scoreboard denotes birdies and eagles. He cranked it up by making five straight 3s, starting on the third hole, shot 32 outbound, three-putted three times in the final 10 holes, and still won. He did this paired in the final round with Payne Stewart, who has two major championships on his resume. And he did it with a head that felt like it was going to explode.

'If I felt like this at Stanford, I never would have left that bed,' he said. 'I got up this morning stuffy, and unfortunately I had to come out here and play. But the good thing is you have to watch out for the sick golfer. For some reason some of the guys play their best rounds when they're sick. Just don't put a needle to my head. It may burst. I can't really hear. I'm so clogged. My throat's not doing good. I've got no energy. I'm dizzy. Other than that, I'm great.'

Again, Tiger drew a zoo – literally. He had eagled the fourth and birdied the fifth to tie Nolan Henke at five under. The crowd was jostling ahead, trying to get better vantage points, when a mass of people cut through the woods between this sixth and seventh holes. This intrusion scared a deer, who attempted an escape through a wetland area. This fired up an alligator, which started chasing the deer and snapping its jaws. The deer escaped but found itself in the seventh fairway, surrounded by 5,000 people. The poor creature must not have known what was worse: the gator, or the Tiger's faithful. Scared out of its mind, the doe fertilized the grass, turned and ran (away from the alligator this time) to safety. Tiger didn't notice the disturbance. He birdied the seventh and eighth holes to take the lead.

The final postscript to this bizarre day involved Taylor Smith, who was told at the turn that his putter grip did not conform to the rules of golf. He asked to play on, pending a meeting with the PGA Tour Rules Committee, and birdied the 72nd hole for what the gallery thought was a tie. That took a little of the joy out of Tiger, who sat in the locker room, his feet up on a bench, his head in his hands, waiting for Smith to finish.

Reilly was in there with him, trying to get a little different quote.

'Oh well. Another win. Some Nyquil. Call it a week,' he said.

Woods didn't say a word until it was time for the trophy presentation, and the news conference, and then back in the locker room again, he sat wordlessly as Reilly tried again.

'So,' Rick said. 'If you weren't sick, how do you think you would have done healthy?'

Again, nothing. Reilly had written an SI bonus piece on Woods in 1995, a real positive story. He talked to him on the phone Saturday night. And Tiger's giving him zero. He got up, headed out the door, leaving Rick there with his pad.

As sick and as drained as he was, Tiger wanted to spend time in the autograph tent. He had blown everybody off all day, and figured he owed it to the tournament. So McPhillips got a cart and the security force got him to the tent and the line formed back toward the 18th green, as long as a full lob wedge shot. Tiger signed. And he signed. And he smiled. And he made eye contact. And he mixed. Earlier in the day, behind the fourth tee, somebody had yelled 'Forget about Shaq. We got Tiger!' Lesley Baker Jr. said, 'What Shaq did for basketball, he's going to do for golf in Orlando. It's a white-dominated sport. That's not disputable. But Tiger's bridging the gap. We're going into the 21st century.' Dr. Bob Sims, a close friend of Earl Woods and the man who hosted the Woods family at his home during the 1996 U.S. Open, said, 'The whole achievement is not surprising, but it is amazing.' Carolyn McCorvey drove over from Merritt Island with her six-year-old son, who is taking up the game. 'They used to say golf was boring,' she said. 'But not with all the money this young man is making.'

So Tiger signed and signed and signed. For a good, solid 25 minutes he signed. And then, as if a clock went off in his head, he got up, put on the blinders, stopped making eye contact, and walked to his courtesy car in the parking lot. Ten more minutes and he would have signed everything. Arnie would have stayed. Jack would have stayed. Tiger should have stayed. But he's only 20, and he was feeling terrible to begin with. At least he sucked it up and made the effort. Twenty-five minutes is better than nothing. A lot of people went home happy. The other ones are going to learn. They have to get in line earlier next time.

Tiger went back to his villa with the rented furniture, too sick to celebrate.

# Twelve

# TULSA TIME

Money was no longer a problem to Tiger Woods. By winning at Disney, he was in the Tour Championship and other perks were now starting to come his way. The Skins Game offered him an invitation to play on Thanksgiving weekend, and the Australian Open paid him a reported $300,000 appearance fee. The Nike and Titleist contracts were just paper money for Woods. This was the real stuff, including the $100 bonuses they paid for birdies in the Tuesday shootouts. He was still very much the Stanford kid, a little green when it came to all that green being stockpiled in his IMG account.

Southern Hills CC in Tulsa was hosting the Tour Championship. When Woods arrived, he was given the keys to a four-door Mercedes Benz courtesy car, compliments of the PGA Tour.

'Wow!' Woods said. 'A Mercedes! I've never been in one!'

'Well, why don't you go buy one?' said Butch Harmon.

'No way!' said Tiger. 'Do you know how much this thing costs?'

Here's a kid with all the money in the world at his disposal, and he was worrying about how much something costs. He was like Arnold Palmer in that respect. Arnold carries around a wad of $100 bills, wrapped tightly in a rubber band. Tiger, according to his friends, is just as tight with his fortune.

He could buy four Rolex watches, but he was wearing the one Disney gave him with Mickey Mouse on the dial. He may order pepper steak on special occasions but he was still partial to fast food, not the fast lane.

After practice on Wednesday, for example, Butch asked Tiger if he wanted to grab some lunch. So they jumped in the Mercedes, and Butch was expecting a nice restaurant, an Outback at least.

Tiger pulled into a Taco Bell.

Butch was in the passenger seat, and Tiger was blasting Montell on the CD player, signing autographs through the drive-in window.

'The hardest part,' Harmon says, 'is listening to that Gawd-awful music he listens to.'

They are in Tulsa now. They started this Magical Mystery Tour in Portland on August 20. Tiger had zigzagged to Milwaukee, Toronto, Quad City, Binghamton, Columbus, (Ga.), Las Vegas, San Antonio and Orlando before this final stop. The original goal was to avoid a trip to Tour School. Then it was to win. Then, maybe, there was the Tour Championship. Now they were here. Southern Hills. The top 30 money winners on the PGA Tour. Tiger Woods did it in seven tournaments. Seven. His tight man, Woody Austin, was grinding all year, playing so many tournaments straight down the stretch that he was a zombie, trying to qualify for Tulsa. Woody played 36 events. He finished 32nd on the money list. Tiger played seven and was 24th going into the Tour Championship. He'd done in seven tournaments what everybody else had all year to do.

It seemed too easy. 'Let's not judge Tiger Woods now,' Mark O'Meara said Wednesday night on the putting green. 'Let's judge him when things aren't going his way, when he's not filled with confidence and enthusiasm. Sooner or later the physical and mental pressure will take its toll, and we'll see that Tiger Woods is indeed human. It may not happen this week, and it may not happen next week. But sooner or later it's going to happen and to me, that's when the true champion is born. Not out of victory. Out of struggling.' In Cleveland, IMG had turned down requests from *Newsweek*, *GQ*, *Fortune*, *People* and *Forbes*. Fan mail was coming in by the sackful, and it wasn't all 'Dear Tiger' stuff. One letter from a Generation X-er began, 'What up, fool?' The Boston Pops extended an invitation to read 'The Night Before Christmas.' Cindy Crawford even wrote, hinting that if Tiger did a deal with Omega watches, she might be available for the commercial shoot.

93

In the media center at Southern Hills, Denise Taylor had her hands full. When Tiger won at Disney, she was deluged with credential requests from *Newsweek, The Washington Post,* the *L.A. Times,* the *Orange County Register* and the *Baltimore Sun. ABC World News Tonight* and *Dateline NBC* had sent crews. 'I mean, it is unbelievable,' Taylor said.

Tiger did his usual thing. The Tuesday news conference. The practice rounds. And an even-par 70 in the opening round, which put him four strokes off the lead held by Tom Lehman and Vijay Singh. He was set up for another top 10 finish. And then, as O'Meara prophesized, adversity came calling.

At approximately 2:51 Friday morning, October 25, Earl Woods was admitted to the Trauma Emergency Center at St. Francis Hospital in Tulsa, complaining of chest pains. Luckily, St. Francis was across the street from the Doubletree, where Tiger and his family were staying. Tiger was up all night. He had a 12:49 tee time. After three hours of sleep, the old Green Beret wished his son luck and told him he'd be watching on TV. Tiger's body went to Southern Hills, but his head and heart were back at St. Francis Hospital. He parred the first, double bogeyed the second, and then went bogey-bogey-bogey-bogey-par-bogey.

Nobody seemed to know what was wrong. There was a press release issued in the media center and Brent Musburger reported it on ESPN, but to the spectators and to playing partner John Cook, it was a mystery.

Going to the 10th hole, Woods mentioned to Cook, 'I just want to get done and go see my dad.' Cook didn't probe and didn't know what that meant, but Tida showed up and that seemed to change Tiger's spirits. He shot even-par 35 on the back for a 78. It was definitely the gutsiest round of golf Tiger Woods had ever played.

'He showed me a lot today and it wasn't golf,' Cook said. 'You can lose your mind out here, and he didn't. He didn't have his head down and sulk. He just tried to fight through it. To hold his demeanor like he did was more impressive to me than some of the drives he tried to hit. In a situation like that, you could stomp off and complain, moan and act like a twenty-year-old but he didn't do that. He tried to make the best of a difficult day.'

Woods didn't spend much time with reporters. The hard part was not knowing if Earl had a heart problem, or a bronchial problem. He still smoked his Merits, and had had bypass surgery

10 years ago. He was 64 now, and slightly overweight. 'There are more important things in life than golf,' he said. 'I love my dad to death, and I'm going to see him right now.'

According to *Golf World* tests revealed some blockage in the coronary arteries and a mild case of pneumonia. Tiger shot 72 and 68 (with a triple bogey) to finish tied for 21st and break his streak of top-five finishes. He ended the season ranked 24th on the money list with $790, 594. His average of $98, 824 per event was best on Tour, better even than Lehman's average when he set the all-time single season earnings record of $1. 78 million.

This chapter was over. Ten weeks. Three wins. The Nike and Titleist contracts. All that money. All those memories, and the three sweetest moments were embracing his father's hand and looking in his eyes on the announcement day at Milwaukee, hugging Tida after Las Vegas and hugging Earl after Disney.

Earl Woods was discharged on Tuesday, and said 'I'll take it easy for about a week, and then get back into my regular schedule.'

## Thirteen

# STAKING A CLAIM

Tom Lehman could see this coming. In 1996, he had won the British Open, the Tour Championship, was the PGA Tour's leading money winner and its Vardon Trophy winner. Yet he had a feeling it wouldn't last for long. After 54 holes of the season-opening Mercedes Championship at the La Costa Resort & Spa in Carlsbad, California, he was tied for the lead with Tiger Woods, who had birdied the last four holes to shoot 65. It took a 30-foot birdie putt by Lehman at the 18th hole Saturday just to pull even, and now they were preparing for a one-hole playoff on a wet Sunday in Southern California to decide it. 'Tiger's performance has got everyone feeling they have to improve or get left behind,' Lehman said.

In Tiger's first two PGA Tour victories, he had beaten Davis Love III in Las Vegas and Payne Stewart at Walt Disney World. Taking on the Player of the Year was just another way to test himself. Instead of being intimidated by the competition, Woods seemed to be thriving on it.

Tiger's run to close out the third round was highlighted by the two shots he hit to reach the 569-yard 17th. In tournament history, only Dewitt Weaver in 1971 had reached that green in two. Around LaCosta, they call this hole The Monster. Tiger whipcracked his 3-wood on the green, and two putted. Tom Lehman, with his thick chest and forearms, had to lay up. Anticipating an 18-hole showdown on Sunday, Lehman admitted, 'If I go out and lose, I'm going to know there's a new kid on the block who's just way better than everybody else. Tom Lehman is player of the year, but Tiger Woods is probably the player of the next two decades. I'm not sure if I feel like the underdog or what, but it's a unique situation. It's almost like trying to hold off the inevitable, like bailing water out of a sinking boat.'

Little did Lehman know how appropriate that metaphor would be on Sunday. With the Bob Hope Chrysler Classic schedule to start on Wednesday in Palm Springs, and with a poor weather forecast for Monday and Tuesday, PGA Tour Commissioner Tim Finchem reluctantly made the call to shorten the Mercedes to a 54-hole event. Only one hole, the seventh, was playable. They would go back and forth on that par three for as long as it took to determine a champion.

Lehman drew the honors. Because the ground was wet, he teed the ball up higher than usual. 'Usually the [sudden death] playoff comes after you've played 18 holes,' he said. 'You want to have some rhythm and some momentum going. My first thought was, "I'm hoping it's a good yardage." You don't want to be in between clubs on something like that. It was a normal six-iron for me, maybe a hard seven.'

With the rain coming down, Lehman took the six-iron, and figured the right-to-left wind would help his natural draw. His swing lacked the rhythm he was hoping for, and the ball came off the toe of the club, high on the face, and nose-dived in the pond. Lehman's broad shoulders slumped immediately, and his chin dropped deep into his chest.

Woods may have been shocked, but he showed no emotion. Instead, he took off his rain jacket, and revealed his bright red Sunday shirt, the color he wore at Vegas and Disney, the color that brings him power according to his mother, Tida. He visualized a high draw that would land right of the pin, away from the water. For most of the week, he had been struggling with his swing, but the extra time on the range allowed him to work it out.

'I was lucky in the fact that I lost the draw,' he said. 'If it was a clear and sunny day in Southern California, the advantage [in having the honor] would have been Tom's. I had no idea how much the wind was going to blow, but when I saw Tom's ball ride the wind, all I had to do was aim in the middle of the green. I still had to execute the shot.'

The shot disappeared in the clouds – Tiger even lost it for a second, because a raindrop hit him in the eye. When it came down and tore a hole next to the pin, the legend of Tiger Woods had once again been injected with magic. 'I overdrew it a little,' he would say.

Lehman went to the drop zone, and nearly holed out a wedge for par, but it wouldn't have mattered. Tiger was in pick-it-up range, just six inches from birdie-two and his third win on the PGA Tour. When he tapped the ball in, that made his winning percentage. 333. It also covered Lehman, who before the tournament noted that Tiger will eventually become one of the best ever, but he still had some earning to do when it came to respect among his peers.

'You have to take your hat off to the guy who hits it stiff when the other guy is basically in the pocket,' Lehman said. 'It was one of those deals where you're either totally overjoyed or really bummed out.'

## Fourteen

# ACE IN THE HOLE

Even when he didn't win, Tiger Woods was the story of the week. He arrived in Phoenix after another controversy, this one involving the Bob Hope Chrysler Classic. It was the thought that Woods would play the Hope as a payback for their appearance on the Mike Douglas Show seventeen years ago. When Tiger took a pass, it hit the hot button of tournament director Mike Milthorpe. 'The biggest thing for me is, if I don't get him to play, all I'm going to hear is, "Why isn't he here?" He's worth a minimum of five thousand tickets a day," Milthorpe said. 'I'm watching a promotion on the Golf Channel [in November] for the Australian Open, and it's Norman versus The Kid. We could have a situation where this is a one-man tour.'

In many ways it had already become that. No Woods was already starting to mean no field. Feeling the heat, Milthorpe lashed out when he should have been more diplomatic. 'Everywhere I go, all people ask is, "Is Tiger coming?" ' he said. 'I hate it. He's bigger than Norman ever was. I certainly know that if Tiger doesn't come, the media isn't going to be talking about how we've got twenty of the top thirty players.'

On the week of the Bob Hope, Jeff Babineau of the *Orlando Sentinel* contacted Milthorpe. 'We wrote Tiger three times, called his father twice, called IMG twice [and] never got a return call or any kind of correspondence,' Milthorpe said. 'I don't mind him not playing. He can go play in Thailand for the rest of his life. I just think if Bob Hope . . . calls you up and asks you to play in his tournament, you say "yes." Mr. Hope is 93 years old and he has done an awful lot for the game of golf. He won't be around forever.'

The reason he said no to Bob Hope's personal request was that his schedule was basically full starting with the Phoenix Open, the third week of the season. He would play Phoenix and Pebble Beach back-to-back, then fly to Thailand for the Honda Asian Classic, and then on to Australia for the Australian Masters. In other words, he was going to Asia and Australia for two huge appearance fees, and 93-year-old Bob Hope would just have to wait. At least, that's the way it came across.

Hope wasn't the only one getting snubbed. Nelson Mandela wrote a personal letter to IMG, extending an invitation to Tiger to play in the South African Open. The conflict was with the Asian Classic in Thailand, which, to be fair, was his mother's homeland.

Although appearance fees are forbidden on the PGA Tour, there are certain incentives that tournaments can offer. The Phoenix Open had agreed to transport 1, 500 underprivileged youths to the TPC of Scottsdale for a clinic held on January 20, Martin Luther King Day. Milthorpe hinted that this was unethical, saying, 'I guess they've got some creative minds in Phoenix.' PGA Tour Commissioner Tim Finchem, doing his best to keep everybody happy, addressed the controversy at the Mercedes Championships.

'Any time you have a player at his level, the tournaments he doesn't play in are disappointed,' Finchem said. 'There's nothing we can do about that. We're encouraged that Tiger has said he'll make an attempt to spread his schedule around. This is not something that is even close to constituting an appearance fee. A lot of tournaments have already asked us what we can do to make Tiger come.'

For almost three days, Tiger was relatively quiet at the TPC of Scottsdale. His opening rounds of 68 and 68 put him 10 shots back of U.S. Open champion Steve Jones, who was on a 62 and 64 tear. Through 15 holes on Saturday, it was obvious that not even Tiger Woods could pull this tournament out, but that didn't mean he couldn't steal a little of Jones's story.

The 16th at Scottsdale is a par-three of 155 yards that was designed by Tom Weiskopf and Jay Morrish inside a grass amphitheater that can hold an estimated 25,000 golf fans. From Friday afternoon through the weekend, it is a giant outdoor party. In *Sports Illustrated* Rick Reilly described it as a giant mosh pit of a par-three, a 'Golfapalooza' and 'Woods-stock.' The locals call it Sun Devil Hill because of the Arizona State students who make it their weekend frat house. Tiger kind of liked the atmosphere. 'I think it's neat,' he said. 'It's untraditional. You don't have these people with handcuffs and mittens on.'

Coming off the 15th green, Tiger told Fluff Cowan, 'Maybe I should run up through there like it's a tunnel at a football game and explode onto the tee box and high-five everybody.' The crowd quieted for only a moment, and Woods nearly backed off in the buzz. All those years of his father's basic training taught him to block it all out and concentrate. He had a 9-iron, and the visualization of a high soft cut. As soon as the ball came off the clubface, there was an eruption, and when the ball hit three feet short of the cup, bounced twice, and disappeared in the hole, the sonic boom could be heard in Tucson. 'Had to be an ace. Had to be Tiger,' Nick Price said back at the clubhouse. It was called the loudest noise in golf history.

On the tee, Woods high-fived Cowan and his playing partner Omar Uresti. Beer cups, programs, cans, baseball caps and cigars rained down, as everybody's arms went up in a touchdown salute. 'Right afterward, I don't really remember anything,' Woods said. 'It was amazing. People were just going crazy. It was ridiculous how loud it was.'

Walking down to the green, Woods gave his 'raise the roof' gesture, plucked the ball from the hole, and threw it to the crowd. It was his second hole-in-one in ten professional tournaments, and although he finished tied for 18th on Super Bowl Sunday, once again, Tiger Woods had stolen the stage.

## Fifteen

# STAR POWER

By the time he reached Pebble Beach for the AT & T National Pro-Am, Tiger Woods had become as big as Kevin Costner. He realized this getting his hair cut at the Pebble Beach Salon one night before the tournament. Peering in from outside the window were guests from The Lodge. A woman in her sixties came in after Tiger left and asked for a lock of the phenom's hair. It was starting to become crazy.

Woods was originally scheduled to play with his father, but Earl's heart condition prevented that. Replacing Earl in Tiger's group was Costner, star of *Tin Cup, Field of Dreams, Dances with Wolves* and *Bull Durham*. As a newly addicted golf junkie, Costner had picked up the game for *Tin Cup*, and was trained by Peter Kostis and Gary McCord. For a beginner, he had some game.

The first two days of the tournament, at Poppy Hills and Spyglass, were chaotic. The PGA Tour's 'No Camera Rule' is not enforced at the AT & T Pebble Beach National Pro-Am, and spectators showed no respect for Steve Stricker, who played with Bryant Gumble in the Woods-Costner pairing. Gumble picked up on it. 'He's a magnet,' Gumble said of Woods. 'The only downside – and it's not his fault – s that I know it can be distracting to other golfers.' It took them six hours to get around, and Woods was frustrated with the swarming galleries. 'They have to realize we're out here trying to earn money,' Woods said.

'There were a lot of cameras clicking. I think it's great that people come out and it's fine if they take my photo, but not while we're swinging.'

When he was playing Poppy Hills, Lehman could hear the gallery screaming five miles away at Spyglass. 'I said, "Whoops, Costner must have made another 3-foot putt," ' Lehman said. Stricker wasn't nearly as amused. 'It was so disappointing,' he said. 'I might never come back here.'

The situation improved slightly at Pebble on Saturday, and Tiger responded by shooting 63 (Stricker shot 72 and missed the cut). He was still seven shots back of David Duval going into the final round, with Mark O'Meara trailing Duval by three. It had reached the point for O'Meara that he no longer attended Orlando Magic games with Tiger because of the accompanying circus. They fish together in O'Meara's bass boat, and play at Isleworth, but he has seen what it's like for Tiger in public and he wants no part of it. 'Everybody looks at him and sees his contracts and says he's a great player, a good-looking kid, all that,' O'Meara said. 'But it's got to be difficult. I don't think I'd want to trade places with Tiger Woods, to be honest.'

But O'Meara definitely wasn't going to back off when Tiger started chasing him on Sunday. 'I was jacked,' he said. 'Tiger's the hottest player in the game. We play a lot of golf together. He says to me, "I just love competition. All I want to do is win. Wouldn't it be great to go head-to-head sometime?" I say, "You may blow it by me by 50 yards and have a better swing, but I'm going to figure out a way to clip you." '

O'Meara and Woods didn't go head-to-head in the final pairing at Pebble Beach, but they were the ones slugging it out for the title. Playing one group ahead of O'Meara, Tiger birdied the 16th, 17th and 18th holes to shoot 64 and conclude a weekend run when he birdied 18 of the closing 36 holes. Tiger hit 7-iron over the flagstick at seventeen, a par-3 that juts out on a promontory by Stillwater Cove and Carmel Bay. In the 1972 U.S. Open, Jack Nicklaus hit 1-iron off the flagstick and in the 1987 Nabisco Championships playoff, Curtis Strange used 3-iron to stake the deciding shot. At the 548-yard 18th, Woods left himself 267 to the stick. Into the wind, and in thick ocean air, that shot was considered impossible. 'That's a long way, a long way,' said Jim Furyk, who was playing with O'Meara. 'I don't think reaching that green in two even entered anyone else's mind this week.'

Tiger had no choice. Behind him, he heard the roars when O'Meara chipped in for birdie at 16, and matched his birdie at 17. To win, he needed eagle.

Since they were playing the lift, clean and place rule, Tiger teed his ball up in the rough, and unleashed a nuclear 3-wood that left him 35 feet from the hole. Never mind that he missed the putt, it was a shot that they'll be talking about for a long time at Pebble Beach. 'I made a good run at it,' Woods said. 'But it was a little too late.'

It was still the story of the tournament, and while it made for great drama – many were calling it the best end to a PGA Tour event they had ever seen – t left Tiger mad at himself for making bogey at thirteen. That made that night's flight to Thailand seem even longer. 'I think it's great Mark won,' he said. 'I love him to death. But I'm disappointed. I should've been in a playoff.'

# Sixteen

# THE ROAD TO AUGUSTA

At 10 p.m. on Tuesday, February 4, 1997, Thai Airways Flight 771 taxied to the terminal at Don Muang Airport in Bangkok, Thailand. Inside the first class cabin, Tiger Woods was startled when the door opened and a TV news crew burst on board to air his arrival live. Queen Elizabeth and President Clinton had been accorded the same honor. Outside, 1,000 of his fans were there to greet him.

Around his neck and arms, hostesses draped traditional Thai garlands. He was met by his mother, Tida, who flew home two weeks early, and two dozen relatives and family friends. A banner was raised that said, 'Welcome Home, Tiger. We Are Happy To See You Back Again.' Riot police and armed militia held back the crowd. A police escort whisked Woods's entourage down a closed freeway to the Shangri-La Hotel on the banks of the Chao Phraya River. The entire twenty-fifth floor was reserved for the Woods party. One newspaper compared it to the arrival of Michael Jackson.

Woods did not disappoint them either in words or deeds. Playing sick with gastroenteritis, taking a helicopter back and forth to Thai Country Club, Woods shot 20-under to win the Asian Honda Classic and overwhelm a relatively weak field that included IMG clients Steve Elkington, Frank Nobilo and Curtis Strange. They were all paid appearance fees, but not as much as Tiger, who was still getting an estimated $300,000. Woods. 'Tiger is basically here for his mother,' said Alastair Johnston, the head of IMG's golf division. 'Yes, the appearance fee was big, but Tiger doesn't take deals just for money. The fact that this is his mother's country tipped the balance.'

Back in the United States, news of Tiger's victory received better play than O'Meara going back-to-back in California by winning the Buick Invitational right after Pebble Beach. Tiger would have preferred taking the first flight back to Los Angeles, but going halfway around the world for just one tournament didn't make sense, so the Asian Honda Classic was packaged with the Australian Masters at the Huntingdale Golf Club. He was quickly learning the demands of international travel, and the price golfers pay for taking appearance fees.

Tiger was in contention after opening rounds of 68 and 70, but ran out of gas on the weekend, shot 72 and 73, and finished tied for eighth, seven shots out of first. There were other, more important, issues on Tiger's mind. His father was scheduled for triple bypass at the UCLA Medical Center, and he was mentally preparing for that all the way home from Australia.

Earl went in for the operation on February 19, the week of the Tucson Chrysler Classic, and there were complications that forced doctors to operate again four days later. He wasn't released until Tiger was playing the Nissan Open in Los Angeles on Saturday, March 1. The travel and the stress of his father's situation were obvious at Riviera, where Tiger snapped at cameramen and was short with the media, many of whom had covered him as a junior.

At his Tuesday news conference, Tiger began to get a sense for what it was like to be a celebrity when an attractive woman from one of the tabloid news shows asked a question on his private life.

'Let me invade your privacy one more time,' she said. 'When you're relaxing, not playing . . . I mean, I know this is for you and it's your passion, but do you have a girlfriend? Do you go to the movies? Who are you as a person? We know you as a phenomenon.'

'Well,' Tiger said, trying to be polite, 'that's for my friends to know.'

Not taking the hint, she pressed on.

'No, tell us,' she said. 'We want to know. We want to know about you.'

Tiger wasn't about to tell her.

'As I said,' he said, 'that's for my friends to know.'

Once the tournament began, Tiger's goal was to play well enough so his father could watch him on television, but with the exception of a few shots, Tiger wasn't a big part the CBS broadcast. Overall, though, the match showed Tiger's maturity. He hung in and shot three-under 281 to finish tied for 20th, 'I'm happy with what I did considering everything that is going on,' Woods said. 'It was hard to get a real deep focus because I was thinking about more important things than a round of golf.'

The Doral-Ryder Open was dropped from Tiger's schedule and Tiger didn't play again until Bay Hill, the third week in March. He offered little at his Tuesday news conference, giving the same stock answers and saying – just as his father taught him – that the surgery was a success and his dad was recovering. Nobody would know until the Masters just how serious that second operation really was.

Tiger had picked up some bad habits playing in the wind overseas, and they weren't totally fixed at Bay Hill. Without his A game, the kid shot 68 in the opening round, and had the other players talking. 'I kind of get the impression that we're all chasing Tiger,' said Tom Lehman, the 1996 Player of the Year. 'I think that he's good for the game. I think that people are aware of the fact that there is a new kid on the block who is extremely talented. And they don't want to step aside.'

It was being called the Tiger Factor, and everybody was feeling it: young, old and middle aged. 'This guy wants to win, and he wants to win badly,' said Mark O'Meara. 'He's got that burning desire. He brings that element in there, and it's convincing more and more young players – shoot, every player – that when he has an opportunity to win, he'd better try to win. You only have so many chances.'

Billy Andrade told a story that occurred after Tiger made the hole-in-one on Saturday at the Phoenix Open. Tiger was 10 shots out of the lead going into the final round when he was approached by Robert Wrenn, a former Tour player working as an on-course reporter for ESPN. Wrenn asked Tiger if he was going to use the final round to work on certain aspects of his game. Tiger looked him straight in the eye and said, 'Next week? If I shoot 55 tomorrow, I might have a shot to win.' Realizing that Tiger was dead serious, Wrenn didn't know what to say.

'This kid is 21 years old, and he's the best player in the world,'

Andrade said. 'He's not happy finishing eighth or sixth or second. He wants to win. And he's pushing us all to think like that.'

Woods ended up finishing tied for ninth at Bay Hill, which showed his ability to post respectable numbers not only when he was fighting his swing, but putting out fires. On the Friday when he was shooting 71, a fax arrived at the press tent of a story from the April issue of *GQ* In it, author Charles Pierce arranged to ride in the limousine taking Tiger from his mother's home in Cypress to the *GQ* cover shoot in Long Beach. Naively, Tiger told several racy, off-color jokes in front of Pierce. Tiger thought they were off the record. Pierce used them in the hit-and-run article anyway, making the point that the language Tiger used, and the jokes he told, were no different than what most 21-year-olds say in the dormitory late on a Saturday night. The problem was that Tiger was no longer a 21-year-old at a Stanford University keg party. On Saturday morning at Bay Hill, IMG went into damage-control mode, issuing a statement through Los Angeles – based spin doctor Linda Dozeretz. It was exactly the wrong thing for IMG to do, because it drew too much attention to the story.

'Thanks to the magazine and the writer for teaching me a lesson,' he concluded. 'I got the message, even thought the writer completely missed it.'

There were many who felt Tiger got what he deserved. After turning down one-on-one interviews with every golf writer except Jaime Diaz of *Sports Illustrated* and Pete McDaniel of *Golf World,* he was convinced by agent Hughes Norton that a *GQ* cover and story would be great exposure and publicity.

And in some corners, the story actually turned out to be great publicity. Many people felt it humanized Tiger, showing him to be normal after all. Others thought it was hypocritical of him to be telling racist jokes when he had been marketed by Nike as the golfer who couldn't play certain courses because of the color of his skin. Either way, it didn't seem to affect his golf. He ended up shooting 71 and 68 on the weekend to finish tied for ninth with Davis Love III, six strokes back of Phil Mickelson. The next day he drove up to Ponte Vedra Beach for The Players Championship.

Earl was worried about the long-term effects. 'That article created a deep hurt,' he told Diaz. 'It disillusioned him and stayed with him a while because he realized he misjudged a situation. He thought, "How could I have been so stupid?" '

Tiger had won his first U.S. Amateur at the Tournament Players Club in 1994, and the questions at his Tuesday news conference started with the golf course itself. But the questioning moved on to such mundane subjects as his golf swing; autograph signings; his play at Bay Hill, his maturity; the upcoming Masters, U.S. Open, British Open and PGA Championships; his relationships with Butch Harmon, Arnold Palmer, Jack Nicklaus, Jackie Robinson, his father and his fan base; and ultimately, the *GQ* article and his ongoing love affair with the media.

Tiger was asked if his growing irritation had to do with being interviewed by people who don't know golf, and he brought up the scene from the Nissan Open press room.

'I don't know if you guys remember, there was a young lady in the back of the room asking . . .'

'Dumb questions?'

'Yeah, she was from *Inside Edition* or *American Journal*. You are going to get some people like that who – she wanted to talk about my private life.'

'Is that what happened in the . . . *GQ* article?'

'I've already answered enough on that *GQ* article.'

Early in the news conference, *Golfweek* columnist Jeff Rude tried to break the ice by asking Tiger if he had any good new jokes, but Tiger wasn't amused. He shot Rude a sarcastic smirk and didn't acknowledge the question with a response.

Other than a player meeting, that was his last trip to the press center at The Players Championship. All his interviews were conducted behind the scoring trailer, and with rounds of 71-73-72-73, he finished tied for 31st, his worst finish on the PGA Tour since turning professional at the Greater Milwaukee Open the previous August. On Sunday, he played with Faldo, and as always, that was an educational pairing. In 11 days, they would be paired again for the opening round at Augusta.

Tiger drove home to Orlando that night knowing he had plenty to work on. The distance control on his irons was off, and he wasn't putting very well, but he would take the week of the New Orleans off to gear up for the Masters. All week he worked at Isleworth, where they shaved the greens down for him. Finally, on the Friday before leaving, he played a practice round with O'Meara.

Mark shot 65. Tiger lipped out two putts, made two eagles, nine birdies and shot 59.

Fifteen minutes after turning in his card, *Golfweek* publisher Ken Hanson, who is a member at Isleworth, greeted Tiger.

'That question Rude asked at the Players was bullshit,' he told Hanson.

Hanson tried to explain that it was just meant to be a funny one-liner, but Tiger hadn't forgiven him for it.

'That question,' he repeated, 'was bullshit.'

Rude got a call from Hanson at his home in the suburbs south of Chicago.

'How upset would he be with me had he shot 65?' Rude asked his boss. 'He should have been dancing with Dom [Perignon]. I guess I should be flattered that he's thinking of me.'

# Seventeen

# SOUTHERN COMFORT

At 3 p.m. on Tuesday, April 8, 1997, Mr. Danny Yates of the Augusta National Golf Club press committee sat behind a microphone in the Masters Tournament press room, leaned forward, and said in a Georgia drawl: 'Well, we've got what y'all have been waiting for all day. So, Tiger, say a few words and we'll let them have a go at you.'

Tiger seemed guarded, but somewhat amused by Yates's delivery.

'Hi and bye. No, I guess, as always, it's a pleasure to be here at Augusta. I'm definitely looking forward to playing.'

'OK. Who's got some questions?'

'Tiger, this being your first pro year on the tour, is it as demanding as you thought it would be?'

'No. A lot more.'

'Travel, media, autographs, what?'

'All of it. You hit the nail right on the head. The golf part is actually the easiest part. That part I love to do. Anything else, outside of the golf course, that sometimes can be a little difficult at times, whether it's people wanting a 10-second little stop with you or an interview for 10 minutes or whatever. It's just people want to get a piece of your time.'

And so it went – over 22 pages of transcribed notes, and it was only Tuesday. For the rest of the week, Tiger kept his head down when he walked under the oak tree outside the clubhouse and tried not to make eye contact with anybody from the news media.

When Jeff Rude called out his name, just to say he was only kidding at the TPC, Tiger kept his stride. He had done his interview.

'I came away from that not only thinking he can't tell a joke, he can't take one either,' Rude cracked. 'I gave him a chance to endear himself by playfully and jokingly dismissing the *GQ* thing with a laugh, but he took the whole thing wrong. He could have said, "I'm out of the joke business. I've proved I'm no Richard Pryor." But he doesn't have that gear right now.'

Tiger was simply not in the mood for any bullshit. He was in what his father called the 'major mode.' It's something he learned playing with Faldo and Nicklaus. 'The week of a major, you have to eat, drink, think, dream – just everything – golf,' he said. 'Obviously, I lack some experience. But being young and having a lot of energy and being psyched to play can also work to my advantage. I can get into that totally obsessed state maybe more easily than an older player, who has done it for years and has more going on in his life . . . But I know how to focus. I've done it before.'

Tiger may have been uptight around the media, but his golf game was close to being right where he wanted it to be. In fact, in the news conference, he was confident enough to talk about shooting 59 at Augusta National, a score that would be four shots lower than the course record. 'I'm here to win the golf tournament,' he said, confidently.

The difference between Tiger at the 1997 Masters and at two previous trips to Augusta was that now he didn't have to worry about his schoolwork at Stanford. He was dedicated entirely to his golf game, so those scores he shot in 1995 (72-72-77-72) and 1996 (75-75) were not true indications of his ability to play the golf course.

It would just be a matter of patience for Tiger. Patience and – as s the case in any golf tournament – putting. 'I just have to go there and play and not try too hard,' he said. Cowan, admitting that expectations are never good for a golfer at the notoriously difficult course, predicted that if Tiger played well here – not necessarily super – he could take the place apart.

At the Mercedes Championships in January, he began working with Harmon on the pace of his putts, specifically gearing up for Augusta. When he was at home in Orlando, he would visit the Golf Channel studios and review tapes of past Masters

Tournaments. He picked up on the way Nicklaus played the course, with safe tap-in pars on the par-3s and par-4s, and a total domination on the reachable par-5s. From Faldo, he gleaned the importance of tee-shot placement in establishing proper angles to those devilish pin placements.

Faldo was asked if he thought it was presumptuous to expect Tiger to tear Augusta up. 'Yes, I think there's a learning curve of playing Augusta and the discipline of playing the golf course, when to hit the ball at the pin and when not, when to make that par and walk. You know, as I said, nothing is impossible, but I think that experience does help here.'

The key would be getting off to a good start and establishing some confidence early. As he's shown in all his wins – amateur and professional – Tiger does have a passing gear. His usual pattern is to come out of the blocks slow (but never shoot himself out of the tournament), establish a rhythm, then blow by everybody on Sunday. At Augusta, the formula was a little different than the norm.

He was given a 1: 44 p.m. tee time on Thursday with Faldo. At Augusta, the tradition is to pair the reigning U.S. Amateur champion with the defending Masters champion, but since Tiger had turned pro there was some question whether the Masters Committee would honor the custom. Normally that late pairing at the Masters is a detriment, because the greens spike up and get harder in the afternoon sun. But this was an unusual circumstance. With the wind-chill, it felt like 34 degrees Thursday morning. By the time Tiger and Faldo got to the first tee, it had warmed up into the 60s.

Faldo and Woods were at the golf course early, going back and forth from the putting green to the practice tee. They were concerned more, it seemed, with their feel than their swings. There's always a big difference in the speed of the greens between Wednesday afternoon (when the course is closed) and Thursday morning. Faldo, especially, was fighting his stroke. With Tiger, it was more a question of distance control with his irons. In 1996, he missed only two of 28 fairways, but was long and left too many times with his approach shots. He needed to be more like Faldo, who had only one putt from above the hole in his final round of 67.

'It will be a difficult draw for Tiger,' predicted Scotland's Colin Montgomerie. 'Nick, I'm sure, is past the stage of worrying who he's playing with. He's his own man and we know that. He'll get on with his own thing. It will be interesting to see what both of them score, but especially Tiger.'

Just before them, former Masters champions Ben Crenshaw, Tom Watson, Jack Nicklaus, Raymond Floyd, Arnold Palmer, Bernhard Langer and Gary Player had teed off in succession. It was prime time at Augusta, and Tiger was right there in the middle of it with Faldo, the three-time champion.

When he came off the range that final time, and walked through the media under the oak tree surrounded by security guards, Tiger looked more like a boxer about to climb in the ring than a golfer going out to play the first round of his first major championship as a professional. He had that mask of intensity and focus on his face, whereas Faldo, paranoid about his putting, was apprehensive.

In truth, Tiger might have been wound a bit too tight. He hit a bad drive down the left side at the first, had to punch out, and made bogey from the front bunker. He missed the fourth green to drop another shot, then bogeyed eight and nine. Four-over at the turn, he steamed to the 10th tee and tried to regroup.

His swing mechanics were off, and then he realized the problem: His backswing had gotten way too long. With Harmon, he had been working on more shoulder turn, which would give him more width, but they had cut down on how far he would take the club back with his arms. Anything too parallel was too long. Seeing his score posted on the giant leader-boards around the course, you couldn't help but wonder: had Augusta and high expectations gotten the best of Tiger Woods? Was he just going to be like the rest of the heirs who never lived up to the predictions?

'I was pretty hot at the way I was playing,' Tiger admitted. 'I couldn't keep the ball on the fairway. From there, you can't attack the pins, what pins you can attack. I was playing real defensive golf.'

The 10th is the longest par-four at Augusta, 485 yards sweeping downhill and to the left. Tiger locked in to his swing though, hit 2-iron and 8-iron to 10 feet, and made the putt for birdie. At the 12th, he flew the green back left with a pitching wedge, but played a beautiful 9-iron chip that he bumped into the bank and released across the green and into the hole. The fortune of that shot carried over to the 13th, where he bombed a high draw around the corner, and reached the green with a 6-iron for his third birdie in four holes.

The 15th was Tiger's place to make a statement. He hit driver and pitching wedge into a hole that is 500 yards long. The pin was cut front left, in a new position designed by Tom Fazio. Tiger didn't even worry about the water, not with a p. w. in his hands. His ball stuck to that green, four feet from the hole, and he made the putt for eagle. Five under in six holes, and not through yet.

One more birdie at the 17th gave Tiger nines of 40 and 30, and at 70, he was only three shots off the lead held by John Huston, with only two other players (Paul Stankowski and Paul Azinger) between himself and Huston. He left a putt hanging on the lip at 18 that would have tied the nine-hole course record, but it was the first time in seven Masters rounds that he was able to break par.

Faldo, on the other hand, three-putted five times on the front nine alone, and shot 75. The kid whipped him by five shots, and looked like he had a good handle not only on his golf game, but the nuances of Augusta. It helps, of course, when you're hitting wedge into most of the par-fours and putting for eagles on the par-fives.

'He obviously played great,' Faldo said, keeping it simple, before heading back to the putting green and the range for more work. 'Good luck to him.'

This night before Friday's second round, at a restaurant in downtown Augusta, Butch Harmon was having dinner with his wife, Lil, his son, Claude, and Cobra Golf founder, Tom Crow. There was a sense of excitement and anticipation. That 40-30 comeback Thursday, at least in Harmon's mind, was decisive. When Harmon stood up and saw golf course designer Tom Fazio and William McKee, the developer of Wade Hampton Golf Club, Harmon made a prediction.

'The kid's going to win this week,' Harmon said.

Now, you have to understand where Harmon was coming from and where he had been: In 1996, as Greg Norman's golf coach, he had endured the most devastating final-round collapse in Masters history. He had made the mistake a year ago, when Norman had a six-stroke lead after 54 holes, of celebrating too early – and certainly Thursday night at a major championship was seemingly not the time to be measuring Tiger Woods for a green jacket.

But there was nobody closer to Tiger Woods and his golf game than Butch Harmon. McKee, who works the range at Augusta as a volunteer, could see the difference in Tiger that night as he hit balls before dark. 'What I saw was focused and charged-up and positive and confident,' McKee said.

No Masters champion had ever started out with a 40, but Woods had a different look on his face Friday. He was visibly much more at ease, because he knew now that he could play Augusta. He had a score to prove it. The key was not getting in his own way. He had to let it happen.

Harmon escorted him off the range, through the clubhouse, under the tree, and onto the putting green. 'I was kidding around when we went through, more to keep him relaxed than anything else, but he didn't need it,' the coach said. 'Yesterday he was very tight, but he was coming into the biggest tournament in the world and everybody's picking him to win the doggone thing. I'd be nervous too.'

Woods's pairing was with Azinger, which was perfect. He made an eagle, five birdies, and his only bogey came at the third, when he drove it pin high on the 340-yard hole but had the ball roll back down a steep bank. His chip released over the green, and he missed a six-footer for par. At 17, he made his only bad play and swing of the day, going at a pin front right when he should have played to the center of the green. With his short game, he got away with it, and wedged up to tap-in distance.

'He makes the golf course into nothing,' said Nicklaus. 'That's why this young man is so special. If he's playing well, the golf course becomes nothing. He reduced the golf course to nothing.'

Tiger hit wedge into the 1st, 5th, 7th, 14th, 15th, 17th and 18th holes. The most he hit into a par-5 was 4-iron. He eagled the 13th by hitting 3-wood off the tee, and 8-iron into the green. 'I'm going to tell you one thing,' said Nicklaus. 'It's a shame Bob Jones isn't here. He could have saved the words he used for me in'63 for this young man, because he's certainly playing a game we're not familiar with.'

Tiger shot 66 and was at eight-under 136, with a three-stroke lead on Montgomerie. Azinger shot 73, and it felt like 83. 'I just got out-concentrated today,' he said. 'He never had a mental lapse.'

That was a tough golf course they were playing. Faldo shot 81 and missed the cut. Norman shot 77 and 74 and missed the cut. Steve Jones, the Open champion, shot 82 and 78 and missed the cut. Mark Brooks, the PGA champion, shot 77 and 82 and missed the cut. Phil Mickelson, winner at Bay Hill and third at Augusta in 1996, shot 76 and 74 and missed the cut. There was one story at Augusta National now: Tiger Woods.

Waiting by the clubhouse was Phil Knight and the Nike entourage.

'Great coaching,' he said to Harmon, throwing an arm-lock around the teacher's thick neck. 'This is what we've been looking for all week. He's making us look smart, isn't he?'

Harmon broke the day down: 'He was a lot looser when he came out to play today,' he said. 'We had a very good session on the range, more kidding around and going over the basics we go over every time. The club was coming up a little steep, and he had to take back the club a little lower and a little wider. That was about it. On the course, I wanted him to watch his takeaway, and the tempo of it. He tends to pick it up when he gets little steep. What we're looking for is a bigger shots shoulder turn, and a shorter arm swing. That gives us the tightness that we like to create the speed, and also for him to get the ball a little lower with his trajectory. As you noticed, he's hitting the ball lower now. Other than that, he hit the ball very well. He obviously is unhappy with something he did, because he told me, "Meet me on the range." '

It was the second shot at 17. Tiger didn't like it. Neither did Butch, but the mistake was certainly correctable.

'Well, that was the wrong play,' Harmon said. 'He's got to play that shot left of the flag. That's a false front on that green, and it suckers you into it. But he didn't like it. I saw him make a practice swing after he hit it, but it was a great round. He's eight under par, and at the end of 9 holes yesterday, he was 4 over. That says a lot for him, number one, about his tenacity and how much he wants to win. That just tells you how good he really is. In the middle of a round he knows his faults and knows the keys he works on for those faults. He was able to turn it around on the 10th tee yesterday, and ever since then, he's 12 under. He's in good shape, but we've got to remember, it's only Friday. We've got two more days and we got to play really good golf to have a chance to win this tournament. That's all we want, is a chance.'

Tiger fulfilled his obligations with television, but stopped at the range on the way to the press center. It was 7: 12 p.m., but working out that shot at 17 was higher on Woods's priority list than pressing newspaper deadlines, so he slow-played the print media. Frank Stone, who works the press room at Augusta as a volunteer, and Carl Reith, a green jacket, hovered nearby, but Tiger wasn't leaving until he was satisfied. Finally, at 7: 35, he made his way toward Stone.

Tida was waiting in the parking lot when Fluff arrived to put the Titleist bag in the trunk of a courtesy Cadillac.

'You did a beautiful job,' she said to Fluff.

'No,' Cowan said, '*He* did a beautiful job.'

At 8 p.m., after a quick pass through the locker room, Jimmy Roberts of ESPN asked Tiger Woods for another block of his valuable time.

Tiger bent his knees, squatting down to Roberts's height. He was loose now. He wanted to stop at a fast-food restaurant on the way home, and then resume his Ping-Pong tournament with Chang.

Roberts was taping a spot that Mike Tirico would use in the studio.

'It is one thing to spend the majority of your life dreaming about leading a major. Tiger Woods, it is another thing to come to the weekend of your first professional major as a leader. Tiger Woods, is there anything about this experience thus far that has caught you off guard, that you haven't expected?

Tiger didn't blink.

'Not really,' he said. 'I've been playing pretty well lately, and playing smart golf.'

Roberts, who trained under Howard Cosell, worked to keep the interview going.

'You're playing medal play, not match play against an opponent,' he said. 'But is there anybody else in the field that you're looking over your shoulder at?'

Again, Tiger did not blink.

'To be honest with you, I don't know who's under par right now,' he said 'I haven't had a chance to take a look at the leaderboards or the scores.'

Roberts knew he had time for one more question.

'Strategy,' he said. 'You were on the range for 20 minutes tonight. Is there anything you were working on? What's to work on at this point?'

'Obviously,' Tiger said, 'I think I can always hit it better, but overall, I'm striking the ball well, and I'm playing well, but more than anything I'm making good decisions, and that's the key to playing well here.'

Roberts wrapped up the day.

'It's a mind game,' he said. 'Halfway home, Tiger Woods is your leader. Mike?'

# Eighteen

# 42 Long

It was 4: 40 p.m. on Saturday, April 12, and Tiger Woods had just hit a 9-iron from the gallery onto the 11th green, 8 feet below the hole. In the tournament office, Will Nicholson, chairman of the Competition Committee, couldn't believe what he'd just seen. 'There's no backing off that shot whatsoever,' Nicholson said. 'It's the wrong angle to go right at the flagstick, but he went right at the flagstick.'

When Tiger ran the putt in the hole, and went to 13 under, everybody – in Amen Corner, and at Augusta National and watching on television – started to realize that it was no longer a question of Tiger Woods winning the Masters. It was now Tiger vs. the tournament scoring record of 17-under 271 established by Jack Nicklaus in 1965 and tied by Raymond Floyd in 1971.

'I think everybody ought to just go on home,' Nicklaus said.

Down in the grandstands at the 12th hole, score reporter Gene Childers wrote a 3 on his clipboard next to the 11th hole, and yelled out above the crowd noise.

'Goodgawdalmighty. Rewrite the record books, boys!'

At 18, he hit sand wedge, and the ball kicked off a bank and trickled down to within a foot for his seventh birdie of the day. Tiger flashed that megawatt smile and the scoreboard operator behind the 18th green posted that final red number, a 15, which tied Floyd's 54-hole record of 15-under 201, and established a nine-stroke lead over Costantino Rocca of Italy. Tiger had shot 65, and made it look easy.

'It's a done deal,' said Jerry Pate, the former U.S. Open champion and CBS analyst. 'This one's over with.'

Tom Kite, the 47-year-old Ryder Cup captain, still held out hope. 'Well, we've got it down to single digits, don't we?' he said. But Colin Montgomerie, who spent the day watching Tiger make birdie after birdie, agreed with Nicklaus: everybody else could go home. 'There is no chance,' he said. 'We're all human beings here.

There's no chance humanly possible that Tiger is going to lose this tournament. No way.'

At the Dubai Desert Classic in late February, Monty had said he wanted to play Tiger in the Ryder Cup at Valderrama, had said the kid only won on resort courses. Friday night, after shooting 67 to earn a spot next to Woods in the final group, Montgomerie hinted that the pressure was on Tiger. On the first tee Saturday, after catching a down slope and skidding a drive past Woods's, he postured to the gallery.

Well, he wanted Tiger, and he got him. 'I appreciate that he hit the ball long and straight, and I appreciate his iron shots were very accurate,' Montgomerie said. 'I do not appreciate how he putted. When you add it all together, he's nine shots clear, and I'm sure that will be higher tomorrow.'

When pressed, Montgomerie said there would be no scenario like the events that unfolded in 1996. 'This is very different,' he said. 'Nick Faldo's not lying second. And Greg Norman's not Tiger Woods.'

There was a big roar in the media center. Golf writers listening to Montgomerie's interview on headsets typed that quote into their laptops, then moved it up high in their stories. There was time for one more question.

'Colin,' a reporter asked, 'you said yesterday that you weren't sure with the pressure going into the third round, as the leader, whether he was ready to stand up to it.'

Colin Montgomerie, now ready to exit, was losing his patience. 'He is,' he said.

Outside the pro shop door, Bob Verdi of the *Chicago Tribune* Mark Whicker of the *Orange County Register* and Rick Reilly of *Sports Illustrated* were interviewing Fluff Cowan.

Reilly asked, 'Getting any goosebumps?'

'Nope,' said Cowan. 'This is what I do for a living.'

'No thrill by it?' said Reilly, pressing for a better quote.

'Not yet,' said Fluff. 'We've still got one day left of golf.'

The caddy went through the clubs: 8-iron into 12, sand wedge into 14, 6-iron into 15, 8-iron into 16, 60-degree wedge into 17 and sand wedge into 18. Verdi joked that Fluff could lighten his load by taking the 3-and 4-iron out of the bag.

Seven birdies. Not the hint of a bogey. A perfect round of golf. And the best shot Tiger hit, in Fluff's estimation, was the one nobody talked about: the pitch from the swale left of the 13th green that set up a 10-foot chance for birdie. Woods missed the putt, but Fluff called the setup one of the greatest shots he had ever seen.

'I was seeing the same thing he was seeing, but I didn't say boo,' Cowan said 'That's the first rule. Don't speak unless you're spoken to. But it looked like if he did what he wanted to do, it was going to work, and it did. He executed it perfectly.'

Golfers were coming off the range, in awe.

'We knew he was good,' said Fred Couples, who trailed by 13. 'But we didn't know he was that good.'

'I think it's too far,' said Rocca. 'Maybe if I play nine holes.'

'I might have a chance,' said Paul Stankowski, who was 10 shots back, 'if I make five or six birdies on the first two or three holes.'

'Is there any way we can get him to go back to school and get a Ph. D.?' wondered Jeff Sluman, who was 12 back.

'It's what we all kind of visualized coming in here,' said Davis Love III, who trailed by 14. 'It's not unbelievable, except that no one else is doing it. He's just blowing everybody apart. He's taken the fun out of it for the rest of us.'

Butch Harmon, Tida Woods and Phil Knight were holding court on the veranda by the clubhouse. A copy of *Golf* magazine was out, and Norman was taking shots at Harmon. Now it was Harmon's turn to fire back.

'Tiger Woods is a much smarter player than Greg Norman,' he said. 'They're both tremendously talented, but Tiger's mental approach to tomorrow is better than Greg's. I don't think you'll see him make mental mistakes. He's so composed. He's made no stupid plays.'

Tida Woods wore a silk shirt with a Tiger on it. She was asked if she was surprised – and she was surprised that somebody was actually dumb enough to ask that question. 'Does it surprise you guys?' she said, and a few shook their heads. 'So why do you ask me those questions?

'This is his ability; you've been seeing it all these years. You've seen him win three straight U.S. Amateurs. This is no different.'

Knight, who paid $40 million for Tiger, stroked his red beard and flashed a billion-dollar grin.

'We expected great things from him,' he said, 'but he's done way beyond what we expected. He's worth what we're paying him. Every penny. When we signed him, one Wall Street analyst, Montgomery Securities, said we overpaid Tiger Woods. I wonder what they think now.'

Back at the house they were renting off Wheeler Road in Augusta, Earl Woods watched on TV. Still recovering from open-heart surgery, he was conserving his strength for Sunday. Damn if he was going to miss this one. 'Each time I see him I'm amazed at how much his maturity has grown,' said his father. 'His attitude is, "I've been there before and I can do it again." '

At Augusta National, the soon-to-be Masters champion was riding to the press tent in a golf cart driven by Dan Yates. Walking alongside was Scott Van Pelt of the Golf Channel.

'Tiger, what the hell are you doing?'

'Scott, I have no idea.'

'What are you going to wear tomorrow? Something red?'

'Yeah.'

'It's going to look a lot like Christmas tomorrow, isn't it?'

'I hope so.'

Frank Carpenter, the Augusta National Club steward, had already been informed to get the green jacket ready.

Tiger Woods wore a 42 long.

# Nineteen

# THE RECORD, THE CORONATION

Lee Elder couldn't sleep. Finally, at 3 a.m. Sunday morning, at his home in Pompano Beach, Florida, he was able to doze off. Two hours later he was up. At 7: 30 a.m. he was on a plane at Fort Lauderdale Airport, bound for Atlanta. At 11 a.m. he was pulled over by a Georgia Highway Patrol officer for doing 85 miles per hour in a 70 mph zone on I-20. 'I've got to get to the Masters to see Tiger Woods win,' he told the policeman. The policeman didn't care. He wrote out the ticket anyway.

Butch Harmon couldn't sleep, either. At the home they were renting in Augusta, he rolled over at 4 a.m. and asked his wife, Lil, 'You awake?'

'Now I am,' she said.

The restlessness of Lee Elder and Butch Harmon was understandable: This was a big day for them, a day that would make the suffering and the waiting and the anticipation seem worth it. For Tiger Woods, it was just another dance with destiny, and he was calm and relaxed in its grip. 'I slept great, like a log,' Tiger Woods would say. 'I have no problem sleeping, trust me.'

At 3: 08 p.m., Harmon and Elder were both near the first tee at Augusta National for the coronation. Harmon gave final instructions, but Tiger Woods's golf game was already on auto-pilot. Elder gave him a hug, which was an inspiration to go out there and do what he had to do. It reinforced in Tiger what his father said when he walked out of the house that morning: 'Son, this will be the longest day you've ever spent on the golf course. Go out there and kick some butt.'

This was the day – April 13, 1997 – that would be a benchmark in golf history, a day when a black man would finally win a major championship in the white man's sport. Right here in the heart of the Deep South. At the Masters, where they once kept changing the rules to keep Charlie Sifford out, where it wasn't until 1975 that a black man named Lee Elder was let in. At Augusta National, where, until six years ago, there were no black members and where now there are only two (Ron Townsend and Bill Simms). Yes, this was more than just about golf. This was the emancipation of a sport and the fall, as Elder would say, of the game's last racial barrier.

The kid had been preparing for this since he was in diapers, watching his father hit golf shots into a net in the garage of their home in Cypress, California. Young Tiger had made a poster of Jack Nicklaus's major championship victories, and had it on the wall in his room. This would be the first for Tiger Woods: One down, seventeen more to catch Nicklaus on the professional side of the poster; he already had one more U.S. Amateur victory, three to two.

He had 18 holes to make it official. But these 18 holes – the final 18 holes of the 61st Masters Tournament – would be 6, 925 yards of victory lap, and when it was over there would be the first of what Nicklaus himself predicted would be 10 green jacket ceremonies. When he put on that jacket at dusk, it would represent a unification, a prayer for the day when blacks and whites and Asians could come together and join in the same celebration. They've always called Augusta National the Cathedral in the Pines. This was the first Sunday when golf really did feel like a religious experience. Non-denominational, of course. A Black-Thai affair.

'This is so significant sociologically. It's more significant to me, even, than Jackie Robinson breaking the [baseball] color line,' Elder said. 'It's such a great day for golf. It's such a great day for all people. I'm a part of history in the past and now I'm a part of history in the present. After today, we will have a situation where no one will even turn their head to notice when a black person walks to the first tee.'

All heads were turned when Tiger Woods walked to the first tee at Augusta. He had on his red shirt and his black pants, and soon a green jacket would complete the outfit. He birdied the second, bogeyed the fifth, bogeyed the seventh and birdied the eighth. On the back, he birdied 11, 13 and 14 to his number, 18 under par, and then he fought to keep it there.

On the 18th tee, a cameraman got him, firing his motor drive at the top of Tiger's backswing and then twice more coming down. His tee shot hooked over the bunker and into the old practice fairway. Tiger whirled on the camera tower, cursing. 'That was a noise that's unnatural,' Woods said. 'Rustling of trees, you don't hear that. But anything mechanical, you hear that; and when they do that on the golf course when it's quiet, it's going to stand out.'

The click of that camera was a blessing; it sent Tiger into the maw of his gallery, allowing him to make that walk up the 18th through a tunnel. He thought of many things after he hit that second shot on the 72nd hole. He thought of his father up there at the 18th green waiting for him; his father, who had just had a triple bypass, who put him through basic training, who dedicated his life to his son's career. He thought of his mother, and the talks she used to give him about sportsmanship and Buddhism. He thought of Jackie Robinson and Charlie Sifford and Lee Elder, and the swath they cut through racism. He thought about the dream he had as a kid, the dream where he won the Masters tournament, and now, here Tiger Woods was, doing just that.

Then he saw the putt that was left, and he realized it wasn't over. 'I've got a tough one,' he said. 'My focus never left me. Even with all the ovations I got and everybody cheering me on, it was a special moment. I knew I had to take care of business first. I was at 18 under par, which is the scoring record.'

He had not three-putted all week, and he wanted to walk off this golf course knowing that could be done. He wanted to walk off with the record and he left himself 5 feet for 280.

This story was too perfect for it to end any other way. He made the putt, did the traditional Tiger Woods uppercut, embraced Fluff, hugged his parents and shook the hand of Tom Kite, the U.S. Ryder Cup captain who finished second at 12 shots back. Then he headed to the Butler Cabin for the green jacket ceremony on CBS, where Nick Faldo put that 42 long on his back.

Next was the presentation on the putting green, a tradition that began long before television. Surrounded by a phalanx of policemen, he walked out of the Butler Cabin and toward the green where he had spent hours earlier in the week getting the speed of the greens. And there, out of the corner of his eye, Tiger Woods spotted Lee Elder and he said 'Wait!' Everybody braked.

'Lee, come here,' he said, and the two men embraced, these two generations of black golfers, the first to play the Masters Tournament and the first to win the Masters Tournament. Tiger whispered in his ear, 'Thanks for making this possible,' he said. There was another tear in Lee Elder's eyes as Tiger surged forward to the green, where the young man accepted the jacket in public from Jack Stephens, chairman of the Masters Tournament. 'I've always dreamed of coming up 18 and winning,' he said. 'But I never thought this far through the ceremony.'

The news conference followed, and outside the interview room, Earl spoke for the first time about his heart operations and about how close he had come to missing this day. During the second operation, in the middle of the Nissan Open, 'They almost lost me,' he said. 'Death was not far away and I was there and I said, "No." When I came back, and I came out of it, my surgeon told me, "You are a true warrior." And I said, "Yes, I have been where the ultimate competition exists. I was competing for my life and I won." '

The 64-year-old Green Beret had fought tougher fights, but this one he fought without Nguyen Phong, the Vietnamese lieutenant he named Tiger after.

'I didn't need any motivation,' he said. 'It's just an inherent will and drive to survive. I have a lot more work to do and many more things to accomplish with Tiger.'

There was a dinner that night at the clubhouse, where he sat at the head table under a picture of President Eisenhower. At the back, near the service entrance, the club's black employees – the waiters and the busboys and the cooks – joined the club members and their wives in the applause.

That night, back at the house they were renting, there was a party for the close friends and family of Tiger Woods. Pete McDaniel showed up from *Golf World* and when he asked, 'Where's Tiger?' Tida and Jerry Chang showed him. They took him to a bedroom, and there was Tiger Woods, fast asleep.

He was hugging the green jacket in his arms.

# PART III

# The Reconstruction

*Whatever he sees as a weakness in his game he turns into a strength.*

– BUTCH HARMON

# Twenty

# HISTORY LESSON

On the plane ride to Augusta, the Monday before the 1997 Masters tournament, Tiger Woods turned to Mark O'Meara and asked, 'Do you think it's possible to win a Grand Slam?' It was a question not many golfers since Jack Nicklaus could ask, but even as a rookie, Woods had charted a course that no other golfer in the last 20 years – with the possible exception of Greg Norman – dared to travel.

The Grand Slam was deemed unattainable in an era where there were no dominating players, an era that will be most famous for players who had relatively short windows of greatness. Tom Watson's putter ran out of fire. Fred Couples had potential, but couldn't deal with the walls closing in on his laid-back world. Nick Price peaked a little too late in life. Nick Faldo won six majors, but the mechanical man eventually broke down. And of course there was Norman, who fell on his sword in several majors and was victimized in two others.

With Norman, there was always the sense that something would go wrong, that he would either block a shot to the right, have somebody hole a shot, or (in the case of the 1996 Masters) suffer a complete meltdown. Over the course of time it was proven that Norman's game was *only* geared to run in overdrive, and winning major championships requires patience, course management, and an ability to consistently hit fairways and greens.

Norman never was able to find that zone where he could simply blow away the field and take an implosion out of the equation. The only exception was when he was working with Butch Harmon, during the 1993 British Open at Royal St. George's and the 1994 Players Championship. Those two performances stood as the most dominating in the nineties, but they are overlooked because of Norman's inability to close.

Nobody, however, put himself in more of a position to win than the Shark, and it was that level of consistency that should be his legacy. In the last 34 years, it was Norman – not Faldo or Price – who had come closest to completing the sweep. In 1986, he led the Masters, the U.S. Open, the British Open and the PGA Championship after 54 holes, the so-called Saturday Slam. That year showed not only just how unlucky Norman was, but also just how tough it is to win a major, let alone four in succession.

In the Masters, he was one of the obstacles that Jack Nicklaus ran over with that final-round 65. He ended up finishing tied for second. In the U.S. Open at Shinnecock Hills, he got into a shouting match with a fan, lost his composure and finished T-12 to Raymond Floyd. At the British Open, he played Turnberry brilliantly, shot a tournament record 63, survived a gale on Saturday and won by five strokes. Then in the PGA at Inverness, he shot 42 on the back side and was impaled by Bob Tway's hole-out from a greenside bunker at the 72nd hole.

Just to prove it could happen again, Larry Mize chipped-in on Norman the following spring at Augusta, otherwise it would have been three straight majors for the Shark when he was healthy and in his prime. 'You can't control what other people do,' Norman once admitted. 'The hardest thing for me to accept out of all the golf was the two back-to-back shots in the majors. The first one was tough, but the second one at the Masters was even tougher. It never happened to anyone ever before, back-to-back. I would have had three straight majors. I think about that, but I don't talk about it. Everybody says, "What if?" But I know it. Those were the two toughest ones to me. You sit here and say, where are you going to be in the archives of the game. Who knows where people put you, but if two shots didn't do that to you, you know exactly where you're going to be.'

With a first, two seconds and a twelfth, it was still the best season anyone had in the majors until Price came along in 1992 and had three top-six finishes in the majors, including a win at

Bellerive in the PGA. Two years later, Price won the British Open and the PGA back-to-back, but went four more years before cracking the top 10 in the majors. Media pressure, equipment changes and the building of a new house contributed to Price's career tailing off instead of moving up to the level that Faldo had achieved early in the decade.

Faldo's run began at the 1987 British Open at Muirfield, where 18 straight pars on Sunday became the stuff of legend. Faldo's swing (as reconstructed by David Leadbetter) helped him go on to win four of the next 20 majors and finish second in two others, including a playoff loss to Curtis Strange at the 1988 U.S. Open. Faldo then went through the publicity grinder, enduring a divorced and a bitter breakup with a girlfriend. While he committed himself to greater heights – going as far as moving to America and visiting Ben Hogan – there was only one more major moment in his career. That, both typically and unfortunately, came at the expense of his foil, Norman, at Augusta in 1996. With six majors, Faldo had one more than Seve Ballesteros, and twice as many as Price and Larry Nelson.

The difference between Faldo and Woods, however, was the big-time game. Faldo was predominantly a predator, feeding off the misfortunes of Paul Azinger, Scott Hoch, Raymond Floyd, John Cook and Greg Norman. In only one of his majors, the 1990 British Open at St. Andrews, did he dominate. His wins were always a matter of attrition. He never had the length of Woods, nor did he have the mental superiority to sustain a competitive edge over his opponents.

The 1990s were also the boom era for golf, when golfers started to make over $1 million a year in prize money and financial security very often took the hunger away. That was the case of Mark O'Meara, who won the Masters and the British Open in 1998, but hasn't been heard from on a Sunday at a major championship since.

When Woods turned pro at the end of 1996, his first goal was simply to secure his tour card. He had met O'Meara previously, through a game of golf that IMG had arranged at Isleworth, and had gotten closer beginning at the Canadian Open in 1996. It was O'Meara who had taken Tiger as his adopted brother, teaching him the ropes, providing both a set of eyes on the driving range and a tremendous family environment at Isleworth, where he bought a townhouse.

By the time they arrived at Augusta in 1997, Tiger had more than secured his tour card. He had won three times on the PGA Tour, including twice the previous fall at the Las Vegas Invitational and the Walt Disney World Classic. In the beginning of 1997, Tiger had come out blazing, with a win over 1996 Player of the Year Tom Lehman at the Mercedes Championships and a hole-in-one at Phoenix that would be immortalized in highlight tapes for years to come.

That he won at Augusta that April surprised no one – including Tiger, who had come to realize that he could win big events in professional golf just like he did as an amateur. The Grand Slam, however, was another matter.

The Grand Slam was golf's 'Impregnable Quadrilateral.' It was won in 1930 by Bobby Jones, but the rotation then consisted of the U.S. Open, the U.S. Amateur, the British Open – which is known in Europe as the 'Open Championship' – and the British Amateur. The Masters was not yet a tournament and the PGA Championship was not considered part of the rota. When Jones won the Grand Slam, there were no professional 'majors,' and the Western Open was considered as important to win as the PGA. Sparked by Gene Sarazen's double eagle at the 1935 Masters, it was golf writers like Grantland Rice and O. B. Keeler who invented the concept of major championships and a professional grand slam. Sarazen's playoff win over Craig Wood at Augusta the following day made him the first golfer to win the modern-day Grand Slam.

Since World War II, Ben Hogan came the closest to winning all four of golf's grand slam events in the same year. With victories at the Masters, the U.S. Open and the British Open in 1953, Hogan never had a chance to complete the slam because of a scheduling conflict between the PGA and the British. Hogan did, however, complete his career slam that year at Carnoustie in the British Open.

There were two other legitimate runs at the grand slam. Arnold Palmer won the Masters and the U.S. Open in 1960, then finished second at the British Open, losing by strokes to Kel Nagle at St. Andrews. Nicklaus also won the first two legs in 1972, and had one Golden Bear's paw around the Claret Jug at Muirfield when Lee Trevino chipped-in on the 71st hole and stole the title.

Woods knew this history, because he charted it, because he knew he wanted to be a part of it, because he had the self-belief that his talent could make it happen. After he won the Masters by the largest margin of victory in tournament history, after he broke the Masters record established by Jack Nicklaus in 1965, after he became the first person of color to win at a club that had long symbolized the prejudice of the Deep South, Tiger Woods had answered the question that he posed to O'Meara on the flight into Augusta.

'It can be done,' he said.

## Twenty One

# REBUILDING STAGE

Tiger knew that to win the Grand Slam, and ultimately run down Jack Nicklaus's major championship record, he would have to make changes to his game and to his mental approach in major championships. Although Tiger won the Masters by 12 strokes and established a new 72-hole scoring record of 18 under par, he knew that his timing was just good that week, that his putter was hot and everybody else was flat-out intimidated. He realized that he lacked the distance control necessary to be a true champion, that the greens he was overshooting would ultimately cost him golf tournaments – and they did one month later at the Colonial Tournament in Fort Worth, where he lost on the back nine to David Frost.

Butch Harmon, his swing coach and trusted counsel, also recognized the flaws in Tiger's seemingly indomitable game. Together they went about the process of starting all over and going back to their first lesson on the tee at Lochinvar Golf Club in Houston the week of the 1993 U.S. Amateur.

'We started after that [Colonial] tournament,' Harmon said. 'We began by talking about it, asking ourselves, what do we need to do to change this? He kept saying, "I can't stand hitting these shots under pressure. It irritates the hell out of me." It was obvious he was having trouble controlling his distance, controlling his trajectory under pressure. I looked at tapes, saw that his clubface was shut at the top, and saw that he was delofting a little coming into ball, and was coming way too much from inside. I started to formulate a plan on what I wanted to do and how I wanted to change it, and from there we started to talk about it. It had to be Tiger's decision to change, obviously.'

Harmon gave Woods a framed picture of Ben Hogan; at impact, Hogan's left wrist was bowed, his clubhead square. He told Woods that to be a consistent ball striker, he would have to find this position. And to find that position, he would have to get stronger and learn to time his downswing better, so that his lower body would not outrace his upper body and his arms wouldn't get 'stuck' behind him. To do that, he had to match speeds.

'He knew it wasn't right,' said Harmon. 'He knew it was a problem up until then, that his body speed was too fast, that his arms were too far behind him, which meant he used his right hand too much and was shutting down the clubface. It was showing up short irons more than anything else was. That's when I told him to bow in the left wrist like my dad talked about. To do that, he had to get stronger.'

Woods won two more tournaments after the Masters in 1997: the GTE Byron Nelson Classic and the Motorola Western Open. Tiger's play in the majors was best remembered for the big numbers he made to derail his momentum and to blow any chance he had to be in contention on Sunday. You can't come back from double and triple bogeys in the majors and expect to win. Tiger finished T-19 in the U.S. Open at Congressional, T-24 in the British Open at Royal Troon, and T-29 in the PGA Championship at Winged Foot, showing flashes of brilliance and impetuousness.

The 1998 season was characterized as the year of Tiger's 'slump.' He won only twice worldwide (just once in the United States), and while he recorded three top 10 finishes in the majors, including a third in heavy winds at the British Open, his year was labeled as a disappointment by just about everyone. Woods had a different take, maintaining that he was a better player than the Sunday he won at Augusta. 'I think my ball flight's improved,' he said. 'I'm able to play in conditions I've never been able to play before. An example was the British Open. The wind was howling. I know that the year prior to that there's no way I could have played that well.'

It was a humbling time, but Woods was earning style points from his peers for the way he was handling the down times. He played all five matches in the Presidents Cup, asking captain Jack Nicklaus to pair him against Greg Norman in the singles. The subsequent 1 p victory against the Shark was one of the few bright spots in a nine-point defeat. 'I became an even bigger fan of him at the Presidents Cup in Australia,' said Nicklaus. 'He could have kept to himself, but he was just one of the guys. He was all for the team, all week.'

When Woods won his fourth event of the 1999 season, shooting 62 – 65 on the weekend of the Buick Invitational, his game was still not where he wanted it to be. The move that he was working on, the synchronization between his upper and lower bodies, the strength required to 'pronate' his left wrist like Hogan, didn't click until a session on the practice ground at Isleworth before the GTE Byron Nelson. It was with one swing of an 8-iron that Woods realized he had it. He picked up his mobile phone and called Harmon, who was at his golf school in Las Vegas.

'He said, "I finally got it. It all starts to feel natural to me." All the work we'd done had fallen in to place,' recalled Harmon. 'The meaning was he didn't have to mechanically do those things any more. It was there. Now he could go play, knowing, "I can win these tournaments." '

When Harmon hit the end button on his mobile phone, he knew the 'slump' was not only about to end, it was about to end with a flourish. 'The rest of the guys,' he said, 'better watch out.'

Harmon was dead right. Starting at the Nelson, Woods's performance was off the charts. Beginning May 13, when he opened the Nelson with a 61, this was definitely a different Tiger Woods – a Tiger Woods with a new coat of armor. He won the Deutsche Bank SAP Open on a golf course that had U.S. Open rough, and headed to Muirfield Village Golf Club with a new attitude to go along with his new swing.

In late March, just after David Duval won the Players Championship to become the No. 1 player in the world, Woods and O'Meara were hitting balls on the range at Isleworth Golf Club in Orlando. With the Masters coming up, it was obviously bothering Tiger that he had been slain by David. 'Listen bud,' O'Meara said. 'The No. 1 ranking in the world is important, but being No. 1 with yourself is more important. It's great to be driven and everything, but you've got to be happy.'

Of course it's easier to be happy when the putts are falling in

The 1997 U.S. Masters, April 13, 1997. Tiger blasting out of a sand trap during the final round. *David Cannon*

The 1997 U.S. Masters, April 13, 1997. Tiger Woods's 2nd shot to 18th. *David Cannon*

The 1997 U.S. Masters, April 13, 1997. Tiger Woods, U.S. Masters Champion. *David Cannon*

The 1997 Mercedes Championships, La Costa Resort and Spa, Carlsbad, California. Tiger Woods and coach Butch Harmon. *Jamie Squire*

At the Johnnie Walker Classic, Blue Canyon Golf Club, Thailand, January 20-25, 1998, Tiger Woods parades trophy with "locals" in attendance. *AllSport*

At the 1999 Masters, April 8, 1999, Tiger Woods looks for his ball on Hole 8 where he took a triple bogey. *Craig Jones*

At the PGA Championship, Medinah Country Club, August 15, 1998, Tiger set to hit a long iron off the sloping fairway of Medinah. *Craig Jones*

At the PGA Championship, Medinah Country Club, August 15, 1999. The second piece of Tiger's career Grand Slam. *Craig Jones*

At the 1999 U.S. Open, Pinehurst No. 2, June 20, 1999, Tiger Woods celebrates holing his birdie putt on the 16th green. *Craig Jones*

The Johnnie Walker Classic at Ta Shee Resort, Taipei, Taiwan, October 9, 1999. Tiger with caddy Steve Williams. *David Cannon*

The 2000 Masters, April 6-9, 2000. *Andrew Reddington*

At the 2000 Masters, April 7, 2000, Tiger Woods plays from the trees on 13. *David Cannon*

The 100th U.S. Open practice, Pebble Beach Golf Links, June 14, 2000. *Jon Ferrey*

The 100th U.S. Open, Pebble Beach Golf Links, June 17, 2000. Tiger on his way to his record-setting U.S. Open victory. *Jaime Squire*

The 100th U.S. Open, Pebble Beach Golf Links, June 18, 2000. The third piece of the career Grand Slam. *Jamie Squire*

At the 2000 British Open, St. Andrews Links, Old Course, July 22, 2000, Tiger hits his approach shot to the 18th green. *Andrew Reddington*

The 2000 British Open, St. Andrews Old Course, July 23, 2000. Faster than Nicklaus—the career Grand Slam. *David Cannon*

The 2000 PGA Championship, Vahalla Golf Club, August 20, 2000. Tiger makes birdie in playoff.
*David Cannon*

The 2000 PGA Championship, August 20, 2000. Tiger poses with his new trophy.
*David Cannon*

the hole and the swing changes start to work in the heat of competition, but Tiger has always listened to O'Meara. Woods learned to chill out, quit slamming clubs, accept his responsibility as the game's biggest star, and enjoy the ride. Once again, M. O. was right.

Arriving at the Memorial Tournament, Woods was much more relaxed than the players had ever seen him. On Thursday, after an opening-round 68, he walked out to the driving range for some late practice. His former caddy Fluff Cowan was there, holding the bag of his new boss, Jim Furyk. There was a perceived tension after the firing, but just to show that it was media driven, Woods walked right up to Cowan, who stuck out his hand. There was never any hesitation. Woods slapped Fluff's palm and smiled as if nothing had ever happened. At the end of the range, Woods hit balls until dusk with only 20 fans watching. For Tiger, this was the picture of serenity.

'I always saw an attack style in his walk,' says Lee Janzen. 'I see a more relaxed walk now. I think he's enjoying himself more. I don't think it has taken away from his focus of what he wants to become, but I think he has a more relaxed confidence about him, that he's really just enjoying himself right now, which could be trouble for the rest of us.'

Even Duval admitted that he saw a change. The uncomfortable vibe that once existed between the two of them was dissipating with time. After finishing third, Duval said, 'I think he's just becoming more comfortable with it all, with who he is and what's demanded of him. He's balancing that out with the golf and he's obviously doing a very good job of it.'

The word 'balance' was the key. Woods had it not only in his disposition, but also in the balance in his golf game. After hitting fairways and greens in Germany, Tiger won the Memorial with his short game. He missed six greens on Sunday, but saved par five times. His flop wedge from 20 yards behind the sixth, from a hardpan lie, under a tree branch, to a green that sloped toward the water, scored a 10 in degree-of-difficulty. Woods left himself 3 feet for par, which he tapped in.

As wondrous as that up-and-down was, the shot that goes on Tiger's highlights video came from behind the 14th green. Missing the putting surface long with a sand wedge from the fairway, he tried to land his third shot in the fringe and have it roll down to the cup. Instead, he left the shot in the rough. 'Now he's going to have a hard time making five,' Nicklaus said from the announcer's booth. Woods responded by chipping his fourth shot down the hill and in the cup for par. The deafening roar could be heard in downtown Columbus as Woods went into a series of fist punches that would have knocked out Mike Tyson.

'I've always enjoyed the challenge of chipping and putting and getting up and down,' said Woods. 'When I was a kid, I had to. I was so wild.'

Nicklaus, the tournament host, was amazed at the all-around prowess of Tiger's game. Jack knew that if he had had Tiger's skill around the greens, he might have won 25 majors. 'He has the ability to do things that nobody else can do,' said the Golden Bear. 'And yet he's got a short game that where if he makes mistakes, he can correct it. That's what's so phenomenal.'

As a golf course designer, Nicklaus was also amazed seeing what a player with Woods's strength can do to his golf course. But if anyone could relate to Tiger's power, it was Jack. Across town at Scioto, the members are still talking about the time a young Bear drove the 375-yard 11th green with a persimmon-headed driver. Where Tiger is longer is with his long irons. At the 539-yard, par-5 11th on Friday, Woods hit 2-iron, 2-iron to 2 feet and tapped in for eagle. 'You tell me how many people in the game can do that,' O'Meara said. 'No one.'

With the U.S. Open coming up at Pinehurst, the combination of Tiger's McGwiresque length ('Chicks love the long ball,' he said) and deft touch would be a decided advantage. Tiger supposedly couldn't win on a U.S. Open golf course, but the No. 2 course would not be set up in typical U.S. Open fashion. There would be considerable run off around the greens, and the one stat that Tiger had improved upon was his putting. He was 147th in 1998, but came into the Memorial ranked 37th. At Muirfield Village, he took only 108 putts for the week, for an average of 27 per round. That number, compared to Vijay Singh's 116 putts, is what won Woods his ninth PGA Tour event and his second of the year.

Woods started putting better after a phone conversation with his father. 'I went back to some of the fundamentals that I used to do as a kid,' Woods said. 'My dad and I had a long talk about that. I've tried to get the picture, putt to the picture, and not worry about mechanics that much. Just make sure you're comfortable and go ahead and be committed. Bury it.'

The final element that made Woods a threat to bury the field at Pinehurst was something that Nicklaus also excelled at: the ability to manage his game. In the 1998 Memorial Tournament, when he finished tied for 51st, Woods made two double bogeys at the 14th hole. In 1997, he made a 9 at the par-4 third. Avoiding a big number in Open conditions will be a bigger test of Woods's patience, but he's certainly advanced on the learning curve. He was evolving from an Arnold Palmer – type who went for everything to a player who tries to play smart like Nicklaus.

'Absolutely he can win the U.S. Open,' said O'Meara. 'He knows how to manage himself better now. I've played with a lot of great players and this guy's got more raw talent than any player I've ever seen. That doesn't necessarily get you wins, but as soon as you learn to master your composure, with that talent, there's no stopping him.'

As a child, Woods put his now-famous poster on his bedroom wall charting Nicklaus's progress in the major championships. Although it was early in his career, Tiger found himself behind schedule after his first nine majors as a professional. Through his first seven grand slam events as a professional, the Golden Bear had amassed three wins, a second, and two third-place finishes. Woods had the Masters win and a T-3 in the 1998 British Open as his only top fives.

In his hotel room near Muirfield Village, Woods read that Nicklaus had 70 top 10 finishes in the majors. That amazed him much more than the 18 victories. 'He's done things that only Jack Nicklaus has done,' Woods said. 'Granted, the bar is set very high. Whether I will ever accomplish it or not, who knows? But it's not the driving force in my life. The driving force of my life it to get my game at a level where I'll be able to compete in each and every tournament I tee it up in for the rest of my life.'

Nicklaus was 22 when he beat Arnold Palmer for his first U.S. Open victory. Woods would be 23 at Pinehurst. There was plenty of time to catch up, but there was no time better than now. 'No, it wouldn't surprise me if he broke my record,' Nicklaus said. 'Not at his age. Not with his talent.'

# Twenty Two

# THE ENDLESS SUMMER

The 1999 U.S. Open at Pinehurst will always be remembered for the putts Payne Stewart made on the 70th, 71st and 72nd holes to win his second national championship. They would become touchstones later that year when Stewart would go down in a plane crash along with business associates Robert Fraley and Van Arden, and a golf course designer, Bruce Borland.

What Tiger Woods will remember from Pinehurst is the two putts he missed at the finish that cost him a playoff. Tee-to-green, he outplayed Stewart and proved that he could handle the physical and mental test of a U.S. Open setup. For the week, he took 113 putts, an acceptable average of 28 per round. Stewart had 111 putts. That was the difference between their aggregate scores of 281 for Woods and 279 for Stewart.

'The rap on Tiger was that he could play Augusta because there wasn't any long rough, but that he didn't have the game to win an Open,' said PGA Tour Commissioner Tim Finchem in an interview the following summer. 'At Pinehurst Tiger played within himself, and came away thinking not only that he'd win an Open, but that he'd win one pretty soon. His game seemed to be rounding into incredible form across the board.'

When he arrived in Chicago four weeks later for the Western Open, Woods had the sense this was going to be his summer. The British Open was returning to Carnoustie, a course so brutally hard that it had been dubbed 'Carnasty.' The PGA would return in August at Medinah No. 3 on the longest layout at sea level in major championship history. The harder the better for Woods.

Chicago was one of his favorite cities in the world. He had good vibes from winning the Western at Cog Hill in 1997, and in Greg McLaughlin, Joel Hirsch and Michael Jordan, he had three good friends who called this their home.

McLaughlin was the tournament director who had given him a spot at the Nissan Open in 1991 and the Honda Classic in 1992. With Stewart, David Duval, Fred Couples, Davis Love III and Phil Mickelson taking the week off, Tiger returned the favor to McLaughlin, who needed star power to beef up his gate. 'If Greg's here, I'm here,' Woods said.

Hirsch first met Woods at the 1993 Western Amateur. Joel was one of the best amateur golfers in the country, and an even finer gentleman. He stood in the back of an interview room during one of Tiger's and Earl's news conferences, introduced himself afterward, and told Tiger that the way he handled the questions was exceptional. Woods was just a high school junior, but Hirsch could see the special nature of this kid.

Through the years they had become friends, playing a practice round once before the Western Open and ultimately becoming closer through a mutual friendship with Michael Jordan. Before the Western, Tiger mentioned to Joel that he would like to get in a practice round at Medinah. Joel was on the executive committee of the Western Golf Association, and was as connected as any golfer in greater Chicago.

'No problem,' said Hirsch. 'I'll get Michael.'

Woods and Jordan had become close through the Nike connection. Tiger had been over to Michael's house in Highland Park and had sat courtside at Bulls games. He and Michael had shared the experiences of stardom together. As Tiger had explained, 'We call each other brothers because Michael is like the big brother. I'm like the little brother. To be able to go to a person like that who has been through it all – and has come out of it just as clean as can be – that's the person you want to talk to. And on top of that, he's one great guy.'

They met for an afternoon round at Medinah, the Tuesday before the Western. Michael had already played in the morning, which wasn't surprising since he normally played 54 holes a day. Tiger arrived early at Cog Hill for his practice round and news conferences, then bolted.

It turned out to be media day at Medinah; so there were television cameras on the first tee when Jordan and Hirsch teamed up to play Woods and Ahmad Rashad. Playing off the tips, Woods wasn't really concentrating even through there was some money on the line. Jordan had teased the kid to the point where Tiger had just given up trying to come back at Michael. Finally they reached the 18th tee, their 27th hole of the afternoon, and Jordan just had to ask the question that everybody in golf had been asking.

'Hey Tiger,' said Michael. 'That Nike commercial: How many takes did it take you to do that. It looked like it was digitally enhanced.'

Woods finally had him.

'Come here, Michael,' he said, shaking his head.

The back of the 18th tee on the No. 3 course at Medinah comes right to the edge of Lake Kadijah. Woods pulled out his sand wedge, and started popping his Titleist Professional 90 up in the air as if it were attached to a string. Finally he whirled on it and sent a powerful draw down toward the water near the second green, some 200 yards away.

Jordan, Hirsch and Rashad just stood there with their mouths open. Tiger returned their looks with one of his smiles.

'It was the only time Michael was quiet all round,' said Hirsch.

Tiger was just as loose and confident that week at Cog Hill. He opened with a 68, shot 66 on Friday to share the lead with Stuart Appleby, moved out in front by four strokes with a Saturday 68, and won by three on July 4 over Canadian left-hander Mike Weir. The $450,000 more than covered his losses to Hirsch and Jordan at Medinah, and sent him off in good spirits to Ireland for a pre – British Open fishing trip with O'Meara, Stewart, Appleby and Duval.

The victory, which moved him back ahead of Duval and into the No. 1 spot on the world rankings, was further proof that the new toned-down swing was deadly when honed. It made him the second-youngest golfer, behind 22-year-old Horton Smith, to win 10 times on the PGA Tour. 'I've taken 10 percent, probably more, off the whole deal,' he said. 'Hence, my mistakes are in better places.'

In his closing news conference, he added, 'Being No. 1 is something I had to be told about. It's nice, but not as nice as winning. Being No. 1 and not winning, like I was doing in'98, that's not great. But I was changing my game then. I knew it was going to take me a while.'

When Tiger returned to Chicago one month later, the mood was decidedly different. His putter let him down in the British Open, where he finished four strokes out of the Paul Lawrie-Justin Leonard-Jan Van de Velde playoff. He had now gone ten straight majors since the Masters without a win. He was now beginning to realize just how mighty Nicklaus's record really was.

If that pressure alone wasn't intense, Woods also had to deal with a controversy. In a *Golf Digest* interview, Duval had stirred the pot on a brewing Ryder Cup controversy involving the PGA of America. Like many players, Duval felt the PGA was making too much on the event ($23. 5 million in profits according to *Golf Digest* at their expense (lose and you get ripped as a choker), and that some form of compensation be made, even if it was in the form of charitable donations.

Woods almost deliberately made himself part of the story, and those who knew the history understood his motives. In 1997, the PGA would not grant his father either a seat on the Concorde or inside-the-ropes access at the course for the competition at Valderrama. These were two liberties that wives and girlfriends get as Ryder Cup perks, but since he wasn't married, Woods felt that Earl should get the same treatment. That had stuck with him for two years, as did some of the comments Mark O'Meara was making about the hypocrisy of the event.

To his credit, Tiger was the only player who jumped in and publicly supported Duval at the PGA at Medinah. Although O'Meara instigated the issue, and Mickelson was just as vehement in his belief that the players were getting ripped off, only Tiger publicly threw himself in front of the controversy. While Duval tried to back pedal on his stance, Woods took on the PGA and wouldn't let up.

In his news conference on Tuesday, Woods knew he had the forum to speak out. Later that afternoon, a supposedly secret meeting was being held between the players who had qualified for the Ryder Cup team and the PGA of America. In attendance would be Ryder Cup captain Ben Crenshaw, and Jim Awtrey, the PGA's CEO.

Once the line of questioning started, there was not much that Julius Mason, the PGA's director of media relations and the moderator for the news conference, could do about it. The more

Tiger was pushed, the further he took it. The further he took it, the better it got. The way Woods handled it reminded Bob Verdi, the former Chicago Tribune columnist, of the way Jordan used to handle NBA labor relations issues.

Q: Tiger, what's your expectation for this meeting this afternoon?

A: Which meeting?

Q: The Ryder Cup player meeting that the PGA officers . . . or that Jim Awtrey is going to be at.

A: Oh, the three o'clock meeting.

Q: Yeah, that one . . .

A: Oh, that one? I didn't know about that . . . [Laughter]

A: My expectations? Well, I'm not expecting a whole lot, just because it's pretty late in the stage of the game. Whether they will come to some kind of resolution and get the heat off of them, I don't know. But maybe the next Ryder Cup, things will be a little different.

Q: Tiger, Duval was in there earlier and was asked to clarify his recent comments about the Ryder Cup. Generally, what's your position on that issue? And what, if any, questions will you bring to that meeting this afternoon?

A: Well, I think for us as players, this is the way I would personally like to see it. I would like to see us receive whatever the amount is, whether it's 200, 300, 400, 500,000, whatever it is; and I think we should be able to keep the money and do whatever we see fit. For me, personally, I would donate all of it to charity. But I think it's up to the other person's discretion of what they want to do with it. With all the money that's being made, I think that we should have a say in where it goes. I know whatever amount I would receive would go to charities that I have worked with in the past, and my own foundation. And just like what I did with the money [I made for the Showdown] at Sherwood. I think that's the way it should be done. The problem is I think you're hearing guys saying, 'Yeah, we need to get paid.' Yes, in a sense I think we do. But I think what you would see is all the players would donate a majority, if not all of it, to charities because this an exhibition. This is not more. And like the media has made it out to be, as well as the fans, this is an exhibition where we're there to have a wonderful time, play with the guys that we know, and still compete at a high level. But it's not going to make or break by career, or anybody else's career. There are tournaments that we play in week in and week out that are going to determine our livelihood and our careers, not just one Ryder Cup.

Q:     The second part of the question was: What questions might you bring to that meeting this afternoon that you want to ask the PGA?

A:     Well, when is it going to happen. How long is it going to take before the revenue sources are going to be distributed into the proper channels, that is, to charity. I know that right now the PGA Tour has a tournament, the World Golf Championship at Firestone. And I asked the Commissioner, I said, 'Well, granted I made it on the Presidents Cup team and I made it on the Ryder Cup team. And you said if I make it on these teams, I would be compensated [in official money] at Firestone.' Well, I asked him this question. 'What if I get injured and I don't play? Do I still receive the money?' And the answer is no. So because of that, that one reason in itself, shows you that it's not being run the way it could be. And on top of that, [the WGC at Firestone] is another tournament that has its own ticket sales, has its own funds and its own revenue sources that it's being derived from. And I understand where the PGA of America's coming from. I understand that, and I understand where the PGA Tour is coming from. But I hope they understand where the players are coming from.

Q:     Tiger, can you ever see a day when sometime in the future you might opt out of a Ryder Cup if the money situation stays as it is and doesn't change?

A:     Well, this is where David [Duval] got in trouble by answering a hypothetical question. Do I see it happening? Well, it could. Will it happen? That's a different story. Will players get fed up to the point where they will not play in a tournament? Well, I presume that it could be a yes, but what has to end up happening is, all of you sitting here today, the press, has to understand what is going on. When the press understands the whole story, not just one little part of it, and we opt not to play, then we'll all have a better understanding why.

The press didn't understand Tiger's thinking and took the side of the establishment. At the annual State of the PGA news conference, Awtrey said it was a 'nonissue,' but Crenshaw continued to make it one, especially in lieu of the comments by Woods and Duval that the Ryder Cup was just an 'exhibition.' In an emotional confession, Crenshaw said, 'I want to say one thing. I'm personally disappointed in a couple people in that meeting. And they know who they are. And whether some of the players like it or not, there are some people who came before them that mean a hell of a lot to this game. And it burns the hell out of me to listen to some of their viewpoints. And I'm not going to say anything more about it. This meeting is . . . it was very good because it clears the air. There was a lot of misinformation and let's not discuss it any longer. Those players knew how I stood before I went in there and that's all I'm going to say about it.'

If Crenshaw had left it at that, it might have died out. But pressed afterward, the captain suffered a meltdown and named names to a reporter from the *Boston Globe*. In the *Sun-Times,* Jay Mariotti called Duval, Woods, O'Meara and Mickelson the Brookline Four. In the Tribune Bernie Lincicome and Skip Bayless characterized the Brookline Four as stereotypical rich, greedy golfers who didn't want to put anything back into the game. Christine Brennan of *USA Today* joined in on the assault. When Tiger came into the press tent after shooting 70 on Thursday, there were follow-up questions on the Ryder Cup issue.

Again, Woods did not back down.

Q: Tiger, you and Davis have sort of really been under the storm this week. How did you feel to get back in between the ropes where you could play your game and have everybody cheering for you and be left alone for three or four hours?

A: It does feel nice. I didn't have to answer any Ryder Cup questions while I was playing out there, or warming up. It was nice to get back in the groove. I hadn't played in three weeks, since basically the British Open. And so it was nice to feel nervous on the first tee and feel the jitters and go ahead and somehow conquer them and get the ball off the tee moving forward somehow. It felt good.

Q: Well, now there's mention of it, do you have any reaction to the comments that Ben . . .

A: God Almighty.

Q: Well, I walked in late. I'm sorry if it's been asked before.

A: I had to open my mouth, didn't I? Sorry.

Q: That's OK. Do you think Ben was talking about you? And any reaction to what Ben said yesterday?

A: From what I've seen he didn't mention any names. And then I was told that he'd mentioned names later on, and I was one of the names. I don't know what that means. But, you know, I've been talking about this since the last Ryder Cup, and I've said the same things, that I wish we could allocate money to charities. And the Presidents Cup, we get $50,000 to be able to donate to charity. Well, the Presidents Cup is not on the same level, financially, as the Ryder Cup. The Ryder Cup's an enormous money maker. And because of that, I think that it is our right to be able to be given funds to help our community. For me in Orlando, plus I also work with a target house in Memphis for some cancer kids that I want to donate money to. And a few other things back in Southern California. Unfortunately, I can't do that. And it is an exhibition. The Presidents Cup we get money to be able to allocate to charities. Why can't the Ryder Cup do the same. It's just unfortunate that this has been blown into the realm that is right now. It's not about being paid. It's about being able to allocate funds. The enormous amount of funds that are being generated at the Ryder Cup through ticket sales, TV rights, merchandise and concessions. There's so much money being made. Why can't we allocate funds to our communities.

The PGA was in the middle of a public relations nightmare, with the world's best player standing up to them at their major championship. It had become a media sideshow, so Mason jumped in and changed the subject.

'I think this is a great time to go through your card right now, Tiger,' he said.

Although Woods couldn't elaborate on it enough just seconds earlier, he was now happy to move on.

'About time, Jules,' he said as, starting with his bogey on the second hole, he dissected a round that was slow in starting but hot at the end with birdies on the 14th, 17th and 18th holes.

Tiger again got hammered in the papers, but didn't seem to care. The PGA had now started, and 19-year-old Sergio Garcia had shot 66 for a two-stroke lead over Jay Haas, Canadian Mike Weir and 1998 Buick Classic champion J. P. Hayes. At 7, 401 yards, the golf course was the longest at sea level in major championship history, and Woods was so long that in pretournament news conferences he talked about driving the first green (388 yards away) with a well-shaped drive and the right wind conditions. All Tiger had to do was keep it in play, because the length of Medinah would eventually wear down 99 percent of the field.

The two middle rounds were where Woods made his move. By shooting 67 on Friday, there were now only two players ahead of him, Haas at 9-under par and Weir at 8-under par. Garcia's loose swing resulted in the Spaniard shooting 73. Hayes shot 76 to blow himself out of the picture. Woods started off the way he finished on Thursday, with three straight birdies and five in the first seven holes. His first two birdie putts were not more than 5 feet combined and he two-putted both of the two par-fives on the front nine for birdie. The surprise awaiting Woods in the paper the following day was his comment that the greens 'were not rolling as true as you'd like to see them in a major championship.'

So now he was not only greedy, he was a whiner, too. In the *Sun-Times* Mariotti wrote, 'Time after time, the most hyped player ever has been in prime position to win majors, only to have his magic putter fail him . . . Hopefully, Woods isn't feeding my suspicions. Hopefully, he isn't creating another set of alibis this weekend in case he doesn't win the PGA Championship.' Tiger either wasn't reading the papers, like he said, or he was using the papers to fine tune his focus. He realized while warming up that his swing was too long at the top, so he shortened his backswing and almost immediately holed out a 300-yard drive on the driving range. That gave him the feeling it was going to be another good day – and it was. He came back with a 68 to tie Weir for the 54-hole lead at 11-under. Garcia and Stewart Cink were at 9-under.

'I was wide, I was tight, I was ripping it,' Woods said.

The news hook was that Tiger had won seven straight times on the PGA Tour with the final-round lead, a streak that extended back to his third pro tournament when he shot 72 on Sunday at Quad City and lost to Ed Fiori. This was already being proclaimed as Tiger's tournament to win or lose.

Garcia as much as said it: 'If he keeps playing like he played today, maybe we will have to look for second place. I'm going to do my best. I'll try to catch him . . . But I know it's going to be very difficult to catch him because, well, if you have a different player, not a player as good as Tiger on top, I think it's a little easier.'

Although he was a tough little man with a background in the Canadian junior hockey programs, Weir didn't seem like a player who would take it low on a major championship Sunday. He had played with Tiger in the final round of the Western Open, and while the lefty shot a solid 70 to finish second, this was a different arena and he had never been in the final group for one of these before.

'I know I am not a household name,' Weir said.

As a 13-year-old he wrote a letter to Jack Nicklaus, asking whether he should remain a left-hander. Nicklaus told him to do what was natural, and he did, earning Player of the Year honors in the Western Athletic Conference for Brigham Young. In 1995 he was on the range at Glen Abbey for the Canadian Open, hitting balls next to Nick Price. The sound of Price's shots was so different, as was the flight of his ball, that Weir decided he had to break down his swing and find something that would carry him to the PGA Tour. Three years later he won medalist honors at the 1998 Qualifying School and, coming into Medinah, he was in the midst of a breakthrough year. At Tucson he was in the last group but drove it in the water on the 72nd hole and shot 73 to finish

T-13. In Atlanta, he was tied for the lead with Cink but shot 72 and finished four back of Duval. 'I was out of college [Brigham Young] in 1993 and it took me five years, getting through the qualifying school, to get here,' he said. 'I can remember many times that I was missing cut after cut on the Australian Tour and you're by yourself over there and you don't have any money and you battle through those times when you're out there on the range by yourself practicing and you can't see a shot 5 feet in front of you. I'll always have those in my memory bank, those tougher times. I think if anything contributes to my determination and not giving up it is because I know how hard it is to get out here. I don't ever want to have to go back to that qualifying school.'

They arrived at Medinah at almost the same time on Sunday, coming in through the employee's entrance at the club. Mike Harrigan, the resident head professional, was interested to see them have a seemingly relaxed lunch together. 'It was neat to see the camaraderie,' said Harrigan. 'It seemed like they were good buddies.'

The challenge on Sunday came from Garcia, the 19-year-old 'Seve Junior' who had won the Murphy's Irish Open the same week Woods won the Western, who had shot 89 and 83 at Carnoustie, and who had provided the last glimpse of innocence in a week where money dominated the story line. At 5'10"and barely 150 pounds, the former British Amateur champion nicknamed 'El Niño' jumped back into the plot on the par-3 13th hole.

Weir was no longer a factor, and was on his way to an 80. Garcia was the closest pursuer, but that was in relative terms; Woods had built his lead to five strokes with seven to play. With such a powerful reputation as a closer, there appeared that nothing could stop him.

Before he teed off, Woods had worked with Harmon on the putting green. Butch's final words to him were, 'If you play your game, you can't be beaten. Now let's go get your second one.' Tiger birdied the 2nd, 5th, 7th and 11th holes. He dropped a shot with a three-putt at the 12th, but was still in control standing on the 13th tee, watching Garcia face an 18-foot downhill birdie putt.

The young Spaniard understood the moment and knew Tiger was there. When his putt went in, the young Spaniard pointed back up to the tee. Woods never blinked, staring coldly down at his target. The hole was 219 yards downhill, over water. It was tough to judge the distance, and Tiger had bogeyed the hole on Saturday with a 4-iron. This time he took 6-iron, but again he airmailed the green.

From deep rough, looking down at the hole, Woods was unable to keep his wedge shot on the green. The double bogey had turned a blowout into the fight of his life. Within three holes, his lead was down to one.

'I wanted him to know I was still there and to show him he had to finish well to win,' said Garcia. 'I did it with good feelings, not hoping that he would make a triple bogey or whatever. I was kind of telling him, "If you want to win, you have to play well." '

This is where the Showdown in Chicago began. For the next five holes the drama produced by Woods and Garcia served as the perfect ending for major championship golf in the 20th century. Woods provided the first miracle, with a shot from underneath the trees to the right of the 15th fairway. Swinging as hard as he had ever swung, and contorting his back so the ball stayed low under the branches, Woods cut a 2-iron onto the green to save par. Just up ahead, Garcia answered with one of the most spontaneously brilliant scenes in the game's history. From behind an oak tree, 189 yards from the green, the Spaniard closed his eyes on the downswing and hit a rising, cut 6-iron that landed on the green and rolled 50 feet from the cup. As memorable as that eyes-wide-shut shot was in the annals of the PGA Championship, nothing topped the reaction. Garcia ran after the ball like a child running through the streets of Pamplona, chasing the ball up the hill to see where it landed, doing a scissors kick in mid-flight and then patting his heart.

'I had a shot,' Garcia said, 'but I had to hit a big slice, and the problem was that on the downswing, I could hit the first part of the tree. If I aimed right, I might hit the second part of the tree. So I opened the clubface, made a full swing, closed my eyes and hit the ball, and went backward just in case the ball hit the tree and [came] back at me.'

The roar hit Woods like he was standing behind a 747 taking off for Madrid out of O'Hare. By the time he reached the 17th tee, the crowd had turned on him. In part because of the Ryder Cup stance. In part because of what Garcia was doing – 'It looked like I was an American,' Garcia said. In part because this was a Chicago crowd on a Sunday after too many beers. It got this way at Valencia CC in 1998, when Billy Mayfair beat him in a playoff at the Nissan Open. There is a faction out there that doesn't like Tiger Woods, and they can be just as nasty as any NBA, NHL or Major League Baseball fan.

'I could tell the crowds were changing when some guy yelled out, "Thousand dollars you don't slice it in the water" on 17,' Woods said.

The 17th green had been changed for the PGA by Medinah club officials. The old green, down closer to Lake Kadijah, was too severely pitched from back to front to be a true test of golf, so the greens committee brought in Roger Rulewich to make a change. At 206 yards, it was a much longer hole now but Tiger was so pumped up that his 7-iron was too much club. Like the shot at 13, he flew the putting surface and came to rest in deep rough, just off the green.

His chip shot hit a dead spot, and he was left with an 8-footer to save par and preserve a 1-stroke lead. 'As I was reading the putt,' Woods said, 'I kept saying, "It's got to be on top of the hole but I know this putt doesn't break as much. There's not enough grass for it to break." '

Woods asked Williams what he thought.

'Inside left,' he said.

It confirmed what Woods was feeling, what the voice inside his head was telling him to do.

'That's perfect,' said Woods.

Woods was in total control of his emotions and his technique. This was the moment his father trained him for, and in a hotel room not far away, Earl was trying to send brain waves to his son, believing that Tiger heard him when he said, 'Trust it.'

Woods knew that the tendency of most golfers on left-to-right putts is to not release the putter blade, and block the putt. When this happens, the putt misses right. 'I released the blade and I don't remember seeing it to start off because I was keeping my head steady,' he said. 'But I remember it from about a foot and a half away, just zeroing in on the inside left of the hole and it fell right in.'

The fist pump was so subtle, so Jordanesque, because as clutch as that putt was, Woods was already thinking ahead to the 18th tee and preparing himself to make birdie, because that's how Earl trained him. Taking 3-wood off the tee to put his ball in play,

Woods walked up the 72nd hole and assessed his approach shot. It was then that he was told: Sergio had made par. You've got a one-stroke lead.

That changed his strategy. He played a commercial iron shot to the center of the green, lagged to tap-in range, knocked his 277th stroke of the tournament in the hole, and celebrated as he had never celebrated before: with a sigh, a deep breath, and the look of a man who had just walked through a mine field.

Jordan and Hirsch were at the Merit Club, on the North Shore. They pulled into the clubhouse after their first 18, and Tiger had his five-shot lead. Hirsch wanted to watch the back nine on TV. Jordan wanted to keep playing.

'Joel, I get too nervous,' he said. 'I can't watch it. I'm going to jinx him.'

They went back to the course, but Jordan couldn't resist. He pulled out his mobile phone and called a friend. The lead had shrunk from five to one. 'Call me when it's over,' Hirsch heard Jordan say.

Earl Woods was never nervous. He showed up that night at the Medinah clubhouse, saw Tiger at a reception, and embraced his son as he had so many times before, on the 18th greens at Augusta, the TPC – Sawgrass, Pumpkin Ridge.

But this hug was unlike all the others. In the sporting sense, this was a close as Tiger would probably ever get to the jungles Earl Woods once escaped. As father and son came to realize, this was the day that Tiger Woods had officially become a man.

Was there telepathy going on? Or had Earl just ingrained in Tiger the belief that he was always there, always telling him to 'trust it,' the way he had when Tiger was a 12-year-old playing the Junior Worlds in San Diego?

Tiger Woods told his father what he wanted to hear.

'I heard you, Pop,' he said.

# Twenty Three

# CLOSING IT OUT

Steve Pate led the search party. It was 11 p.m. on the night of September 26, and Tiger Woods was passed out on his hotel bed at the Four Seasons Hotel in downtown Boston. The United States Ryder Cup team had just staged the greatest comeback in Ryder Cup history, coming from four points down on Sunday to defeat the Europeans, and now Tiger's teammates were looking for him. They wanted to roust Tiger, make him chug champagne and join the celebration that was raging in the team room.

'I just crashed,' said Woods. 'That whole week took so much out of me. I was wiped out.'

So much had been made of this Ryder Cup, and Tiger's importance in it. He was expected to lead this team but for the first two days, he was bearing the brunt of several awkward pairings and an inspired European team.

It wasn't until the very end of the final practice that captain Ben Crenshaw told Tiger to play a few holes with Tom Lehman; they would be partners in the Friday morning foursomes. When Sergio Garcia and Jesper Parnevik took them down, Crenshaw tried Woods and David Duval. Lee Westwood and Darren Clarke beat them 1 up. Woods was 0 and 2 after the first day, and coming off a 1-3-1 showing at Valderrama in 1997, was definitely feeling the heat.

On the second day, Crenshaw tried Woods with Steve Pate, and they had to fight hard for a 1 up victory over Miguel Angel

Jimenez of Spain and Padraig Harrington of Ireland. The captain tried to ride that pairing into the afternoon, but Woods and Pate lost the last match of the afternoon, 2 and 1, to Colin Montgomerie and Paul Lawrie.

Crenshaw came into the interview room that night and was so emotional that his thoughts became incoherent. His voice cracked and his eyes misted. Down 10 – 6, he waved a finger and left behind a warning. 'I'm a big believer in fate,' he said. 'I have a good feeling about this. That's all I'm going to tell you.'

What Crenshaw could sense was a difference in the attitude of Woods and Duval, how they had come to not only understand the Ryder Cup experience, but to cherish it. They both stood up during private dinners and spoke with conviction of their passion for the game, their teammates and their country. That Saturday night, back at the team hotel, they looked at the pairings and swathe potential for victory that no one outside their team room saw.

Their part in Sunday's victory was somewhat overlooked in the bull rush onto the 17th green after Justin Leonard's 45-foot bomb sealed the victory. Woods had one of the day's easiest pairings, and took care of Scotland's Andrew Colthart 3 and 2. Duval's 5 and 4 victory over Parnevik, who had gone 3 – 0 – 1 as Sergio Garcia's partner, was more emphatic.

'This is all for Ben,' said Woods outside the locker room.

It took Woods nearly four weeks to recover and regroup for the conclusion of the season, but by the end of October, Tiger was talking hat trick. The National Car Rental Golf Classic at Walt Disney World was the first leg of a monster fall schedule that had him going around the world in 30 days. His itinerary included the Tour Championship in Houston, the WGC – American Express Championship in Spain, the Johnnie Walker Classic in Taiwan, the World Cup in Malaysia, two exhibitions in Japan and the PGA Grand Slam of Golf in Hawaii. For Woods, there was no such thing as playing out the string – not when there were two $5 million events coming up at Champions and Valderrama.

The Disney tournament, played 10 miles from his house, was one of his favorite stops because it was low-key and convenient. In 1996, Woods had won his second professional tournament on the Magnolia course, outplaying Payne Stewart down the stretch on Sunday to qualify for his first Tour Championship. The circumstances were now much different.

Woods was in a position where he could set his own schedule, taking blocks of time off to avoid burnout and allow him to peak for the majors. Two weeks after the PGA, he racked up his fifth victory of the year by defeating Phil Mickelson in the NEC Invitational at Firestone. Disney was his first tournament, other than the Ryder Cup, in the two months since Akron.

Woods, commuting from his townhouse at Isleworth, won for the second time in four years at WDW, and for the sixth time in 1999. He won by shooting a final-round 73, which was enough to hold off Ernie Els and move past the $4. 7 million mark in yearly earnings. He also won for the sixth time in his last nine events. Starting at the Deutsche Bank – SAP Open in May, Woods has finished 1, 1, T-3, T-7, 1, T-37, 1 and 1.

'Playing at home is great because you don't have to look at the remote . . . you know what the numbers are,' said Woods, and these numbers were premium channels: Not since Tom Watson in 1980 had anybody won six times in one year on the PGA Tour. (Nick Price's five-victory season in 1994 does not include his British Open triumph at Turnberry.) Watson (32) and Price (37) were in their primes when they took it deep. Woods didn't turn 24 until December 30 and by then he could have caught Jack Nicklaus, whose back-to-back seven victories seasons in 1972 – 1973 included Disney titles.

'I'd like to get seven, and then eight would be nice,' Woods said.

Woods got his sixth at Disney by opening with three-straight rounds of 66 that were a mix of his A and B games. Els played with Woods on Saturday and raved about the control Tiger had over his golf ball – 'I was totally in awe,' Ernie said. Woods, who didn't birdie a par-5, thought he played better Friday. He went home after the third round and hit balls until dark trying to match his arms with his lower body.

His ball-striking on Sunday won the tournament. He three-putted three times, and missed a 6-footer for the lead on the 15th hole. Through his lapse, he lost a two-stroke lead to Bob Tway, gained it back, fell into a tie with Els, and then reassumed a one-stroke margin when Ernie blew a down-grain birdie putt at the 17th nearly off the green, and missed the come-backer for par.

For all the money that Woods has stashed and invested, he couldn't buy a putt. The difference was that when he needed to cozy a 35-footer on the 72nd hole, Woods did what all the great ones do: He lagged it to 2 feet, tapped in, and got off the green before it bit him back.

This win was a textbook example of the new Tiger. He basically didn't beat himself the way Tway (triple bogey at the 12th) and Els (lay up into the pond at the par-5 14th) did. He had control over his emotions, his swing and his ball flight. When the fairways were muddy and the ball was picking up mud, Woods lowered his trajectory. When his ball had a gob of dirt on it, he slowed down his body speed and dead-armed shots into greens. These were the subtle traits of a genius, and they serve to highlight his amazing record for protecting a final-round lead; he had won for the third time this year with an over-par round on Sunday, and he was now an unbelievable 10-for-11 on Sundays. That percentage (. 909), against the level of competition that exists today, is Woods's gaudiest stat.

Although he now had a half-dozen victories for the year, Woods was seeing just how hard winning really was – even for a player of his mental strength and immense athletic ability. There was a greater sense of humbleness to him: At Disney there were no end-zone dances after a big putt – in fact, when he made a 40-footer to close out Saturday's round, his reaction was absolutely sheepish. He said all the right things in the news conferences, signed enough autographs to fulfill his obligations, and competed as true champions are supposed to compete. At 23, he had grown into his role quite nicely.

And nobody seemed to be enjoying it more. 'When I was in junior golf, I thought that I could never love the game as much as I did then, until I got out here and starting playing more,' he said. 'For some reason, I love it more. I never thought that would be possible. I thought that I'd reached a level in which you can't love the game more than that, but I love to play, I love to practice, I love to compete. I can honestly say I love it more now.'

Tiger's next stop was the Tour Championship at Houston, which will forever be remembered, not as the week Tiger won his seventh tournament, but for tragedy. Monday brought the shocking news that a Lear jet, chartered from Orlando and believed to be carrying Payne Stewart, was flying out-of-control across the Midwest. Everyone aboard was believed to be either unconscious or dead. The place finally crashed in Aberdeen, South Dakota, with the body of Payne Stewart inside. For the next six days, the sadness was too overwhelming to overcome. Traveling back to

Orlando for Friday's funeral, and then back to Houston for the conclusion of the tournament, Woods shot 67-66-67-69 to win by four strokes over Davis Love III.

Although he was one of five players in the 29-man field who did not participate in wearing knickers on Sunday as a tribute to their fallen colleague, Woods grieved in his own way and memorialized Stewart with a more dignified image – by raising the crystal trophy skyward and looking to the heavens during his victory speech. 'You don't have to wear knickers to honor someone,' Woods said. 'I'm comfortable handling things internally. I don't need to show the pain I feel inside.'

From Houston, Woods led a transatlantic air caravan of golfers headed to Valderrama for the final big-money event of the year, the WGC – American Express Championship. Woods was now defined as a man on a mission. He came to the approach shot on the 71st hole leading by one stroke over local favorite Miguel Angel Jimenez. In the Ryder Cup, Woods putted off this green and into the water at a pivotal moment, and now he faced 100 yards after two well placed shots down the fairway.

Woods took a 9-iron, wanting to chip the ball without much backspin. 'That way,' he said, 'I thought I could take the pond out of play.' The shot seemed perfect, leaving a pitch mark 15 feet behind the hole. The ball checked and then started its trickle back toward the hole. From the fairway, Woods watched as his ball kept rolling in slow motion past the pin, off the green, and into the pond.

Afterward he was told by Sergio Garcia that the green had been triple cut. 'Combined with the pin placement and the wind,' said Woods, 'that meant there was almost nowhere to hit it.'

When he walked off that green after holing out with a triple bogey 8, his lead had disappeared and there was one hole to play. From the gallery, Woods could hear the murmurs of those gleeful over his misfortune. With that in the back of his mind, he parred the 18th for a 68 and waited for Jimenez to finish. 'The fact they were cheering [when my ball went in the water at 17] had nothing to do with the Ryder Cup,' Woods would later say. 'I think it had to do with a person from their own country, who is obviously playing well, and in a big event, now being in the lead. [Jimenez] had a tremendous year in Spain; two wins and a second, I think. And I think that obviously they wanted him to win. But I also had a lot of fans pulling for me, as well. So when the ball went in the water, it was disappointing to hear the sounds, but understandable.'

Jimenez came to the 72nd hole leading by a stroke. He then did what Miguel Angel Jimenez is supposed to do in that situation: He pulled and hooked his drive, made bogey, and lost to Woods in a playoff. It was an escape made possible only because Woods kept his composure after the triple bogey. If he had let the partisan gallery at the 17th green get to him, he never would have made par at the 18th, which put just enough pressure on Jimenez to force him into that bad drive.

Woods became the first golfer since Johnny Miller to record eight victories in the same season. With his second $1 million first-place check of the season, he also went over $6. 6 million in PGA Tour earnings, which was more than the combined earnings of David Duval and Davis Love III, Nos. 2 – 3 on the money list.

It was as dominating a year as anyone has ever had in golf. Byron Nelson, Jack Nicklaus, Arnold Palmer and Johnny Miller – all of whom had monster seasons – were asked to weigh-in and give historical perspective.

Nelson, who won an amazing 11 straight in 1945 and 18 overall that year (plus seven runner-up performances), sounded genuinely pleased that Woods kept his streak alive. He doubted, however, that even a player of Tiger's skill could summon the mental and physical strength necessary to win seven more in a row.

'I'm not saying anybody can't play better than I did, but there's so many things the boys have to do now,' Nelson pointed out from his home in Roanoke, Texas. 'They have the press, and their sponsors . . . I had one sponsor, Wheaties, and they paid me $200. That was it. Golf just wasn't that big then.'

It wasn't as global, either, which makes Woods's accomplishments all the more remarkable. 'I think that he very well could challenge Jack, but there's so many good players now from all over the world,' Nelson added. 'Jack mainly was beating Americans. Now you've got guys from all over, like [José Maria] Olazabal.'

The day after Tiger won his fourth straight, Nicklaus was at Bear Lakes Country Club in West Palm Beach, Florida, watching his son Gary in the second stage of PGA Tour Qualifying. Between the ages of 32 and 33, the elder Nicklaus had won seven tournaments (including two majors) in 1972, and another seven tournaments (including the PGA) in 1973. Tiger was now 23. 'I think he's had a great year,' Nicklaus said. 'How great is it? That's hard to say. The competition was great and he played great, but when I played, I never compared it to Nelson or Hogan. Tiger's year stands on its own two feet. He played great in all the significant tournaments. He's won four in a row, and nobody's ever won four in a row in 46 years. That's pretty good. I never did it.'

Palmer won eight tournaments in 1960 and then went back-to-back with seven-win seasons in 1962 – 1963. He was most impressed with Tiger's winning percentage (. 428), but didn't want to sell short the level of play during previous generations. From his summer home in Latrobe, Pa., Palmer said, 'I don't know if it's any better today than what guys like Nicklaus or Miller or some of those guys I played against did, but certainly the depth is there today. I think Tiger's exhibited some exceptional strength in his golf, and there is no question about it: He has the ability to get stronger when he needs to.'

Miller wanted to point out that beating Nicklaus, Lee Trevino, Raymond Floyd, Hale Irwin and Tom Weiskopf in 1974 – the year he won eight tournaments – represented just as strong a group as Tiger had to beat 25 years later. He also noted that Woods never had a great head-to-head showdown, that his wins 'came against a bunch of Jimenezes' instead of against Colin Montogomerie, David Duval, Ernie Els and Phil Mickelson.

It was Miller who once criticized the American players on the PGA Tour for not having a killer instinct, blaming the U.S. Ryder Cup losses in 1985 and 1987 (and the tie in 1989) on the fact that there weren't enough wolves in the pack. Now he was saying that the lone wolf has turned everybody else into sacrificial lambs. 'The big guys didn't dominate except for Tiger, and that opened it up to Tiger,' Miller said. 'I don't want to take anything away from Tiger, but it wasn't a great year for the superstars.'

Miller, taking a break from his duties as NBC's analyst at his home in Napa, California, said he could see Woods averaging five wins a year for the next 10 years, and adding eight professional majors to the two he already owned. That would still put him behind Nicklaus's pace, but he'd only be 33, with at least 10 good years left. 'I think it's getting to the point where he's scaring the field, which is where Nicklaus was, and where Palmer was and where Watson was,' Miller said. 'Tiger is moving into that realm.

Before everybody knew his potential was phenomenal. Now they're saying he's unbelievable. You're not supposed to say that when you're competing against somebody. You can think it. But you don't say it – even if it's true.'

Miller was talking about the quotes coming from Montgomerie, Love and Els, all of whom had conceded that Tiger was on a different planet. Said Love, 'That day I played 27 holes with him in Houston [the third round of the'99 Tour Championship] was the most frustrating day I had all year. I got out of my game, was swinging too hard, making bad decisions . . . I lost my rhythm. Maybe it doesn't happen on the first tee, but your mental outlook changes.'

Five of Tiger's last six victories had come against players ranked in the top 15. There was Vijay Singh at the Memorial, Sergio Garcia at the PGA, Phil Mickelson at the NEC Invitational, Els at the National Car Rental and Love at the Tour Championship. Els, who had lost a seven-shot lead to Woods at the Johnnie Walker in 1998, had gone from 'next great player' to president of Tiger's fan club. 'Nobody can touch this guy now at the moment,' he said. 'He has gone to another level that I don't think the rest of us can really find right now.'

The win pool had definitely shrunk. Els, Singh, Garcia, Mickelson, Love, O'Meara, David Duval, Justin Leonard and Tom Lehman did not record a win from the time Woods won in Germany until the end of the year. With Woods capturing victories in 10 of the last 14 events he played in, guys were basically playing for second every time Tiger teed it up. Trampled in this sprint was Duval, who seemingly had Player of the Year honors locked up with four wins (including the Players Championship) going into the Masters.

'Are we able to beat him?' said Lehman. 'Definitely, but I know I've got to do things better. I get sloppy, my course management gets bad, I get angry – all the things you can't allow yourself to do. I've thrown away shots and thrown away tournaments, and I've played enough with Tiger to see the way he plays. He's incredibly talented, yet he doesn't beat himself. When he hits a bad shot, he recovers. When he hits a good shot, he takes advantage of it.'

O'Meara swathes coming during their matches at Isleworth Golf Club in Orlando. From that day in May when all the swing changes finally clicked, Tiger was a different golfer. 'I don't even [practice] with him anymore,' said O'Meara, only half-joking. 'He's too good for me. It's pretty amazing, with all the expectations placed on him, that he's just become that much better.'

Woods realized the edge he had on Love, Els, O'Meara and even Phil Mickelson, who had become parents and lost some of their former edge. Tiger was in no hurry to get married, let alone have children. The only golfer with the same single-mindedness was Duval, and David had now shown the same ability to deal with all the baggage that comes with being No. 1.

'I think what ends up happening is that when players have been out here for a long period of time, it's very easy to get in a rut of just playing golf and forgetting that when you first came out here, you had your specific goals and you were trying to accomplish them,' said Woods. 'The guys who are secure on the tour by virtue of enough wins of the top 50 in career earnings, it's easy to get in a rut of just playing golf and not focusing on winning championships.

'But also, too, your life changes over time. Guys come out here without having kids, and when they get married and settle down, that becomes their priority. Because of that, golf takes a back seat until they realize something's changed, that they're not playing well, that they're not devoting enough time to it. They need to devote more time, but by then, they let a few years slide by.'

There was also a sense of patience in Tiger that was manifested in the way he went about playing each shot, and each hole. As his agent, Mark Steinberg, pointed out, there was a bit of 'I told you so' coming from Woods, who knew all along that the 'reconstruction stage' he and Butch were working on would ultimately make him built to last.

'That's the thing, I did it slowly,' said Woods. 'I could have done what Nick [Faldo] did with David Leadbetter [in the mid-1980s] and completely lose my game for a year and a half, two years, then try to come back. [But] I don't know if I could have done it that way. It might have sped up the process, but in the meantime you lose a lot of confidence.'

Woods now had the total package that would allow him to be more consistent. The big numbers that destroyed his chances at Congressional, Troon and Winged Foot in the 1997 majors were now taken out of his game. Physically and emotionally, he now appeared in total control of his golf ball and his temper. His highest rounds after the May epiphany were a pair of 74s at

Carnoustie at the British Open. He wasn't slamming clubs as much, and he was able to win in all climates, on all grasses, by shooting low on Sunday, or by grinding out a score right around par. He was able to win the PGA with a closing 72, the NEC with a 71 and Disney with a 73 – all by one stroke.

At the same time, he could go four rounds in the 60s, as he did at the SAP Open, the Tour Championship, and the World Cup, and win going away. It was at the point where he was making the game look easy, and he seemed to be enjoying it so much more. 'The game's still elusive, there's no doubt about it,' he admitted at the American Express Championships. 'Is it easier? It's easier from the standpoint I'm not playing as many trees as I once was. That makes things a lot easier. I'm not putting myself in the trouble that I used to, because my swing has improved. And I think that goes for anybody whose swing improves. You start to put yourself in situations where you're not in the same old predicaments. And I've been able to do that very well this year. My swing has really come around, thanks to basically two years of a lot of hard work. It's nice to have the shots that I have in my repertoire right now that I can rely on. Just in case if one doesn't work I can go to that one, and if another one doesn't work I can go to another one. It's nice to have that variety.'

It was at Valderrama that the difference in Woods's game was in the spotlight. The last time Woods played that course, during the 1997 Ryder Cup, he was airmailing greens and was unable to work the ball through the course's cork trees. Just two years later, heavy winds blowing in off the ocean and the tight, quirky course did not bother him. 'If you watch me play now versus in'97,' Woods said during that tournament, 'you'll see that my trajectory of my golf shots are much flatter. And they don't have, I guess – I guess you say they don't have a peak in them that they used to. My angle of attack is different and a little shallower, hence I don't spin the ball up in the air as much, therefore I can keep the ball flatter, longer, in the air. I can hit the ball and bore it through the wind better.'

What gave Woods an added advantage at courses like Augusta, Firestone, Valderrama and Champions is that he has the natural ability to hit the ball high. Growing up in Southern California, he had to hit those shots to hold greens. 'The great thing is where I came from is that I can always hit the ball high at any given time,' he said. 'That's easy for me to do. I think that's more of an advantage, because now play the ball lower, but I can always throw the ball up in the air on hard greens, without having to change my swing. Other guys who are naturally low-ball hitters have a difficult time getting the ball in the air because they feel very uncomfortable playing different types of courses because of that.'

After his victory at Valderrama, Woods continued his world tour by traveling to Taiwan (where he finished sixth in the Johnnie Walker Classic), Malaysia (where he won the individual title and led the United States to victory in the World Cup), Japan (where he conducted clinics and an exhibition for Nike) and Hawaii, where he won the PGA Grand Slam of Golf.

When the season finally ended in December, Woods had 11 wins, over $7.6 million in worldwide prize money, the Vardon Trophy (with the lowest stroke average in PGA Tour history at 68. 43) and the PGA of America and PGA Tour Player of the Year Awards. Still, there was more for him to accomplish, and he could sense it. Much, much more.

## Twenty Four

# THE INNER CIRCLE

On December 29, 1999, the day before his 24th birthday, Tiger Woods shot 65 in the opening round of the Williams World Challenge, an event he was hosting at Grayhawk Golf Club in Scottsdale to benefit the Tiger Woods Foundation. It had become clear now that Tiger was not only hitting the shots, but calling them as well. He had evolved from a boy to a young man and his father, Earl, had cut the strings and allowed his child to start making decisions on his own. It was Tiger's show now, his life.

'I raised Tiger to leave me,' was Earl's mantra, and part of his Plan. It was the circle of life: Tiger could feel his dad letting go, and enjoyed the independence. Instead of talking every night, they would go weeks without communicating. Technically, Earl was chairman of the Tiger Woods Foundation and president of the Tiger Woods Corporation, but he was traveling less, and thus being quoted less. It was his mother, Tida, who was now there waiting for him behind the green when he won; Earl was in a hotel room or rented house, watching on television.

The old Vietnam vet was not well. At 68, he had survived three open-heart operations and prostate cancer, but he refused to change his diet, or stop smoking and drinking. He still lived in the family house in Cypress, California, the same house where he took Tiger in his diapers to the garage, sat him in a chair, and had him watch his Pops hit golf balls into a net. Tida now lived in a home Tiger had built for her down Interstate 5 in Tustin. She would go clean the old house, but had quit trying to convince Earl that his life would end if he didn't quit his habits.

There was nobody whom Tiger loved and respected more than his dad, and it killed him to see his father walk so stubbornly toward death. At the same time, the whole experience was an awakening. It made Tiger realize it was time to move on, to accept more responsibilities, to make some changes that were necessary for the long-term benefit of his life and career. His father had trained him to be a general, and generals have to make cold decisions. Tiger made two of them by purging superagent Hughes Norton and caddy Mike 'Fluff' Cowan. These were moves that had Earl's approval, but ultimately the call was made by Tiger.

Historically, Tiger and Earl never hesitated in making changes to the structure of their organization. Tiger may be big into loyalty, but as the firing of Norton and Cowan proved, loyalty doesn't always go both ways in the Woods camp. Sports psychologist Jay Brunza, the caddy for Tiger's first two U.S. Amateur victories, was the first to go. He was followed out the door by lawyer John Merchant, the former USGA executive who was the first head of the Tiger Woods Foundation. After Norton was relieved of his duties, there were even whispers that the next person to get the eject button would be Tiger's swing teacher, Butch Harmon.

Norton and Cowan were replaced by Mark Steinberg, a more likeable, more media-friendly personal manger and Steve Williams, an unapproachable caddy who had previous experience carrying for big-ego stars Greg Norman and Raymond Floyd. Earl gave both of these decisions his blessing, but the cuts were ordered by his son, and were the truest indications that Tiger was ready to do it on his own.

'Earl's role is very important in Tiger's life,' said Steinberg. 'In addition to Earl basically running the foundation on a day-to-day basis, he is kind of the surveyor of Tiger. When we have big decisions that come up, the three heads come together and we discuss those issues. Whether it's the General Motors contract, or an issue coming up with Tiger, Earl provides some wisdom that sometimes Tiger and I don't see the side to. He's not involved on a day-to-day as much as he used to be, but he is still involved in the big-picture scale.'

'Steiny' and 'Stevie' became part of an inner circle that now featured Joanna Jagoda, the first public love of Tiger's life, and Greg McLaughlin, the former executive director of the Western Golf Association. Along with instructor Butch Harmon, Stanford teammate Jerry Chang, junior high school friend Bryon Bell and Greg Nared of Nike Golf, the inner circle of Team Tiger was closely bonded and hard to penetrate. 'I've always surrounded myself with people I could trust,' Woods said. 'I've done that since I was a very little kid. I've had my close friends and I've always kept them. My same friends I've known since grade school are still my best friends. I have a few people that I confide things into, but there are people I call good friends, and then there are my best friends.'

Trust is big with Tiger. It takes time to earn it, and once it's lost, it's usually lost forever. In the case of Norton, the dismissal was characterized by the Woods camp as an eventuality of the relationship, that Hughes had taken Tiger this far and it was simply time for a change. In actuality, the cut was quite deeper for Norton, who had been on the trail of Tiger since he was playing junior golf, and used his signing as a rebirth of his career at IMG after Norman let him go.

Norton's strengths were as a negotiator, and what he asked for Tiger at both Nike and Titleist were unprecedented. In signing Tiger to $100 million worth of endorsement contracts, Norton had immediately put Woods in the Jordan League. But Earl Woods thought Norton took too much credit for those deals and was too 'out front' as Tiger's representative. Publicly, it was Hughes who took the blame for the mismanaging of Tiger's schedule the first year of his professional career.

'There is a difference between the two of them,' said Earl. 'Hughes is a money, bottom-line guy. Money is not that important to Tiger. He cares about humanitarian work. There is a clash there. Tiger is not one who wants to be the top money winner, or the top money endorser. That is not what's important to him.'

What was important was history, and the chasing of a record. As Jordan had told him, 'Hey man, the business is great. But you'll be remembered for one thing: what you do on the golf course. Years from now, people won't be talking about the endorsements and the smart deals you made; they'll talk about how many tournaments you won, how many majors you won. Your name will be made that way.'

Tiger listened to the advice of Michael and his father, making the cut of Norton from his team. This put IMG in the awkward situation of replacing the man in their organization who discovered Woods and devised the scheme to pay Earl as a 'talent scout,' but business was business and Alastair Johnston, head of IMG's golf division, had a solution. Behind the scenes, Johnston and Mark McCormack had been grooming Steinberg with their high-profile LPGA superstars Annika Sorenstam, Karrie Webb and Michelle McGann. Besides being incredibly sharp and media savvy, Steinberg was also just 30 years old and had a background in athletics. In 1989 he had been on the bench of the NCAA Final Four Illinois team that included future NBA stars Kendall Gill, Nick Anderson and Kenny Battle. He was a much better fit for Phase II of Tiger's development.

The first thing Steinberg did was work more closely with Tiger, Earl and Butch on melding Tiger's playing schedule with his commercial endorsement obligations. 'One of the things Tiger and I were joking around about the other day was the tour schedule,' said Steinberg at the end of 1999. 'It's telling us a new season is starting. But for him, it's not like the Tour Championship ends the end of October, and he's got until January first. That's ludicrous. He took more time off in that Ryder Cup area than he did from the end of the year to the start of the year. I told him don't worry about getting off to a good start, just continue doing what you're doing. This is one long season. The next 30 years for you could be one long season. I don't say that to freak him out. I'm just saying, hey, take your large blocks of time off throughout the year. Let your off time come in May, in August and December.'

Steinberg only added one major deal to Tiger's portfolio, but it was a blockbuster – totally outside the box when it came to conventional thinking about the core of Tiger's fan base. In the fall of 1999, General Motors announced that it had signed Tiger to a five-year deal that would pay Tiger $30 million to endorse Buick. As this contract was being consummated, Steinberg was renegotiating with Nike. In *Golf World*, Ron Sirak reported that Woods had earned $50 million in 1999, and that figure would grow to $65 million in 2000.

Best of all, from Tiger's standpoint, was that the business of being an icon had not interrupted his preparation for competition. Steinberg had accomplished what he set out to accomplish, and was making it clear that the final call on all decisions was being made by the man at the top: Tiger, not Earl. 'I have no game plans that are railroaded with Tiger,' said Steinberg. 'He is more involved in business than people can ever imagine. He really gets involved in all aspects of his business. He wants to know how a deal works, why a deal works and the reasons behind it. We don't spend two hours on every little point that we do, but he really wants to be involved.'

Inside the ropes, Tiger's support came from Williams, an outdoorsy, fit, New Zealander who had replaced the legendary Cowan early in the 1999 season. This change had been orchestrated by Harmon, but it was Tiger who wanted to make the change because Cowan had become too much of a media celebrity. In many ways, Williams was the anti-Fluff. In tremendous physical shape, he usually dashed off into the gallery as soon as the rounds ended and was waiting either on the driving range, or the putting green, for Tiger. He also took a no-nonsense position in dealing with the media. Whereas Cowan was always accommodating to the press, Williams refused interviews because he knew his job depended on it.

It also bothered Woods that Cowan made disclosures about his pay scale in a *Golf Digest* interview with three other tour caddies, saying he made $1,000 a week, plus the standard percentages for wins [10 percent] and top 10 finishes. He also increased his income by doing commercials for ESPN, Choice Hotel and the World Golf Village, creating an overexposure that led Tiger to question his effort.

What finally severed the Woods-Cowan relationship was the Nissan Open in 1999. First Woods reportedly pulled up to the clubhouse at Riviera and saw his caddy conducting interviews. Then, when his yardages didn't match up, Tiger took over his yardage book and told Cowan that he would be taking high school buddy Jerry Bell to LaCosta the following week for the Andersen Consulting Match Play Championship, a tournament that would mean a $1 million payday for Woods and potentially $100,000 for Cowan.

The change was made by Harmon the week of the Doral-Ryder-Open. The first choice was Greg Norman's caddy, Tony Navarro. Harmon knew that Tony was untouchable, so he went after Williams, who was working that week for Floyd. There was a tremendous buzz in the caddy yard, and there was speculation that the job was going to Greg Rita, who had major championship wins for Curtis Strange and John Daly. What complicated the process were the contracts that had to be signed with Williams, and the various equipment and clothing companies involved with Tiger.

'This is not a normal caddy's job,' said Harmon. 'This is a worldwide job where you're put in situations that you've never been in before.'

Williams made his debut in March at Bay Hill. Floyd had endorsed him by saying, 'Steve was the only caddy I've had who didn't choke,' and this would be particularly important on a bag that would be in contention almost every time out. In the 35-year-old Williams, Woods also had someone he could train with, use as a bodyguard, and, most important, share the same wavelength on yardage and club selection. This was extremely important, especially when Woods went through a much-publicized golf ball change, going from Titleist to Nike before the Deutsche Bank SAP Open in May of 2000.

'I can't say enough about Stevie,' said Woods. 'He's so positive out there, keeps me upbeat. We have a good time out there, whether I'm playing good or bad, it doesn't matter. We're going to enjoy each other's company.'

Joanna Jagoda, a law student at Pepperdine University, was the most mysterious component in Tiger's support group – which is the way Woods preferred it. They met at the 1998 Nissan Open while she was a student at the University of California at Santa Barbara; one of her college friends was dating Bell, who was now getting ready for med school and caddying that week at Valencia CC in the northeast corner of the Los Angeles metroplex. Tiger and Bryan traveled up to UCSB shortly after that tournament to attend a party, and that's when Woods and Jagoda first connected. Her first tournament with him was the GTE Byron Nelson Classic that year, but by the Presidents Cup in November she was appearing at functions and hanging with the rest of the wives and girlfriends who traveled to Australia.

It said something about Woods's character that he would pick such a well-grounded young woman to accompany him on this journey through fame. Yes, Jagoda was blond and attractive, but she was also intelligent and with goals of her own. Friends said she brought a sense of normalcy to his life.

'All the great players found by accident or otherwise that a great partner off the golf course provides balance in life which allows them to have peace of mind on the golf course,' said the Golf Channel's Peter Kessler. 'I don't know Joanna well, but I'm always impressed by her character, her poise and her sense of perspective despite the ferocious hurricane that surrounds her boyfriend.'

The final official addition to Team Tiger was McLaughlin, who came on board as executive director of the Williams World Challenge. McLaughlin was the first tournament director to consider giving Woods a spot in a PGA Tour event. In the summer of 1990, he proposed to the board of the Nissan Los Angeles Open that an exemption be granted to Eldrick 'Tiger' Woods, a 14-year-old phenom from Cypress, California. The board voted McLaughlin's proposal down, but McLaughlin pitched Woods again in 1991. This time the board approved the exemption and McLaughlin had a friend for life.

Their relationship developed through the'90s. Woods moved on to the Honda Classic and McLaughlin arranged another sponsor's exemption. McLaughlin moved on to the Western Golf Association, and took care of Tiger and Earl when they traveled to Point of Woods in Michigan for the Western Amateur. McLaughlin later went to Chicago, where Woods won the Western Open at Cog Hill in 1997 and again in 1999.

Surrounded now by a support group that he was comfortable with, Woods approached his 24th birthday on December 30 as a young man seemingly much older than his years. The next night, he enjoyed a New Year's Eve benefit concert given by Natalie Cole at the Princess Hotel in Scottsdale, Arizona. His mother and father were there, as were Steinberg, Jagoda, McLaughlin, Nared, O'Meara, and Chang. There was much to celebrate, much to anticipate.

'I see a huge difference [in attitude] between 1997 and 1999,' said McLaughlin. 'The swing changes are one thing, but he just seems to be much more with it. He manages the whole thing a lot better now than he did a couple of years ago. That comes with experience, age, maturity, whatever you want to call it.'

Tiger Woods was now ready to embark on a year that no golfer – perhaps no athlete – had ever experienced. He would take his game, and his popularity, to unimaginable heights. Once again, he would raise the bar.

# PART IV

## The Greatest Year Ever

*The guy's a freak, you know?*

– ERNIE ELS

# Twenty Five

# NEW BEGINNING

The Williams World Challenge was a made-for-TV event, a Silly Season filler for NBC, which no longer had an NFL package and was looking for alternative programming for its holiday viewers. The tournament would start on a Wednesday or Thursday, take Friday off for New Year's Eve, and then return on the weekend. For NBC producer Tommy Roy, it was a chance to showcase a young man who had become one of the most dynamic sports performers in the world. For Tiger Woods, the host of the event, it was an opportunity to get ready for the 2000 season by testing himself against an all-star cast. David Duval, Sergio Garcia, Davis Love III, Hal Sutton, Justin Leonard, Vijay Singh, Phil Mickelson, Tom Lehman and Mark O'Meara had all come to Grayhawk Golf Club in Scottsdale, Arizona, which was a testimony not only to the power Tiger had over the *Golf World* but the corporate world as well. Williams, a communications and energy services company, put up a $3. 5 million purse with $1 million going to the winner.

Woods came to Arizona having not played any real golf in two weeks. But he was taught by his father not to accept defeat on any level – o matter what the stakes – so this wasn't going to be a week where he shook hands at corporate receptions and slapped golf balls around without caring. Being in contention on a week-to-week basis is what he had been striving for by going to the swing change; now that Tiger was technically sound, he wanted to keep on improving.

That's what the end of the 1999 season was all about, and that's what he wanted to build on in the new year. He didn't want to lose his momentum, his edge, or his aura of intimidation – a aura he would never acknowledge publicly, but in his heart knew existed. 'It's almost as if he had to defend why he didn't win more last year,' said his agent, Mark Steinberg. 'It was a very soft "I told you so" this year. He didn't come out and stick his finger in everybody's face and say I told you so, but if you think about it, it really is an "I told you so" kind of story. He wasn't b. s-ing people when he said he was going through swing changes.'

Woods brought his Hogan face to Grayhawk. Waiting on a tee box, a woman spectator asked him, 'Why don't you smile more?' Woods politely answered, 'Ma'am, right now I'm nervous. I don't know if you can smile when you're nervous. You may have that skill, but I don't. I'm trying to win a tournament. I'm giving it everything possible I have right now. I'm trying to get myself to where I have a chance to win. That's how I know how to play.'

The only player to beat Woods on a Sunday in three-plus years had been Ed Fiori, the sawed-off Texan who caught him in Quad Cities in his fourth pro tournament. It had become the most pivotal moment in Tiger's personal time line, because it showed Woods how anybody could have a hot week and beat him. 'The biggest thing that happened to me was losing to The Grip,' he would say. 'If I had won that tournament, it might have been different. I probably would have perceived it as being too easy.'

In his mind, Woods began the 2000 season already one leg upon the Grand Slam. He won his second major championship in a grueling battle against Garcia at Medinah, and figured with the two Millennium Opens at Pebble Beach and St. Andrews, going for four straight was more that a legitimate goal – it was a definite possibility. In his conversations with Butch Harmon, Woods was now talking about running the table. 'He says he's only got to win the first three, then [he] will have won four in a row,' said Harmon. 'He may be the only one in the game to do it. He believes he can do it, I tell you that.'

Woods wouldn't say this in his news conferences, but he knew – just as everybody knew – that he'd be the odds-on favorite to win again at Augusta. With that new game of his, with that distance control, that control of emotions, and control of everybody's psyche, his chances of going two legs upon the slam were pretty darn good. With a few breaks, he'd be money.

Motivation would not be a problem. The income he was earning off the course had not affected his desire to get up every day and try to improve upon what nobody else could touch. It was a scary prospect for the rest of his competition, to face that kind of talent and have it want to kick your butt every day. With Tiger, there would be no chance of a letdown. As Harmon said, 'Tiger doesn't sit on what he's done. He wants to improve on what he's done and get better. He will get better. He's still just a young man.'

Coming up that big at the end of 1999 had definitely revealed a side of golf that had never been seen before, at least not since the days of Byron Nelson. Winning 11 straight – as Nelson had in 1945 against the likes of Ben Hogan, Sam Snead, Jimmy Demaret and Lloyd Mangrum – was perhaps the one record Tiger Woods would never break, but he did have four-in-a-row working on a carryover of seasons.

Whether it was official or not, The Streak was something he wanted to run with. He was not afraid of taking it deeper, of pushing himself into the realm that Johnny Miller talked about, where it reached a point in certain tournaments where everybody was playing for second. There was too much fun in being the Michael Jordan of golf, being the man, dealing with the pressure on a week-to-week basis better than anybody else had ever dealt with it, answering the call time and again in a league where four wins in a year was once considered a career season. Tiger was now doubling that and thinking he could take it to double digits.

What would keep him going? That was a stupid question. 'Strictly winning, simple as that,' he'd say with a blank expression. 'You always want to win, that's it. Nothing more. Obviously I'd like to possibly one day come close, if not surpass Nicklaus's records, which would be nice. But I think if I go out there every tournament with the intent of winning, then that will take care of itself.'

His attitude was right where it should be: he took nothing for granted yet became more and more confident with each passing tournament. It was a dangerous combination, because nobody was going to outwork him and nobody was going to take more heart into the arena. All he had to do was bring his game that week, and there he'd be, going to Pebble and St. Andrews with the same attitude he brought to the end of 1999. Imagine going into the Opens thinking 'sweep.' What a buzz that would create.

He had raised the bar in 1997. He raised it again in 1999. And now he wanted to raise it even higher in 2000. 'You know, to be honest with you, I don't think you're ever finished,' he said in a reflective moment at the end of his record-breaking year. 'As soon as you feel like you're finished, then I guess you are finished, because you've already put a limit on your ability and what you can attain. I don't think that's right. You should always strive to become a better player.'

The X Factor, as Woods knew, was that this was golf. Nobody has ever dominated – not in the way he had the potential to dominate. Golf is such a 'feel' game, that to find that feel on the right four weeks, even for a Tiger Woods, is next to impossible. As good as that 'feel' felt at the end of 1999, Tiger wanted to make sure he didn't lose it for 2000. 'Right now the moves I've been working on are becoming more natural,' he said. 'But there are always going to come periods of time when it's not going to feel natural. You're going to slip back to your old faults, which I've done in the past. I don't care who you are, when you change your swing, you're always going to revert back to your old tendencies. I still do that. That's just the way it is. We're all comfortable with our natural shots. I sometimes think, "Am I close to getting there?" I don't know. But ask me in about 20 years, I'll probably have a better answer for you.'

Right now all Woods was worrying about was having the type of total game he wanted to have with him, for those days when his A game was lost somewhere and he wanted to turn 74 into 69 the way Nicklaus did time and again. That's how you win tournaments. He had proved at the Memorial that his wedge was every bit as good as Phil Mickelson's, that he could be beat tee-to-green by a world-class ball striker like Vijay Singh and still come out on top. But what really turned Woods into a dangerous finisher was his putter. By improving from 147th in 1998 to 24th in 1999, Woods was now considered a complete player.

The turnaround on the greens was attributed to an idea Harmon planted in his head just after leaving Augusta. After months of trying to coach Tiger on the greens, Harmon finally conceded that Tiger had too many technical thoughts running through his head, that it had taken the feel out of his stroke. 'Before he took time off [after Augusta], we started talking about putting,' Harmon said. 'I told him, "Do me a favor, don't listen to me, O'Meara, your dad. Just go putt and putt like you did when you were a kid. Get your motion back." '

Ultimately, Woods started 'releasing' the putter head, producing a more natural roll on the ball. Instead of lipping out or losing speed, the balls were diving in cups – 'burying,' as he liked to put it. The touchstone was the putt he made on the 71st hole of the PGA Championship. Statistically he had stepped it up, but nobody was making them when they needed to, nobody was thinking 'make' with as much confidence as Tiger. Everybody talked about his prodigious length, but it was his short stick that was winning tournaments and building a portfolio. By making that gut-twister at Medinah, it kept Woods on schedule with Nicklaus, and allowed him to think about the Grand Slam in different terms.

Tiger's goals for the millennium season were to drive the ball better, hit 75 percent of his fairways, and putt more consistently throughout the entire year. Before the Williams World Challenge, he had traveled to Titleist's test facility in Carlsbad, California, where he worked on the computers in Scotty Cameron's putting lab, and to Harmon's golf school in Las Vegas. At the Williams, where he finished T-10, Tiger was trying to quiet his right foot on the downswing with his driver. He was also in the midst of an off-season training program: he'd run in the morning with his caddy, Steve Williams, and lift weights after his rounds. He was like any other athlete training for the season, except nobody had ever prepared for a golf year like this.

Woods played golf year-round with the passion of a football or basketball player in the playoffs. He wanted to stay focused and motivated, and to do that he'd have to come out hot and then pace himself for those 16 days when it mattered most, for those 288 holes that would determine a season. If he came out and hammered everybody in California, it would send an early message to the rest of the guys that it could be a long year – for them.

Tom Lehman, a Minnesota boy who made it late in life, won the Williams World Challenge for the $1 million Christmas Bonus. Honestly, while he had long since passed the point of needing the money, it couldn't have happened to a nicer guy. Tiger shot 70-71-76 to close out his week in a tie for 10th. There was obviously some work to do before Kapalau and the

Mercedes Championships at the start of the year, but he was closer than this performance indicated.

'The start of the year is the key,' said Harmon. 'He doesn't want to let down. He wants to come out with intensity. In all honesty, if he comes out on the West Coast and starts winning again, I don't know what these guys are going to do. Nobody thinks he can keep up the pace he kept at the end of this year, but then again I've learned to believe that this kid can do anything.'

## Twenty Six

# STREAKING

The new year started the same way the old one had ended, with the continuation of a winning streak that had begun at the 1999 NEC Championships. On January 9 at Kapalua, the second of three World Golf Championship events staged by the PGA Tour in conjunction with the World Federation of Tours, Woods won a thrilling duel against Ernie Els, sinking a 40-footer on the second playoff hole for his 16th career victory. That it occurred prime time back in the East on ESPN was even better. Technically, it was his fifth straight win, breaking Hogan's 1953 winning streak. Officially, as Woods acknowledged, it was only one-for-one. He had 10 to go. 'Season's over,' Woods said. 'To do it in one year is more difficult than having it spread out from one year to the next.'

Els had become the poster boy for the type of excellence the PGA Tour used to stand for in the B. T. (Before Tiger) Era. He won his first U.S. Open at Oakland Hills in 1994 at the age of 24, came back three years later and beat Colin Montgomerie and Tom Lehman at Congressional for his second Open title, but since then he had been lapped (11 victories to 3) by Woods. He spent the off-season at his winter home in South Africa, recommitting himself to the game. He had not won in the United States since the Nissan Open, and admitted to his wife on the plane flight to Hawaii that to beat Tiger he had to work harder, get tougher mentally, and not be psyched-out the way some players obviously were. 'I have to set my standards higher than I ever did. I have to because I've got a guy who's better than me, so I've got to push myself to another level in order to play with this guy.'

They were in the last group on Sunday, a pairing John Hawkins described in *Golf World* as 'the collision we've been waiting for, an epic duel of major championship intensity on a mountainside considered too idyllic for such heavy substance.' Watching the finish in the locker room were Harmon, British Open champion Paul Lawrie and his agent Adrian Mitchell, and Gary Planos, the director of golf at Kapalua. Said Planos, 'Everybody was glued to the tube, going nuts.'

Els threw everything he had at Tiger, but Woods kept answering. Ernie outdrove him on the final hole of regulation, but Woods countered with a 3-wood that Planos, who was now on the course, will never forget. 'It seemed like it was in the air forever, and all of a sudden the ball landed softly and stopped 12 feet from the hole,' said Planos. 'Andy North, who was doing the telecast for ESPN, patted me on the back and said, "Do you have a good enough golf tournament?" ' Els then responded with a 286-yard 2-iron that stopped 10 feet from the flag.

The drama became so intense that at one point ESPN on-course reporter Charlie Rymer caught the attention of the Golf Channel's Scott Van Pelt, who was standing behind the 18th green between Ernie's wife, Leizl, and Tiger's girlfriend, Joanna. It was Tiger's play. 'Right after Ernie makes his putt (on the first playoff hole), Rymer turns around at me with this bug-eyed expression and every hair on his arm was standing on end,' said Van Pelt.

Planos had the Mercedes M-Class SUVs lined up for the drive up the hill to the 18th tee. Els was in for a long ride. 'Tiger walked over to me, and he had a smile on his face,' Ernie said later in the year to Michael Wilbon of the *Washington Post* 'He wasn't tense or anything and he said, "This is great, let's keep this going." We were having the times of our lives.'

The first playoff hole was just as gripping. Ernie was trying to go for the power slot on the 663-yard par-5, but hung on and ballooned his drive high and right. Tiger ripped his ball and had a 2-iron into the green. From 325 yards, Planos didn't think that Els had a chance of getting home. 'Ernie got up there and hit a rocket,' said Planos. 'It rolled in there 15 – 18 feet and none of us thought he could get it back there [to the flag].' Woods hit a better shot, but it took a bad kick and he had a tough two-putt down the hill.

Over his first putt, Tiger knew the grain would grab it and kick it left. He still didn't compensate enough, and had 7 feet remaining to save the birdie. Els had a chance to end it, but he missed and that gave Tiger life. This wasn't quite like Medinah on Sunday, but it was another chance for Tiger to prove he was the best player in the world. The ball went in, and Rymer's arm hairs stood at attention once again as the gallery, media and tournament officials either ran or drove their golf carts towards the first hole.

Planos had never seen anything like this on Maui. For 17 years, Kapalua had hosted a season-ending pro-am, but the atmosphere had always been more like a family vacation than a golf tournament. In 1999, when The Plantation Course was awarded the Mercedes Championships, David Duval won by nine strokes. As he hustled toward the first green, watching the gallery assemble and the players hit their tee shots, he wondered how much longer this would last. On the East Coast this was going into primetime and the ratings were soaring toward an ESPN record. Van Pelt was trying to collect his thoughts, knowing he had to file his report on deadline.

When Planos saw where Woods and Els hit their approach shots, he headed to the second hole to make sure the marshals were in place because there were no gallery ropes up the left side of the hole and 10,000 people were ready to make a stampede. Woods and Els both had putts in the 35 – 40 foot range, downhill and into the grain. 'Nobody makes those putts,' he thought. After he made sure that everything was in place, Planos walked back up the hill to the first green, and could hear the crowd noise build as Tiger's putt worked its away across the Bermuda grass toward the hole. Just as he walked through the gate, the crowd erupted and girlfriend Joanna gave him a high five.

'My first thought was that this was a great bit of sports history, like Ali-Foreman at the Thrilla in Manila. That was when Foreman was hitting Ali as hard as he could and Ali kept saying, "Is that all you got, George?" Honestly, that was the best finish I'd ever witnessed. I never saw two guys eagle the last hole, go to a playoff, then birdie it. It meant nothing in the grand scheme of things, it was Kapalua, yet it meant everything.'

That night, Van Pelt called Els in his room to praise him for his effort. The Big Easy just laughed. 'Cuzzie,' he said. 'What the heck am I supposed to do? The guy is just an animal.'

# Twenty Seven

# OUTPLAYED, OUTMATCHED

The bigger he got, the more pressure there was on Tiger Woods to play every week – to the point where it became almost comical. The first question he was asked at the Williams World Challenge news conference was about his decision to play the Phoenix Open, but Woods already knew his schedule and he wasn't going to divert from it. Being able to be peak at the right times had become one of his trademarks and after Kapalua, he would take three weeks off to hang out at his West Coast apartment in Manhattan Beach, California It was his way of preparing for a four-tournament stretch beginning at the AT & T Pebble Beach National Pro-Am.

The Streak was now getting more play nationally. Byron Nelson's phone at his ranch in Roanoke, Texas, started ringing constantly; most of the calls were from golf writers wanting Lord Byron to lend some perspective to Tiger's chase.

For starters, Nelson won all of $52,000 in 1945. Tiger made $522,000 just for winning at Kapalua. Nelson only had Americans to beat. Golf had since become a global game and Woods was taking on the world. Nelson had also assembled his streak in relative obscurity. There were no major championships that year; World War II was ending and tournament golf was a series of barn-storming stops made by men from the trunk of their cars.

Woods was about to make golf larger than any other sport, first by winning the AT & T in the most phantasmagoric way possible, and then by returning to Pebble Beach four months later to begin the greatest summer in golf history with a record-obliterating performance in the 100th U.S. Open.

The rush started on the 15th hole at Pebble on Monday afternoon, February 7. Once again the AT & T had been hit hard by the elements, but the tour was committed to a 72-hole finish. CBS provided rare network coverage of a non-major golf tournament, but many affiliates around the country carried local programming instead. Tiger trailed rookie Matt Gogel by five strokes going into the final round, and eight with seven holes to play. The Streak appeared to be over to everyone but Tiger, who was still trying to get something going. Then, with one swing of a pitching wedge, everything changed.

Tiger, trailing by four strokes at the time, landed his shot 10 feet right of the hole, The combination of spin and contour sent the ball juicing toward the cup for an eagle 2; the ballgame was now on. Playing behind him, Gogel was already running on fumes. Woods saw the scoreboards, that he was now just two strokes back, and kept pouring it on. His approach shot into the 16th was artistically better than his shot at the 15th. The full swing sand wedge left a pitch mark 2 feet from the cup, nearly rolled in for back-to-back eagles, and stopped 3 feet from the hole. Birdie. Woods was now just one back.

After a par at the 17th, Woods knew he needed one more birdie. The par-5 18th was playing long, so Woods laid up and stuck a wedge to finish off a 64 and post a 273 total, 15 under par. Needing a 4 at the 18th to tie, Gogel made 6 for a 40 o the back side. In his office at the Washington Wizards office, Michael Jordan was calling columnist Michael Wilbon at the *Post*. The cover of *Golf World* said it all: AMAZING 'This ranks up there,' Woods said of the comeback. He had tied Ben Hogan's record of six-straight PGA Tour victories, set from June 14 – August 22, 1948, and admitted, 'It's definitely more intriguing.' Hogan had the Inverness Round Robin in there, but it counted, just as Nelson had the Miami Four Ball. Woods had all stroke play tournaments in his run, and while the calendar had turned and there were other unofficial events in the mix, Tiger was now more than halfway to Nelson's mystical 11 straight.

Streak watchers were looking at Tiger's schedule, trying to figure where the 11th straight would come. Knowing he would play the Buick Invitational and the WGC – Andersen Consulting

Match Play Championship, and figuring he would play the Nissan Open at Riviera and the Bay Hill Invitational, Woods could conceivably go for No. 10 at the Players Championship and No. 11 at the Masters.

Now, instead of downplaying The Streak, Woods seemed to be embracing it. 'If I had lost but we had won the team thing [with amateur partner Jerry Chang], I was going to try and claim it,' he said. 'Hey, Byron won some four-ball championship in there.'

The number of press credential requests for the Buick Invitational tripled overnight. Rick Schloss, the media coordinator for the Buick Invitational, now had 300 people covering the event, including writers from the *Christian Science Monitor* and *Wall Street Journal* 'It was like one big slumber party,' said Schloss. 'I told everybody right from the beginning of the week, we all had to get along like one big happy family.'

As defending champion, Tiger cooperated by putting on a show. Seven back with 12 holes to play, Woods pulled even for about five minutes, forcing Phil Mickelson to birdie three of the final six holes for the win. There was some debate as to whether having high school classmate Bryon Bell on the bag instead of Steve Williams made a difference, but Woods was trying to help his childhood buddy get through medical school, and besides, he didn't do a bad job in 1999, when he won and broke Tiger's losing streak. 'Bell deserved to defend, too,' said Woods.

Despite playing poorly by his standards, Tiger shot the day's second low round (68) and provided good theatre (and good ratings) for CBS, which outdrew the NBA All-Star game on NBC. The Streak had ended, but not without a fight. 'It was kind of a miracle to even be under par the way I was hitting it today,' he said. 'Through 13 holes I hit six greens and I was five under. That's not bad. I just wasn't hitting it good enough to give myself a viable chance down the stretch, and it finally caught up with me.'

With the pressure off but the competitive edge still on, Woods traveled 20 minutes up Interstate 5 to the LaCosta Resort & Spa for the WGG – Match Play Championship, a event he was bounced from in 1999 by the eventual winner, Jeff Maggert. Early in the week, Woods flatly denied a British tabloid report that he and Jagoda had become engaged, saying, 'Let's put an end to this crap right now.' He then stepped to the first tee in his first match against Michael Campbell, got in the New Zealander's face, and said without anyone else hearing, 'I heard you want a piece of me. Now you've got me.'

Campbell, who had resurrected his career with three wins in Australasia, had just been trying to pump himself up in the week leading up to his match with Woods. He never recovered after Tiger's birdie-birdie start, losing 5 and 4. The next four opponents in Tiger's path kept their mouths shut, but all went the same way as Campbell. Retief Goosen of South Africa and British Open champion Paul Lawrie of Scotland took Woods to the 18th hole before losing; Maruyama and Davis Love III went out early. That left Woods in the final against Darren Clarke, Harmon's lager-drinking, cigar-smoking Northern Irish protégé.

In the Ryder Cup, Clarke had teamed with Lee Westwood to beat Woods and Duval in a four-ball match, so he knew that Tiger wasn't unbeatable. To get to the finals at LaCosta, Clarke had knocked off Paul Azinger, Mark O'Meara, Thomas Bjorn, Hal Sutton and David Duval, but he figured to meet his match against Woods. Warming up that morning before the match, Clarke lit his first cigar of the day and yelled down to Harmon, who was hard at work with Woods, 'That's OK, Butch, I don't need any help.'

Ranked 19th in the world, and known to be an underachiever, Clarke made six birdies in the morning of his 36-hole final against Woods and found himself no better than all square. While Tiger beat balls during the lunch break, Clarke smoked a big fat stogie and rested for the remainder of the match. In the afternoon session, he made four birdies in a five-hole stretch and closed out the match, 4 and 3.

Woods took the loss like a gentleman, taking his hat off to shake Clarke's hand. 'Darren obviously has the ability to play great golf,' he said. 'It all depends on how dedicated he is. Butch has been trying to get him to work a little harder. He does it at times and he's able to play great golf.'

To say this was a victory for the Everyman was a stretch, but it definitely played big in Europe. Tiger was entered the following week at the Nissan Open but it was his fourth straight week of tournament competition and the fire just wasn't there. He finished a respectable 18th and took two weeks off, skipping the start of the Florida swing to recharge himself for the first major of the year. The Masters was now in his sights, so it was time to start working on the kind of shots he'd need to win his second green jacket.

After making eight birdies in 12 holes in the semis against Love, Woods fought his swing and kept himself in the match by sheer will. If it wasn't for his putter, Woods would have gone out early, but as he would prove later in the year, the putter was the most important club in his bag. 'I did a lot of it with smoke and mirrors today, with a lot of hands and timing it well,' he said. 'Darren just flatout outplayed me.'

For Clarke, it was time to celebrate, and that sounded like his favorite cardiovascular sport. That, and curling pint mugs. 'Just goes to show after all that hard work I've put in in the gym this winter, my right arm is definitely stronger,' he said, laughing about the dust that had settled on his exercise equipment back home in Portrush. In many ways this was the anti-Tiger, but the game of golf is not always won by dedication and hard work. Sometimes it just takes nerve and a hot day. Darren Clarke definitely had that working in his $1 million match against Tiger Woods.

'I saw a Darren Clarke I hadn't see before,' Harmon said. 'I knew he was capable, but he did to Tiger Woods what Tiger Woods has been doing to other people. He kicked his butt and looked him right in the eye as he was doing it.'

# Twenty Eight

# NO LOVE

Moving back East, to his home at Isleworth Golf Club in Orlando (and to greens he could actually putt on), Woods set up camp for the spring. Nick Faldo used to refer to this time of year as 'the run unto Augusta.' For Woods, the run-up would start at the home course of four-time Masters champion Arnold Palmer, the Bay Hill Club and Lodge. Bay Hill was not Tiger's favorite course, but he had already won the events hosted by Byron Nelson and Jack Nicklaus, so he was going for the 'legends sweep.'

Palmer had been hard on Woods and his conduct, but the King was now giving Tiger his blessing. 'I think Tiger has done a tremendous job in the last two years, two and a half years. I think he has started to handle himself a lot better, with you guys, the press, and I think that's a good sign. I think it will help his golf and his regularity on the tour.'

During his heyday, Palmer took with him to the course the same daring and confidence that had become the trademarks of Woods. Tiger played smarter than Arnold, but had the same explosive ability to rip off low rounds and as a result of that, the same commanding presence when he walked onto the first tee of a tournament.

Palmer won 27 times from 1960 through 1963, including five major championships. His 1960 season, where he won eight tournaments – including the Masters and U.S. Open back-to-back – was one of the greatest years of all time. He was then 30, at the height of his career. Forty years later, sitting in the press tent at Bay Hill, the 70-year-old Palmer remembered those days as if they happened yesterday. He was now gray, distinguished, and a recent widower. His wife, Winnie, had died the previous December after a battle with cancer, and it was good to get his mind on something else. The thought of what he did in the early sixties made him flash back to a time when he was doing what Woods was doing in 2000. 'I felt like I could win every week,' he said. 'I didn't tell anybody, I tried to keep it to myself. But I had confidence in my game and there was a period of time when I was astonished that I didn't win more than I did.'

What Woods had accomplished didn't surprise Palmer. ('I don't know that I've ever seen anyone go through the ball quite the way he does and with the speed that club head is going through.') What did surprise him somewhat was Tiger's ability to play well on days when he didn't have his best stuff. Those were the days that Palmer had trouble mastering, when his machismo would get in the way of his management. Woods would never pump four balls out of bounds (two in the driving range, two into the street) the way Palmer did at the 1961 Los Angeles Open. Palmer would probably never rely on his wedge for that closing birdie, as Woods did on the 72nd hole at Pebble Beach.

Woods had learned how to play within himself, and not let the adrenaline short-circuit his brain or his behavior. 'Just knowing what happened to me at times when I wasn't playing my best golf, probably has to happen to him a little bit, too,' said Palmer. 'And that is you just have times when things weren't clicking and body chemistry isn't working the way it should and you're going to hit some bad shots. I think the guy that probably did that the best was Byron Nelson. Having known Byron for as well as I have for a lot of years, I've talked to him about it. He admitted that he had ups and downs on certain periods of time, but he also said that, without much disagreement, he was sick in his stomach almost every time he went out to play golf before he teed it up. That kind of tells you something that the intensity was so high all the time, but that it never kept him from being consistent.'

There was no greater measure of Tiger's consistency than his No. 1 ranking. IMG founder Mark McCormack and PGA Tour Commissioner Tim Finchem were at Bay Hill to commemorate that and to present Woods with the McCormack Award, named after the originator of the world-ranking concept.

It was McCormack who saw this all coming, who encouraged Hughes Norton to pursue Tiger as a junior golfer, who sold the USGA on the concept of paying Tiger's father a fee to be a 'scout' for IMG, who 40 years ago had created his agency by signing Palmer to a representation contract that would give birth to the largest and most powerful sports management group in the world.

A villain to some (because he corrupted golf by bringing in corporate sponsorship), a visionary to others (because he had grown the game as much as any businessman and administrator), McCormack had restructured his golf division in the early 1990s, after a series of high profile defections including Greg Norman, Nick Price and Raymond Floyd. By promoting Alastair Johnston ahead of Hughes Norton, it lit a fire under Norton and led to the signing of Woods, which was IMG's all-time greatest coup.

As a contemporary of Palmer's, and a historian of the game, McCormack had seen golf evolve for over five decades and reach the millennium at a height either equal to or greater than the other spectator sports. The reason for this was the man to his right on this day at Bay Hill: Tiger Woods.

'It's a particular honor today to sit here next to a gentleman who is rewriting the record books of golf as each year goes on,' he said. 'In every generation of golf since I've been involved in this sport, everybody always said there will never be another Hogan, Snead and Nelson; that there will never be another Palmer, Player, Nicklaus; there will never be another Ballesteros or Watson; nobody can ever dominate again. But this young man has once again proved everybody to be totally wrong. He has dominated the sport in the past year or so in a way that's just breathtaking. And he's handled himself with great dignity around the world, becoming a great ambassador for the U.S. tour and himself. What he's done to bring golf into places of the world that it's never been seen before is absolutely incredible. I think when it's all written at the end of the day the contribution that Tiger Woods has made to golf is something that perhaps is something that nobody else has ever done. It's an honor for me to be here and be a part of the ceremony.'

Although Woods 'slumped' in 1998, he still rode the big lead he created in 1997 and maintained the No. 1 ranking for 43 weeks that year. Although Duval overtook him for 15 weeks, Woods eventually regained the No. 1 ranking and held the position for

37 weeks over the course of 1999. Bay Hill marked the 100th week that Woods was the No. 1 player in the world. In four days, he would prove not only the validity of that ranking, but the power that he held in the world of sports.

Bay Hill is always held at the peak of March Madness, the NCAA Championships. Tiger was one off the lead after an opening round of 69, causing Colin Montgomerie to walk into the locker room and declare, 'The tournament is over.' He took over on Friday with a 64, and was two strokes upon Love going into Sunday's final round.

In the locker room on Sunday, Tiger arrived wearing more subdued colors. Rather than the traditional blood-red shirt, he was attired in black and gray. Bill Fields, covering the tournament for *Golf World,* ran into Woods in the locker room before the final round. Tiger had his Nike hat on backwards, which led Fields to say, 'It's the other guys who need a rally cap.' Woods didn't say a word, but when he lifted his head, that klieg-light smile of his said it all.

Love had become one of Tiger's whipping boys and was accused of going 'soft' since winning the PGA in 1997. Winless in 23 months, nursing a bad back, and talking about the purchase of a new Harley-Davidson, he had lapsed into the type of lowered-standards syndrome that typified professional golf before Tiger turned professional.

'My expectations were a lot higher than what I've done,' Love admitted. 'Everybody looks back and says they could have done better. We all give them away sometimes. I don't feel I've played as good as I can play, whether it's this year, last year, or the first year I was on tour.'

Love started with back-to-back bogeys on Sunday, but fought back and was only two strokes down after the 11th hole. The 12th at Bay Hill is a reachable par-5. Tiger made 4, Love made 5 and was done after missing a 30-inch par putt on the 14th. What surprised Woods was the way Love backed off after that, as if he were playing for the second-place check.

Was he? There were varying theories. Even Love hinted that he was a softie. 'Every time I played with Freddie [Couples], my wife would look at the pairings and say, "You've got Freddie," ' said Love, 'and I knew what she was thinking.'

Love, with 12 wins through the Buick Challenge in 1997, was top5 in the world and higher than that on the talent meter. His swing was long and wild when he came out of North Carolina in 1986, but he had managed to gear it back and was just gaining confidence when his father, *Golf Digest* instructor and former touring professional Davis Love, Jr., was killed in a plane crash outside Jacksonville. Davis, who loved his father and counted on him for guidance in many things – one of the most important being his swing – was crushed.

Davis Love Jr. had been one of the most highly thought-of men in the game. It took Love three years to put the loss behind him professionally. With three wins in 1992, including a clutch performance at the Players Championship, Love was 28 and still approaching his prime. He followed with two wins and a second in 1993, but the imprint he left on that season was a Ryder Cup clinching comeback against Italy's Costantino Rocca at the Belfry.

Love's problem was the majors. He didn't record a top 10 finish until the 1995 Masters, when Ben Crenshaw beat him. (Ironically, both players [as well as Love's father] had been taught by legendary instructor Harvey Penick, who had died on the eve of the tournament. Love still played well enough to win and came back the next year to nearly win the U.S. Open at Oakland Hills. A three-putt at the 72nd hole cost him a playoff. With a downhill birdie putt on a slick green to win, Love somehow lagged it short of the hole, and missed the 2-footer for par that would have sent him out the next day against Steve Jones.

The 1997 PGA was Love's greatest moment, with two closing 66s at Winged Foot and a rainbow over the 18th green on Sunday as he holed out for victory. The rain – pouring down on him, his mother, Penta, and his brother, Mark – seemed like tears from heaven.

But since that day, through Bay Hill, Love had only won once and was 0 – 5 against Woods in head-to-head confrontations. 'Remember when Tiger used to grade himself?' said Love in a closing thought. 'He's about an A-minus right now every week and an A-plus some weeks. If Ernie Els played up to his potential every week or I did, or Fred Couples, we'd shoot low scores week after week. Just mentally right now, he's got the advantage.'

When Woods turned pro, Harmon told him, 'Davis, when Tiger learns to control his distances, nobody is going to beat him.' Love saw the 'Before' (Las Vegas in 1996) and the 'After' on several occasions. Even the 'Before' version was better at times than anybody had seen before. 'When Tiger first came out, I said,

"This guy is not anywhere near as good as he can be." People didn't believe me.'

They certainly did now.

'His nickname should be Laser Woods,' said Billy Andrade. 'His shots never leave flags. He steps up, laser. Next shot, laser. I never played with Hogan, Nicklaus, Palmer or Snead in their primes, but it is unbelievable to see the shots Tiger plays. He hit as many great shots as Olin Browne and I hit good ones.'

Loren Roberts, a two-time Bay Hill winner, played well enough to shoot 11 under and finish tied for fourth. But the game he was playing was definitely different than the game Woods was playing.

'The face of golf is changing,' Roberts said. 'These guys are reaching all the par-5s in two, hitting three-woods in there that stop like my wedge shots. I'm glad I'm almost 45 and not 25 hitting it this short. Tiger hit eight-iron to the [530-yard, par-5] fourth hole one day, and four-iron to the [570-yard, par-5] 12th. What was he, 13 under on the par-5s? I can't beat that.'

The win was Tiger's ninth in 15 starts, and his 18th tour victory, which tied him with Greg Norman on the all-time list. Tiger had not only outdrawn the NCAA, but the NBA as well, gathering a 5. 3 overnight rating while the Knicks-Lakers game registered a 4. 0. It didn't matter if it wasn't very competitive down the stretch, that Love had backed off. It was Tiger. He wasn't bigger than the game, but he was the show. Some guys had yet to accept that.

Some already had.

## Twenty Nine

# SUTTON IMPACT

There was no Davis Love waiting for Woods the following week at the Players Championship. Instead there was a southern man who wasn't going to let himself get psyched out, who was one of those next Nicklauses to come along and run headlong into the wall of expectation. In Hal Sutton, Woods had to face the Louisiana version of Darren Clarke – in physical stature, anyway. Sutton was not the partier that Clarke was, but they were built similarly: like linebackers or fullbacks on a pretty good high school team. You wouldn't take either one in a race, but if you needed the first down or a stop on the goal line, Sutton and Clarke were the guys.

Mentally, they were totally different in their approach. Northern Ireland's Clarke wasn't intimidated because he knew Woods well enough to 'slag him off.' While Woods and Sutton were Ryder Cup teammates and respected each other, this fight was more intense just because of what Hal kept saying in his news conferences to pump himself up.

It started with a response to Colin Montgomerie's opinion that the Bay Hill tournament was over in most player's minds on Thursday after Woods opened with a 69. 'The view in the locker room – without anyone saying it out loud – was [that] the tournament was finished,' said the world's third-ranked player. 'It was like, "Who is going to finish second?" ' That really hit Sutton's hot button. Asked to comment on Montgomerie's comments, Sutton snorted, 'He was in a different locker room than I was,' adding, 'I tell you this: Praising Tiger all the time is certainly [creating] a defeatist attitude. There are a lot of people who don't think they can beat him right now down the stretch on Sunday. There's a lot of doubt in their minds.'

Sutton told a story about the first two rounds of the Nissan Open at Riviera. Woods was just out trying to recover from the match play loss to Clarke, and suck up enough juice to finish out his fourth straight West Coast tournament. Sutton used those 36 holes as a personal test. 'I think it was important that I send him a message,' Sutton said. 'One, that I could beat him, playing with him. And two, that he knew that I could beat him playing with him.' Woods shot 68 and 70. Sutton shot 69 and 67, but hardly sent a message. Woods was basically oblivious to Sutton and to the 'game within the game' Hal was playing.

It was that way for the first two days at the TPC, as Tiger had enough to worry about with a swing that wasn't quite on plane. With a double bogey in each of the first two rounds, and a pair of 71s, he trailed Sutton by four strokes. That's when he made his move, shooting 66 on Saturday to create a final-round pairing with Sutton, who had shot his third-straight 69. It was Tiger's first round under 70 at Sawgrass in 15 tries.

Woods had expected to play better at the Players Championship. His first U.S. Amateur came on the Stadium course in 1994, but his first three TPCs developed into weekend practice rounds for the Masters. This one turned into a three-day weekend.

Seventeen years ago Sutton came to this tournament as a rookie in a pair of red Sans-a-belt pants – and won. He won the PGA that year at Riviera and was named the 'Bear Apparent' by *Golf Magazine*. Blond, good-looking, the son of a Louisiana oil man, Sutton went through a multitude of swing instructors and wives until he settled on his college coach, Floyd Horgen, and a young Texas woman named Ashley. They brought normalcy back into Hal's game and his life, as did his three daughters.

What Sutton showed Woods was an example of how potential can turn into what Hal himself once characterized as a 'pity party.' Now he was back with a vengeance, after a 3-1-1 Ryder Cup; he needed to make up for lost time. Although they weren't paired for the third round, Sutton was now aware of Woods and Woods was obviously aware of Sutton since he had closed the lead to one stroke. 'I was trying to answer everything he did,' said

Sutton. 'I am not going to roll over and play dead.'

The final round took two days to complete, and while the golf was good, the quotes were better.

Sutton: 'You've got the greatest championship in the game and you have the best player in the world right there on my tail. That doesn't mean he is going to win tomorrow, even though everybody else in the world is trying to figure out a way for him to go ahead and do it.'

Woods: 'I'm going to go out there and play my own game and see what happens. Obviously Hal may think a little differently. That's fine. He needs to motivate himself the way he needs to motivate himself.'

Sutton had a three-stroke lead when play was suspended on the 12th hole Sunday because of a thunderstorm. Everybody said the suspension favored Tiger, in that it broke Hal's momentum and lengthened the golf course. If there was a good omen, it was in Hal's favor. It just meant one more night of thinking about Tiger. Also, when he won in 1983, it was on a Monday.

The next day, after he won, Sutton admitted, 'I will tell you the truth. I got nervous as heck. I have been as nervous as heck for the last two or three days. The other night, I was sitting in the bed, I thought: Well, you know what, I am not praying to him, so he is not a god for sure. When that realization came over me, it was like: OK, this is OK. He is just human like I am, so we can handle this.'

Woods had three-putted the 12th hole on Monday morning, cut a three-shot deficit to one with an eagle at the 16th, and made Sutton work for two closing pars and the largest check in PGA Tour history ($1. 08 million). Afterward he admitted it was OK to praise Tiger now, because he didn't have to go hit another shot with him.

Then, there was time for one more lecture.

'I thanked the crowd for keeping the respect and the integrity of the game, because Tiger Woods is not bigger than the game,' Sutton said. 'And you all do a damn good job of making him bigger than the game. That is what makes it tough. That is why a lot of people get against him at times because they pull for the underdog. I beckon you all to let's keep that respect in the game.'

Tiger acknowledged that he wasn't bigger than the game, but Sutton felt that the media had built him up to be larger than life. His delivery was just a little over the top, so the spirit of the message was not well taken in every corner of the interview room. In his *Sports Illustrated* game story, Alan Shipnuck subtly described Sutton's 6-iron to 6 feet on the 72nd hole as 'his most eloquent statement of the week.'

'Let's go back to the Arnold Palmer days, to the Ben Hogan days, to the Jack Nicklaus days,' Sutton said. 'None of those guys were ever bigger than the game. The game is the biggest of all.'

What Sutton was saying was true – yet, these were unique circumstances. These weren't the Palmer days, the Hogan days or the Nicklaus days. Even with Sunday's rain interruption, the PGA Tour event had once again outdrawn the NBA, and the reason for that wasn't Hal Sutton, as courageous as he was at the TPC. The reason for that was one young man named Tiger.

# Thirty

# ACCESS DENIED

In the week between the Players Championship and the Masters, Woods worked on the shots he would need to hit at Augusta. The high draw, the shot Woods called his sweeper, would be needed off the tee. From the fairway, Woods would then hit his high cut to hold Augusta's greens. It was the same formula for every player, but Woods seemed to be dialed in at the right time. 'My game is very solid right now,' he said before leaving Sawgrass. 'Believe me, I'm ready.'

There was no golf course that favored Woods more, but since his 12-shot victory in 1997, Tiger had finished T-8 and T-18 in his two trips back to Augusta National, and had not broken 70. That would be like Elvis missing the top 40 for two straight years during his prime.

In 1998 his game was still in the repair shop, and he had to deal with an assortment of distractions ranging from a death threat he received via the Internet, a Friday pairing with Fuzzy Zoeller and Colin Montgomerie, and a ride in a police car to Mark O'Meara's house. Considering their history, the Zoeller pairing was especially taxing.

On the Sunday in April 1997 when Tiger was completing the most historic afternoon in American golf, Zoeller was asked outside the Augusta clubhouse by a CNN camera crew what he thought of Tiger's performance. Zoeller, the 1979 Masters champion, had just exited from the locker room and was on his way to the parking lot.

'The little boy's playing great out there,' he said. 'Just tell him not to serve fried chicken at the [Champions] dinner next year.' Walking away, Zoeller stopped to deliver the kicker, 'Or collard greens or whatever it is *they* serve.'

Known for his politically incorrect humor, Zoeller was trying to be funny. The Woods camp and the African-American community did not take it that way. The sound bite was found by a producer, and the tape didn't air until a week after the event. Zoeller tearfully apologized during a news conference at the Greater Greensboro Open. Woods was in Portland, in a meeting at Nike with Phil Knight and his agent, Hughes Norton. Knight reportedly commented, 'That can wait.' Norton and Zoeller also had a history, so there was no hurry to issue a statement accepting the apology. Players sided with Zoeller, feeling that was just Fuzzy being Fuzzy. Kmart had already canceled his $1-million-a-year endorsement contract.

Tiger and Fuzzy met face-to-face at the Colonial Tournament that year, but it still wasn't over. John Daly tried to put together a practice round for them at the U.S. Open, but Woods declined. The following April at the Honda Classic, Woods announced his menu: cheeseburgers, grilled chicken, french fries and milkshakes. Zoeller, who had just shot 69 and was 4-under for the tournament, was asked by the local media in South Florida to comment.

Zoeller went off. 'I didn't write it, boys,' he said. 'You're the ones who buried me, and I appreciate it. But it's over with, it's done, water over the dam. For some reason out there, shit sells. I don't understand why that is, but it does . . . I would hope the people remember the good, but they tried to tear it all down last year. I've lost my respect for you guys. Now I understand why athletes don't talk to you guys . . . It will never die. They're beating on me right now for Augusta. They've been beating on me since California. And I won't mention anything. I won't say a word.'

Closure finally came through fate, as both Woods and Zoeller shot 71 to be paired together. You would have thought it was Nelson Mandela and F. W. de Klerk walking side-by-side for 5 1 2 hours. Afterward, Woods called it 'just another pairing' and tried to put the issue to bed. 'It's the press that wants to keep talking about it,' he said. 'No offense, but I think it's in your ballpark now. Fuzzy and I buried it a long time ago.'

Zoeller took the same position. 'It was a beautiful day,' he said.

'He's just like everyone else. Don't make a big deal out of this.'

The difference between Woods's score of 285 (3-under) and the 270 (18-under) he posted in 1997 was a combination of tougher weather and some inconsistent ball striking. He took exactly the same number of putts both years (116), but he hit 11 fewer greens in regulation. The best part of the week was being able to put the green jacket on O'Meara, who birdied the last three holes to win.

There were no distractions in 1999, but Tiger's putter let him down. He led the greens hit in regulation category, but was 55th among the 56 players in the field who made the cut. It was one month after the tournament that Butch told him to forget everything that he, O'Meara and even his father had taught him about putting: Just go out and be a natural.

Coming back to Augusta for the third time since his victory, Woods was the prohibitive favorite. Asked about the Grand Slam he said, 'I won, what, eight last year? If I won the right four of those, I'd be doing all right. If you put yourself in there enough times, you never know.'

Woods had a 10: 38 a.m. pairing with Stewart Cink and amateur Aaron Baddeley, the 19-year-old Australian Open champion. Conditions were best described as being on the edge. The wind was swirling, then gusting, and then flat calm, making club selection guesswork at best. The Cup and Tee Marker Placement Committee had tried their best to set pins in some borderline locations. The rough, added in 1999, was also deeper and there were some new shelves that golf course designer Tom Fazio had sneaked in during the annual summer tweaking.

Woods bogeyed the fourth with a 4-iron over the back of the green, and a 5-iron into a greenside bunker at the fifth. He came back with two birdies and was even par in the middle of the 10th fairway, after drawing a beautifully shaped 3-wood off the tee. With a 7-iron into the green, Woods got too steep on his downswing, stuck the face of his club into the ground, and fanned a high trajectory shot that plugged in the right front bunker. With the green sloping away from him, he hit a shot that trickled down to the collar, and he three-putted for a quick double bogey.

Holes like this are going to happen at Augusta, where one mistake can lead to a chain reaction faster than at any other major championship course. Woods shrugged it off, and headed on. At the 12th, the scariest par-3 in the world, Woods had 135 yards to the front edge and after conferring with caddy Steve Williams, selected 8-iron. He hit a shot that was later described as being 'pretty solid' but the ball hit a wall of wind, landed on the front bank, and rolled into the water. From there he wedged on and compounded the error again by three-putting for a triple bogey 6.

Again, Woods remained composed. You get bad breaks in golf and you get good breaks. The key is not letting the bad breaks get inside your head. 'I told Stevie coming off 12, if we just get to two over par or three over par, we're fine. We'll just keep plugging along and make the putts when we can. If I can give myself legitimate chances, I'll be all right.'

With birdies coming in at 12 and 16, Woods posted 75. The lead, held by Dennis Paulson, was 68. Tom Lehman was at 69. Nobody else broke 70. As disappointing as those two swings were at 10 and 12, the second day was probably the round that cost Woods the tournament. Vijay Singh, the eventual winner, and Ernie Els, who would finish second, both shot 67. David Duval, who was in the hunt until the 13th hole on Sunday, shot 65 and took the lead at 138. There were 17 scores in the sixties, but Woods fought his putter and shot 72. After two rounds he had 64 putts, and trailed by nine strokes.

The good break came on Saturday. With a 10:10 a.m. tee time, Woods shot 68 and was in the press room just as a violent storm swept across the course. The leaders were just getting started as Woods went through his card with Billy Morris, the publisher of the *Augusta Chronicle*. Woods, irritated by comments made by Mark Lye on the Golf Channel's *Viewers Forum*, wanted to prove that he was not out of the tournament. He pointed out that Paul Lawrie made up 10 shots on the weekend to win the 1999 British Open at Carnoustie. 'I am not out of it,' he said.

By the end of the day he certainly wasn't. When play was suspended because of dark, Singh and Duval were just short of the 15th green. They would have to go out on a cold Sunday morning to complete their third rounds, then wait around for six hours to complete the final round. Woods would get to sleep in.

'I'm not saying you can go out there and shoot 69 and win being that far back, but it's possible,' he said. 'People have gone low here and shot 63s. You just need one of those magical days to do that. But I just figure if you're that far back with all the trouble there is out there on the golf course, that you can go ahead and shoot 30 on the back nine. In the past, 30 makes up for more than just six shots.'

It had taken him 10 rounds to break 70 again at Augusta, but now he was back in the flow. With a 33 o the front nine Sunday, he had put himself into second place. What hurt him most on Sunday were the three putts that Singh made at 15, 16 and 17 to close out the third round, and the three putts he hit that grazed the edges at 10, 11, and 13 in the afternoon of the final round. Those six strokes were the difference in Vijay's winning total of 10-under 278, and Tiger's 284. Although his weekend aggregate of 137 was the lowest of any player in the field, Woods had dug himself into too deep a hole early, and left Augusta without the green jacket once again.

'Even though I didn't get off to a good start on Thursday, I still had a chance,' he said. 'I'm proud of that – the fact that I got back into the tournament and had a chance going into the back nine on Sunday. I just didn't win.'

Jack Nicklaus had once predicted that Tiger Woods would win 10 green jackets before he retired, an achievement that looked like a lock after the 1997 runaway. He was now 1-for-4, and at a point in his career when a fifth-place finish in a major was considered a disappointment. It showed just how high the bar had been raised.

# Thirty One

# NEW BALL GAME

Drifting down the Green River in Park City, Utah, Tiger Woods contemplated his next three weeks of tournament golf. He was in the middle of his annual spring break, the window in the schedule where he would kick back and start preparing for the U.S. Open. It was here in the mountains where he could escape with Mark O'Meara. In some of the little towns, they didn't even recognize him. He enjoyed the anonymity.

The other thing he liked about Utah was the fishing. Like anything else he does in life, Tiger wants to win, and this was one area where Mark O'Meara still had the upper hand. They had started on the Lake Bessie Chain at Isleworth, and had fished the previous summer before the British Open in Ireland. Tiger was catching on, but O'Meara just loved schooling him on the water, figuring it probably wouldn't last long. 'He may beat me in golf, but I'm kicking his butt in fishing,' says O'Meara. 'He gives me a few shots on the course and I give him a few fish on the river.'

Tiger's first tournament back after the Masters was the GTE Byron Nelson Classic at the TPC at Las Colinas in Irving, Texas. He won the Nelson in 1997 one month after winning at Augusta at a time when Tigermania was at its loudest decibel. What sold him on the event, though, was the Four Seasons Hotel. The security was good, and there was an underground walkway to the health club, where nobody asked him for an autograph while he worked out. It was a nice little package, and he liked supporting Nelson's tournament.

The Nelson was also the venue where it all came together for Woods in 1999. Just before leaving Orlando he found the key to his new golf swing, and off he went on the best one-year ride in golf history. In the 12-month cycle that began at Las Colinas, Woods had played in 22 tournaments around the world, won 12 and earned more than $9. 3 million. Now it was time to start what Woods considered a new season.

'Many great players have sustained it for years,' Woods told Doug Ferguson of the Associated Press on the Tuesday before the event. 'They may not have finished in the top10 every week, but when they're not playing well, they still have a chance to win. And that's where you want to be.'

In his three weeks off after the Masters, Woods didn't touch a golf club other than a catalog shoot. He was rusty in the opening round and shot three-over par 73 on the TPC course. In danger of missing only his second official cut as a professional, Woods came back with 67 at Cottonwood Valley and called Butch Harmon in Las Vegas. Harmon flew into Dallas on the red-eye, straightened Tiger out, and Woods shot 67 and 63 to miss the Jesper Parnevik – Phil Mickelson – Davis Love III playoff by one stroke. If he had made a 15-foot birdie putt on the 72nd hole, Woods would have been in sudden death and then CBS would have probably not cut away because of its commitment to *60 Minutes* and its sweeps-period miniseries *Jesus*.

'We wanted to address a couple of things right away,' Harmon said. 'The Open is coming up in a month and with Tiger going to Germany next week, we didn't want to have two weeks worth of bad habits to fix when he got back . . . Mostly, he just totally relaxed during the month off, which is an absolute necessity sometimes. But now, we had to get a few things worked out. We focused on his posture, which was better today. He straightened up quite a bit.'

Woods flew home after the Nelson knowing he would be making a move that would create a buzz in the *Golf World*. He said nothing about it in his conference call with the national media to promote the PGA Championship, but Wally Uihlein and Bob Wood knew what was going on. So did upper-level management at both Titleist and Nike, the two major players in Tiger's equipment portfolio. The news was that Tiger would be switching from the Titleist Tour Professional 90 – the ball that helped him win 18 tournaments, two major championships and three U.S. Amateur titles – to the new Nike Tour Accuracy ball, which he had been testing since January.

This day had been coming since last summer's Nike commercial aired during the U.S. Open. Uihlein, the president and CEO of the Acushnet company, had signed Woods to a $20 million contract with Titleist when Woods turned professional in 1996. He was going to sue Nike over the implications of the ad – that it was a Nike ball Tiger was tapping off the face of his wedge – but he held off until after the majors, not wanting to distract Woods from more important matters. The suit was filed in the fall, and Tiger's contract was reworked so that he would be paid $50,000 for every tournament where he used the Titleist ball. The deal was also restructured because Uihlein was in the loop with Mark Steinberg on the impending deal with Buick, and the switch in logos on Tiger's golf bag. All that would be left between Tiger and Titleist would be his 975D driver and 3-wood, his Scotty Cameron putter, and his prototype blade irons that were patterned after the Mizunos he used as an amateur.

The Nike Golf people were ecstatic. Wood, who is Uihlein's counterpart at Nike, saw this as a banner day for his division. Titleist was the industry leader in golf balls, but Nike was coming on strong with a non-wound ball that was being produced in Japan for them by the Bridgestone Corporation. They had their first victory when Paul Azinger won the Hawaiian Open, but with Woods in the fold, the potential was limitless.

Woods began secretly testing a prototype Tour Accuracy the week of Azinger's victory at Waialae. It was all done at Big Canyon CC, near Tiger's home in Manhattan Beach, Calif. The point man for Nike was Kel Devlin, son of former touring professional and ESPN golf analyst Bruce Devlin. Kel played college and pro golf, so he had knowledge of what a tour player is looking for, as well as a lot of respect for Tiger.

They would meet again over the course of the next four months, at Isleworth and at Nike's quarterly meeting in Beaverton, Ore. Devlin would have a launch monitor with him, a device to measure clubhead speed, launch angle and spin rate. Woods was so adroit with his golf swing that he could give the readings without even looking at the launch monitor. Devlin, tour rep Mark Thaxton, and Nike's engineers would leave those sessions spellbound at

Tiger's ability to know exactly where the clubhead was at impact, and what unmarked Nike prototype he was using just by feel – and sometimes sound.

'The amazing thing was that he asked more technical questions about product than any golfer I've worked with,' said Devlin. 'He wants to know spin rates, launch angles, initial velocity. He'd ask, "Is this ball doing this compared to the ball I used to play?" He was a sponge for information.'

The session at Isleworth the week of the Honda Classic was the most memorable. Chris Zimmerman, the company's Director of Sales, suggested that the Nike Film and Video crew tape the test, which, because of a strike by the Screen Actors Guild, eventually turned into the first Tiger-Nike golf ball commercial. In it, Woods is spinning sand shots to show the feel around the greens of Nike's new non-wound ball.

Devlin still talks about the footage that isn't shown in the commercial, the stuff shot on the range. 'After 5 – 6 shots, he'd start playing games,' said Devlin. 'He'd say, "OK, I'm going to cut one here, so my spin rate will be 400 rpms more than if I hit a draw." He'd wind up, and it would be 400 rpms more. He'd hit a shot and be within 100 rpms of what the ball launched at. Every once in a while we'd slip in a different ball. He'd say, "That was a different ball. It felt harder." Or he'd hit one off the bottom of the club and he'd say, "My swing speed was 128 MPH but since it was off the bottom of the club, the swing speed was 1 MPH less, so the spin rage was probably 3, 100." He'd be nailing it.

'Then he said, "OK, I'm going to crank it up, give it 5 MPH more swing speed." Sure enough, it would register 5 MPH more in swing speed. Everybody sitting there dumbfounded. There was a road on the back of the range at Isleworth. We asked him, "How far to the road?" He said 290, and then he cranks on it and flies it right to the middle of the road. Then he says, "OK, I'm going to hit it over the road now," and he bombs it an extra five yards over the road.

'He's got so much control on what he does with the golf club, it's incredible. He's worked so hard at getting the right launch angle and the right spin rate on the driver, that it's made him a better driver. He launches it at 12 degrees with a spin rate of 2, 800, which is perfect. Add in 130 MPH clubhead speed, and it translates to 300 yards pretty easy.'

Still, Nike wasn't prepared for Woods to move to its ball until after the majors. Their goal was nine months, sometime during Tiger's next down time in September. But Tiger was so into it, and the non-wound ball could be tweaked more easily by the technicians than the wound ball, that by the Byron Nelson, Woods had made up his mind that it was time for a change. The Friday before he left for Germany, Woods called Devlin from the Byron Nelson. 'Get on a plane,' he said. 'I'm going to tee up the ball.'

## Thirty Two

# THE PLAYABILITY TEST

On Tuesday, May 16, Tiger Woods, Joanna Jagoda, Mark Steinberg and Steve Williams flew in a leased Gulfstream jet from Orlando to Hamburg for the Deutsche Bank – SAP Open in Germany. Tiger was in a fantastic mood. He felt good not only about the Nike ball, but about life in general. The tournament's sponsors had given him $1 million to play this tournament in 1999, and he responded by winning his first title on the European continent. His record-setting year, which included the major championship at Medinah, had only ramped up his appearance fee numbers and five-star treatment.

From his suite at the Atlantic Hotel, he could overlook Lake Alster and take in a fireworks display that was part of Hamburg's cherry blossom festival. If he wanted to take a drive, there was a Maserati waiting in valet parking. Part of the appearance fee deal called for him to participate in a bizarre rooftop closest-to-the pin promotion to benefit a local youth charity. That would be no problem, not after opening the tournament and debuting his new Nike ball with a 70.

Woods had played that day with Colin Montgomerie, who was using the Callaway ERC driver that was banned in the United States by the USGA because the face didn't meet its 'trampoline effect' standards. Even with the hot club, Monty wasn't in Tiger's zip code, and this pleased Woods immensely.

In his news conference that day at Gut Kaden Golf and Land

Club in Alveslohe, Woods said, 'The feel of it is very similar to what I've been accustomed to. It flies a little different in the wind. I don't know how to explain it.'

The lighthearted rooftop competition would involve nine star players hitting golf balls across the four-lane Monckebergstrasse to an artificial green atop a parking garage. Lee Westwood was trying to activate his cell phone to ring in the middle of player's backswings. Jesper Parnevik hit a bump-and-run shot. Even the usually serious Tiger was showing a side that only O'Meara, John Cook, Stuart Appleby and Ken Griffey Jr. see in their battles at Isleworth.

'ERC wedge?' he said to Montgomerie.

Sergio Garcia got it also. When the Spaniard came up just short of his target, Woods started yelling, 'Throw a shoe! Throw a shoe!' It was a reference to the controversy the young Spaniard had created at the previous year's World Match Play Championship at Wentworth, when he took off his Adidas golf spike and flung it up the fairway after a poor drive.

When it was Tiger's turn, he landed a shot 3 feet, 3 1 2 inches from the cup to win the competition. The next day he shot another 70 at Gut Kaden, bogeying two holes coming in to fall four strokes behind Miguel Angel Jimenez of Spain. The Deutche Bank field included all of Europe's Ryder Cup team. While Darren Clarke said, 'Tiger's the man to beat . . . He can fly bunkers the rest of us mere mortals can't,' there were others who felt their turf needed protecting.

Westwood turned out to be the man. Struggling in the months leading up to the event, he shot 69 and 64 on the weekend to beat Woods, who closed 67 and 70 for a fourth-place tie. Woods had the lead going into the final round, but lost it with a blocked 7-iron into the pond at the 11th hole. The double bogey cost him the tournament, but not any respect. 'There was the feeling that we didn't want the Americans coming over here and us being rolled over,' said Westwood. 'It's nice to show that there are an awful lot of good players here and that people can't come over and beat us on our own field.'

Woods shrugged it off and flew to Ohio for another title defense, this one at Jack Nicklaus's tournament, the Memorial. It was a big week at Muirfield Village Golf Club in Dublin, which was celebrating its 25th year of hosting the event. Jack was the honoree and Arnold Palmer would be there, along with Gary

Player. It was the type of week that Tiger always stepped up for, and after that back nine in Germany it would be good for him, and Nike, to produce a victory.

'Whatever equipment gives me the best shot to shoot low numbers,' Woods said, 'that's the equipment I'll play.'

There were some who were questioning the move to the new ball. Hal Sutton, for example, made the switch from a wound ball to a non-wound ball, and although his commercials give the Spalding Strata credit for his resurgence, there was also a learning curve involved in the transition. 'That can be a very dramatic change in a person's life,' Sutton said. 'I doubt very seriously that he's spent a lot of time in a lot of different elements in a lot of different competitive situations.'

Harmon, who was at Muirfield Village, was also concerned. 'I had some trepidation,' he said. 'He had won 18 tour events with the other ball. But he wanted something that would spin a little more around the greens.' Woods admitted, 'Any time you hit a two-piece ball versus a wound ball, you're going to feel a dramatic difference. But the performance, the cover of it feels very similar to [the Titleist Professional]. Obviously it's going to fly a little bit different . . . not necessarily higher or lower, but there's a different arc to it. Wound balls tend to spike up more and two-piece balls tend to be more flat.'

Woods was slow out of the gate, shooting 71 while Harrison Frazar took the lead at 66. Frazar, a college teammate of Justin Leonard at the University of Texas, was still looking for his first tour win. Although Tiger was five strokes back, only seven players had produced better scores.

Muirfield Village had been lengthened by Nicklaus, but that played into Tiger's wheelhouse. 'They think that by making the course longer they are making it tougher' said Steve Flesch, the promising left-hander who is middle-of-the-pack in driving distance with a 274-yard average. 'But all they're doing is making it easier for the long hitters. It's a little frustrating, but it makes you work harder. Somebody's got to figure out a way to raise their game.'

While they were figuring it out, Woods was taking his own level up a notch. Beginning on the fifth hole of the second round, and ending with the eighth hole of the third round, Woods played 22 holes in 15-under par. The shot that had his playing partners shaking their heads was a 234-yard 3-iron he hit off a downhill lie on the 563-yard seventh hole Saturday afternoon. That shot, which singed the cup as it went by, set up a 20-foot eagle that Tiger drained. On the next hole, he hit 7-iron to a foot and tapped it in for birdie. 'It's not that he was six-under over six holes,' said Frazar, who shot 43 on the back side for a 78. 'It's how he did it. He hit shots I don't know any other human can hit.'

Watching this in the clubhouse was Leonard, who in 1992 had won the U.S. Amateur. Looking for his first top10 of 2000 and having a quick lunch before heading to the range for more work, he looked at a television screen and saw Woods starting the back nine. Sitting next to him was another former U.S. Amateur champion, Scott Verplank. They just about choked on their shrimp cocktails.

'He just flew it over the tree!' said Leonard, incredulously, as Woods carried an oak tree 280 yards off the tee at the 10th.

'I just try to get it past the tree,' said Verplank. 'He just flew it past it by 30 [yards].'

So obsessed is Woods by perfection, that he came off the course that day after shooting 63, saw Harmon, and said, 'Meet me on the range.' He went out the next day and shot a cleaner 65 to open a six-stroke lead. 'Phil's win [at the Colonial] and the fact that he matches his three victories probably inspired Tiger,' said Harmon. 'He has no animosity toward Phil, but when a player wants to be the best, those things can motivate.'

The final round was pushed into Monday because another series of storms had moved in over central Ohio. Woods shot a closing 70 with a bogey at the 72nd hole when one of those new Tour Accuracys flew the 18th green, hit a cart path, and landed among the spectators. For the first time in his career, Woods had defended a title. But more importantly, he would be going into Pebble Beach on a high.

The new Nike ball held up under tournament competition – he was 30-under par in eight rounds with it – and with a little help from Butch, his game was just about dialed in.

'It wasn't but about three years ago, we all as players were saying that those days – when somebody was going to kick butt and dominate – were gone,' Azinger said. 'But you know what? They've returned, with a vengeance.'

# Thirty Three

# 'BUTCHIE'

After he won the Memorial by five shots, Tiger Woods traveled to Las Vegas for a few days of work at the Butch Harmon School of Golf. This was his final tune-up before the summer, and despite finishing no worse than fifth in his last seven events, there were problems that had crept into his game – like the blocked 7-iron on the 11th hole in Germany – that he could not afford to be carrying into Pebble Beach for the U.S. Open.

It didn't take much for Harmon to straighten Woods out; then again, since the swing change took hold in May of 1999, it usually takes just a few words to put an image in Tiger's head. When he shot 64 in 35 MPH winds at Rio Secco the week before the Open, Woods knew he was ready. So did Harmon.

'The mechanics have gotten so good,' said Harmon. 'His set-up posture is perfect, the plane of his swing is perfect, the path of his downswing. Everything about it is textbook. Some players get in a zone, play good for a while, but they never swing like Tiger's swinging now.'

Much has been said and written about the theory he imparted, the swing changes he choreographed, but Butch has always been able to *communicate* with Tiger and therein lies the secret to their bond. From the day he walked into the clubhouse at Lochinvar Golf Club in Houston, Butch knew what to say and how to say it. Watching them together before Tiger tees off is a flashback to the days when Angelo Dundee would put his hand on the shoulder of Muhammad Ali just before the bell rang; the last word from Butch is usually a detonation device.

'Here's a story that I've never told before,' Harmon said at the beginning of the 2000 season. 'We're at the Amateur at Pumpkin Ridge for the'96 U.S. Amateur. Tiger was five down after 18. His posture was messed up. We fixed that, and I was trying to think to myself, "OK, I've got to tell him something. I know he's pissed off," so I put my arm around him and said, "Had you noticed that every time Steve Scott wins a hole, that cute little girlfriend of his is laughing at you?"

'Tiger turned to me and said, "You noticed that, too?" I knew that's all I had to say. I remember after he made that putt on the 35th hole, he literally sprinted past me going to the 18th tee. He slapped me on the butt and said, "She ain't smilin' now!" He never missed a step.'

Harmon gets off on stuff like that because it's inside golf, and nobody is more inside or understanding of the game than Butchie is. Here's a man who grew pupas the son of a Masters champion, who learned the game at places like Winged Foot, Seminole and Thunderbird, who worked as a club pro in such distant corners of the golfing world as Morocco and Texas City, Texas before he found fame and fortune.

The Woods-Scott story is one of his classics. It's the type of story Butchie's father would have loved telling in the grill room at Winged Foot during his three decades as the club professional there. There was nobody better at holding court or giving lessons than Claude Harmon. As his namesake son, Claude 'Butch' Harmon listened and learned with great alacrity.

Claude didn't live to see what Butch has done to help Tiger reach his potential, but if he did, you can bet he'd have a one-liner to capture it.

'I just wish Dad could see this,' said Butch's brother, Dick, who has been the head pro at Shady Oaks in Houston for the past 25 years. 'I know how proud he would have been with Butch's efforts.'

Growing up in Westchester County, N. Y., Butch was some-what of the black sheep in the family. While Dickie, Craig and later Billy settled into premier club jobs, Butch took years before he finally found himself. Those who know Butch know what Billy means when he says, 'Butch's biggest battle has always been himself.'

Butchie, known for his hot temper, was a 150-pound halfback for New Rochelle High. He could run the 100-yard dash in close to 10-flat, and destroy a set of clubs in less time than that. Some Butch Harmon stories are priceless. He'd show up on the first tee at Winged Foot with the scuffed-up remains of a beautiful Hogan persimmon driver that his father had given him. Looking at the spike marks on a club that had been perfectly finished, Claude would just shake his head, nod at the driver and tell Butchie, 'Re finished by Foot Joy, I see.'

Dave Marr was an assistant under the elder Harmon at both Winged Foot and Seminole, and it was his theory that Butch was the way he was because Claude was so tough on him; it was a way of rebelling. In that respect the name 'Butch' was a perfect fit. He certainly wasn't a country club kid from Westchester named Claude. He was Butch or, to those closest to him, 'Butchie.'

His parents thought boarding school was a way to break him, so they enrolled Butch at Villanova, an institution run by Catholic priests in Ojai, Calif. One day Claude Harmon Sr. got a phone call. One of the priests had picked up Butch and thrown him against a wall. Butch had countered with a left hook.

'Why did you punch a priest?' asked his father.

'I don't know,' said Butch, 'but I guarantee you that guy will think twice before he picks up another kid by the shirt and throws him against the wall.'

Although he had a cutting wit, Claude Harmon was a gentle man who never used a four-letter word unless it was g-o-l-f. Thinking that his son might have reformed, he gave him a set of clubs that he had used to finish third in the 1959 U.S. Open at Winged Foot. Butch took them to the University of Houston for less than a semester, where he snapped the shafts and threw every one of them in a lake. When he returned home and told his father he was joining the Army, Claude zinged him with one of the all-time best spontaneous comebacks in golf history. 'Why not join the Navy,' Claude told Butch, 'so you could get my clubs.'

Harmon went to Vietnam and came back to America wanting to play the tour. His golden moment was a victory in the 1971 Broome County Classic, a one-day tournament that would be the forerunner of the B.C. Open.

Butch soon realized that he didn't have his father's skills, that he wasn't going to win the Masters or set the course record at Seminole. So he decided to follow in Claude's footsteps another way, building a career as a club professional. His first big job was at Royal Golf Dar Es Salam Golf Club in Rubat, Morocco, where he was the personal instructor for King Hassan II.

While his brothers had high-profile jobs – Craig was at Oak Hill, Dick at Thunderbird and River Oak and Billy at the Vintage Club and Newport CC – Butch bounced around from jobs in Iowa to Texas City, Texas. His father, who had one of the quickest wits in golf, saw the bayou muni Butch was tending to and remarked, 'All you need is a tattoo parlor in your pro shop, and you'll be set for life.'

But Butch was a fighter who had the family name and his father's knowledge of the golf swing. This knowledge could make him a hot property in the new era of touring pros latching on to coaches or teachers. Seeing the success Dickie had with Lanny Wadkins, Butch carved out a relationship with Davis Love III, who was looking for a set of eyes after his father went down in a plane crash in 1989.

The success Harmon had tightening up Love's long and loose swing led to a bond with Steve Elkington, the Australian who was close friends with one of his father's contemporaries (Jackie Burke, who was based at Champions Golf Club in Houston). Butchie now had some momentum going. Through Elkington, he was introduced to Greg Norman on the putting green at the TPC of the Woodlands during the 1991 Shell Houston Open. Norman was in between instructors and totally lost with his game. Unable to get a 2-iron airborne, Harmon imparted some of his father's basic principles on the Shark, and within two years Norman was winning the British Open again and setting a scoring record at the Players Championship. This led to Harmon getting a job at Lochinvar, an all-men's club on the north side of Houston. It also led to a 1993 visit from Earl Woods.

'What we always used to say about Butch was that if you put him in the middle of the desert, somehow he'd get back,' says Billy Harmon.

The Harmon-Woods relationship started at Lochinvar the day Tiger was eliminated in the second round of the 1993 U.S. Amateur by Paul Page, a Walker Cupper from Great Britain. Earl had walked some holes with Butch at Champions, and made the call based on Greg Norman's reputation of being the best driver of the ball in the game. Tiger was hitting the ball all over the map.

Over lunch at Lochinvar, they discussed Tiger's golf swing, what Tiger was trying to accomplish and what Butch had seen at Champions. When they finished eating, Butch asked Tiger if he wanted to hit some balls, and it wasn't long before they were on the practice tee: Butch with his video camera, Tiger with his clubs.

'Tiger showed me some of the shots that he could hit, and I made some suggestions to him at the time that would make him more consistent,' Harmon said. 'It was nothing special, but I guessed he liked the results that he saw.'

To cut down on Tiger's wildness, Harmon suggested a wider stance for a better foundation, a wider arc at the top of his backswing, and less hip turn, which would prevent his club from going past parallel. It was similar to the work Harmon did with Love, since Davis and Tiger were built similarly.

Harmon kept telling Woods that in order to get to the next level, he had to control the distance of his shots, and work the ball depending on the conditions or the shape of the hole. Tiger came back the next day, and they worked again. For the next year, they would get together only twice, but not a week would go by without a phone conversation, or a month without Tiger mailing Butch a tape of his swing.

Butch's first question was always, 'Where's the ball starting out?'

From there, he knew what Tiger was doing wrong and could correct it over the phone. From those early days of their relationship, he knew that Tiger was a special talent who would have to work through a learning curve while living up to a set of expectations that no golfer since Nicklaus had had to live up to. Harmon watched the Amateur from Anaheim, where he was attending the PGA West Coast Merchandise Show. As he saw Woods walk up the 18th fairway, there were tears in his eyes; he was happy not only for his pupil but also for what Woods's success means for golf. 'This young man is one of the best young players to come out of this country in a long, long time,' Harmon said. 'That's the good news. The bad news is that he has to live up to it now.'

Three years later, Harmon parted ways with Norman to work exclusively with Woods. Their breakup was bitter, and came during a practice round before the 1996 PGA Championship at Valhalla. Officially, it involved Harmon trying to negotiate a clothing deal with Reebok after Nike had approached him with a contract to wear its clothes. (In his defense, Harmon was attempting to stay loyal to Greg.) Unofficially it had to do with ego, and Tiger's rise in popularity during Norman's decline. Greg had also lost faith in Harmon after his Masters collapse to Nick Faldo, and felt his clubface had become shut at the top under Harmon's tutelage.

Long-term, Harmon wouldn't have been able to juggle his time between two superstars. With Norman now out of the picture, Harmon could dedicate his time to Tiger, and the construction of his golf school at Rio Secco Golf Club in Las Vegas. Soon his teaching rates would rise to $500 an hour and his success with Woods led to a contract with *Golf Digest*, two book deals, an instructional video series, a regular spot on the Golf Channel's *Academy Live*, a clothing contract with Canadian designer Jack Victor, and a deal with SkySports to do analysis at 10 events. Tiger didn't mind, just as long as he was Butch's No. 1 priority. He even blessed Harmon's teaching relationships with Mark Calcavecchia, Se Ri Pak and Darren Clarke.

The bigger Tiger got, the bigger Butch got. In November 1999, a Las Vegas golf magazine sent a photographer over to Rio Secco to shoot Harmon dressed in a king's crown and robe. Harmon complied, but he never lost sight of the real king, never forgot that the kid was the show. 'We take a lot of heat [from other coaches],' Harmon admitted. 'You hear a lot of, "There's Butch Harmon, trying to be in the spotlight." That's not what it is all about.'

There was a time, though, when it looked like Butch's days were numbered. The rumors were hottest in summer 1998, when Tiger was still struggling with the swing changes being implemented by Harmon. On the range, players were saying that Tiger was getting advice from Hank Haney passed down to him by Mark O'Meara. After working with Greg Norman for five years, Harmon knew how temperamental superstars could be. Now, though, he also had to deal with Earl Woods, and that's a job in itself.

Butch was just as bull-headed as Earl, and the chemistry of that relationship took an ego check by Harmon for it to work. He understood, just as everyone associated with Tiger understood, that while Earl was taking more of a background role, he still wielded the second-most power in the unit. If you got on Earl's bad side, you were history.

Early on, Butch tried to establish some ground rules. 'I told Earl up front that it wasn't going to work if I tell Tiger something and he disagreed with it and told him to do something else,' said Harmon. That may have been the edict, but Earl pulled rank in summer 1998 when he felt Tiger's putting stroke had become too mechanical. Butch acquiesced, knowing to pick his battles as long as he had Tiger's ear and his respect.

He loved the kid, and while the kid was his meal ticket, there was much more to the relationship than the typical player-instructor bond. Earl knew this, too. There were times when he had to play Lieutenant Colonel, and since they were both in Vietnam at the same time, Harmon knew his role was subordinate. Ultimately their problems were resolved and Butch not only survived, but gained more power and a higher profile as Earl traveled less and took more of a backstage role in the production.

Earl and Butch actually played off each other's strengths. Earl was basically a loose cannon, a guy who would pop off and then say he was misquoted. This was hurting Tiger, detracting from his image and his accomplishments. Harmon knew how the game worked, how Tiger should play it, and was secure enough in his beliefs to tell Tiger what he sometimes didn't want to hear. He brought to the lesson tee a chest load of war stories and a wealth of knowledge that dated back to the Hogan era. With his background at Seminole and Winged Foot, he also brought a touch of class that Tiger soaked up.

The kid also loved Butch's inherited sarcasm, a sense of humor that was passed down from Claude. They could be boys together, giving each other the business without it affecting their work relationship. 'Butch is obviously my instructor, but he's more than that,' said Woods. 'He's a friend. And, you know, we almost act like brothers around each other. We understand when it's time to work, we become teacher and student, whereas outside of that, we become brothers again. He's got a wonderful feel of how I am by being on the range and seeing how I am that day. It's a weird relationship, because we know when to switch on and off and evolve in and out of it.'

They had certainly evolved as a team, and were about to celebrate their greatest hour. On the Medinah flag that hangs in Butch Harmon's home in Las Vegas, there is the inscription, 'We've got two now. Thanks for all your help. Tiger Woods.'

It was now time to go out and get No. 3.

# Thirty Four

# A WEEK AT THE BEACH

On Wednesday morning, June 14, 2000, Tiger Woods, Mark O'Meara, and John Cook went out to play an early practice round before the 100th U.S. Open. This was standard operating procedure for Tiger; sometimes he'd go out at 6 a.m. to get his work in before the crowds arrived. Not even the Payne Stewart memorial service on the 18th green at Pebble Beach would keep him from this. And when he was asked about his absence afterward, he had the perfect answer to deflect any criticism. 'I figured I've gone all through it with the [previous] memorial services, and I felt by going, it would be more of a deterrent for me during the tournament, because I don't want to be thinking about what transpired,' he had said. 'It all depends on how you are personally. If that's how you want to put closure to it, that's how you want to put closure to it. I handle things a little differently.'

Ten hours after that service he was still at work. If you walked down by the pro shop at dinnertime you would have seen Tiger Woods on the putting green, trying to find something that just wasn't quite here, the final component that would be required to tackle golf's ultimate examination. Stroking putt after putt, it wasn't until almost two hours into the session that something finally clicked.

For the most part, Tiger's putts were going in the hole. What he didn't like was the way they were going in the hole. They weren't going in the cup with the right speed, or the right roll. To a golfing impresario, this was more than a mere nuisance. Tiger wasn't releasing the putter, and on the Poa annua greens at Pebble, he'd need to put a pure stroke on the ball for it to go in. Late in the day these greens would be as bumpy as moss, and Tiger counted on playing late at least three days. 'I was making quite a few putts in practice rounds, but the ball wasn't turning over the way I would like to see it roll,' he said. 'I worked on it for a couple of hours and found that my posture was a little off. My release wasn't quite right.'

He had spent three days in Las Vegas before the Open working on his game with Butch Harmon. Really, it was more a matter of safeguarding than fixing. They spent most of the time replicating the shots he would need at Pebble Beach, starting with the tee shot at the first and finishing with the approach to the 18th. 'We just had to shape some shots, curve the ball a little differently for some of the holes out there,' Harmon said. Once Tiger got the putting stroke in order on Wednesday night, it was just a matter of going out and trusting it.

On the practice range Thursday morning, Tiger was loose. He talked to Harmon about the Los Angeles Lakers and staying relaxed. His 45-minute warm-up was perfect. His alignment and posture didn't need adjustment, the synchronization between his upper and lower body was in synch. 'We didn't talk about mechanics at all,' Harmon said. 'Everything was totally clicking.'

You couldn't write this in the *New York Times*, but Woods, *really* won the tournament and the third leg of the Grand Slam on Thursday with an opening round 65. Miguel Angel Martinez, the Spaniard, shot 66. John Huston, the Floridian, shot 67. But when the kid went out and shot 65 with just 24 putts, that was the ballgame. Six birdies, 12 pars and no bogeys: the start of the greatest summer in major championship history. The beginning of the end for the field. 'We're all looking for one score all the time – and that's his,' said Colin Montgomerie.

Mark O'Meara was upon the driving range that day, waiting, knowing that nobody had a chance this week. He played three practice rounds with Tiger before the Open. Tiger missed one shot. One He was now telling Hank Haney and Bernie Nichols about it. Haney is his coach. Nichols is the former NHL star.

'Johnny Miller came up to me on the 16th fairway on

Wednesday,' O'Meara said. 'So how is the kid playing?' he asked me.

'I told him, "Johnny. I've played the tour for 20 years now and Tiger is the best player I have ever seen. He doesn't have the best record year, but he's already the greatest player of all time."

'So Johnny says, "But how is he hitting it?"

'I said, "Didn't you hear me?" This guy has everything. He drives it longer and straighter than anyone in history. He can hit it high or low. He can hit cuts and draws. He has more imagination around the greens than almost anyone. And he's putting great right now. How can he lose?'

Woods had the 8: 40 pairing with Jesper Parnevik and Jim Furyk, two grinders, one colorful, one intense. Both had wins in 2000, Jesper at the Bob Hope and Furyk at Doral. They were bunched into the heart of the morning star groups; Phil Mickelson Jose Maria Olazabal, Lee Westwood, Hal Sutton and O'Meara were playing just ahead of them while Sergio Garcia, David Duval, Tom Lehman and Justin Leonard were just behind. As far as the weather went, they got the best of it.

Marking his ball on the first green, Woods saw the blanket of fog moving in. He started with birdies at the fourth and seventh holes for an outbound 33, and then cruised home with birdies at 10, 13, 14 and 18. His driving distance number (297. 8) looked like the weight of a modern-day NFL offensive guard. He had four putts inside 18 inches. He also made a six-footer, two eight-footers and two 12-footers to save par.

In the three previous Opens played at Pebble, nobody shot as low as Tiger took it, not Jack Nicklaus, Tom Watson, Lee Trevino, Johnny Miller, Tom Kite, Hale Irwin, Arnold Palmer or Curtis Strange. Tom Kite's lowest score, when he won in 1992, was 70. Conditions were different, but not much more difficult. With the blessing of the USGA, golf course superintendent Eric Greyrok started putting a liquid potassium fertilizer on the rough six weeks out, so there were spots where it was possible to whiff shots just 2 feet off the fairway. Tiger called his best shot of the day a gouged sand wedge from the right rough at the 11th. 'That was probably one of the worst lies I've ever gotten,' he said.

For security reasons, two Monterey County Sheriffs and an FBI agent accompanied him. He had come to Pebble Beach for State Amateurs and AT & T tournaments, he'd had days when he shot lower, but this round set a tone. Johnny Miller predicted it

35 minutes into the NBC/ESPN telecast. 'When I saw Tiger on the practice green, I could tell he was in that zone,' Miller said on air. 'He's going to do something this week that people will be talking about one hundred years from now . . . Tiger is going to break every U.S. Open record in the books. This is going to be the week that he says, "See you guys." '

Woods had it working every way imaginable; his game was in shape, his mental picture clear, and all the stars were aligned to handle the elements he could not control. For example, it couldn't have worked out better for Tiger when Jeff Maggert stood on the 10th tee at 3: 45 and asked for a USGA rules official. Maggert couldn't see the fairway because there were waves of fog rolling in, and as is his right, he refused to play his tee shot. Players in his group, Fred Couples in particular, were irritated because they knew the logjam this would create. Woods was already through his round and his news conferences when play was officially suspended at 3: 57. He was back at his room when the round was called for the day at 6 p.m. That would turn the second day into turmoil, with play resuming for 75 players who had not completed the opening round. Woods would get to sleep in, work out, and be fresh for his eventual second-round tee off. Skip Bayless of the *Chicago Tribune* called the fog bank, 'Tiger's vapor trail.'

'June gloom,' is how Tiger described it. 'This is what happens every June. The fog, the low clouds roll in. They burn off early in the afternoon and you have a wonderful summer – generally that's the way it is along the coast.'

The irony was that upon the driving range, near the polo fields, it was a beautiful afternoon. Tiger had taken advantage of the nice weather to gloat about the 65 a little, mess around with O'Meara, and then work on his game. This was not the cleanest 65 in the world. His putter had saved the round.

The Thursday weather report was the headline in the Friday morning *Monterey County Herald*: Tiger hits a new low. Tiger not only had the round of the day, but the quote of the day. Asked about Parnevik's orange shirt, Woods had said, 'Well, he was noticeable out there,' adding after a pause, 'You could see him in the fog, that's for sure,' and then finishing up with, 'He was our beacon, so no one would hit into us.'

By the time Tiger finally got to the practice green behind the first tee, it was late in the afternoon. Jack Nicklaus was coming up the 18th hole for the final time in the U.S. Open. He had reached the 18th green with two thunderous shots, and the roar could be heard upon the first tee. 'We heard this huge roar coming up, and I though someone had holed it from the fairway,' said Woods. 'But I thought about it and said, "Jack is due to finish any time now." If this was his last U.S. Open, it would be nice to actually have seen it. But I had more important things to take care of.'

Nicklaus had paused to sit on the fence behind the 18th tee to collect his thoughts. He then split the fairway, and hit a 3-wood some 240 yards to the front edge of the green. From there, two putting for the closing birdie was too much to ask. Nicklaus had tears well up in his eyes. He left the 50-footer for eagle almost 5 feet short, and left his 154th stroke of the tournament short and in the jar. In the NBC booth, Dan Hicks asked his audience, 'Where are the Golf Gods now that you need them?'

While one in particular was just teeing off, Nicklaus walked off the course and into the arms of his wife, Barbara, and his family. 'Well, that's the end of it,' he said. 'I'm ready to let it go, and I'm ready to let it go for a very good reason. I really don't think I can compete anymore.'

Jack had bristled when Bill Fields of *Golf World* asked if he had any regrets about playing years after he threatened to be a serious threat in his favorite tournament. He was now 60 – with an artificial hip, bad feet, and a backswing that was cut off – but Fields's question had hit a sensitive spot. He had shot 73 and 82 – his worst 18-hole score in the U.S. Open. But he still came away from it with a masochistic desire to come back, mentioning that he could win the Senior Open and qualify for the 2001 U.S. Open at Southern Hills.

He had won the National Open four times, once at Pebble (1972). Earlier he called this tournament 'the total examination of the game of golf,' adding, 'It probably does more to make a man out of you than any other tournament.'

There was a sense of urgency to Tiger's demeanor as he played the front side. He didn't want to be impatient, because once again he got a break with the weather. At the same time he wanted to get in as many holes as possible, knowing the pace of play would be miserably slow. In the 12 holes he got in before dark, Woods showed flashes of brilliance and his first two signs of being human. His first bogey of the tournament didn't come until the fifth hole, the par-3 Nicklaus had dramatically redesigned along Stillwater Cove. With a 20-minute wait on the tee, Woods hit his first real bad shot, a flared 8-iron that left him a tough bunker shot, over a grass overhang. He came right back from that with back-to-back birdies at six and seven. His iron from the right rough at the sixth was a shot that only Woods could hit; from the deep grass, up the hill at the par-5, to 15 feet for eagle. He followed that up with a 60-degree lob wedge to 15 feet at the seventh. In two passes Woods had shown off his strength and his distance control.

Some of that good work was lost with a bogey at the ninth, and now it was getting dark. Woods, wanting to finish the day with a surge, finished birdie-birdie, knocking a 3-footer in at the 11th and a 30-footer from across the green at the 12th. When Woods made that final putt, the bemused looks on the faces of Parnevik and his caddy, Lance Ten Broeck, said it all: 'The only thing that can stop Tiger from winning is Tiger,' said Parnevik.

NBC had already announced it would return at 6: 30 Saturday morning with bonus coverage. While network executives wouldn't admit it, a big part of this decision was made because of Tiger. In the words of NBC Sports chairman Dick Ebersol, 'In the TV age there have been two other people who have attracted viewers beyond their sport. They are Muhammad Ali and Michael Jordan. Tiger Woods is clearly the third one.'

Woods had a three-stroke lead at sundown over Jimenez. He was at 9-under par, threatening to become only the second player in Open history to reach double digits. Behind Jimenez, Denmark's Thomas Bjorn and Argentina's Angel Cabrera were his closest pursuers, at 2-under. While Tiger kept saying, 'there's a long way to go,' the consensus was that NBC would soon be televising a blowout. In the rules trailer behind the 18th green, USGA committeemen were amazed that this setup was yielding so many birdies to one player – Woods now had 10 of them in 30 holes.

Saturday morning at the 100th U.S. Open will always be remembered for the drive Woods hit off the 18th tee, and for the stream of expletives that came out of his mouth as his Tour Accuracy ricocheted among the rocks. It was 8 a.m. Pacific time when Tiger lost both his ball and his composure. In the NBC truck, executive producer Tommy Roy and director Tom Randolph knew immediately they would have a situation; it put a pallor over the morning telecast. 'Sporting events are not done on taped delay,' said Roy. 'With the WWF you're expecting that. All others are done live. The only other kill switches used today are in NASCAR, where you're listening in to a driver and a crew chief. Even then it's a kill switch, not on a delay per se.'

Mark Steinberg had heard the tirade, and was waiting for Woods outside the scoring trailer. As the crafter of Tiger's image, he knew an apology needed to be issued. 'It was in the heat of the moment, and unfortunately I let it slip out,' Woods said. 'And I regret doing it.' NBC and the USGA received calls from irate viewers but for Tiger, this incident – like the Payne Stewart memorial and Nicklaus's final walk up the 18th in a U.S. Open – could not make him lose his focus or concentration. As he said, he had more important things to take care of.

Even with a bogey at the 18th, Tiger broke a 97-year-old record held by Willie Anderson for the largest 36-hole Open lead (six strokes over Bjorn and Jimenez) and he had tied the scoring record of 134 held by Nicklaus, T. C. Chen and Lee Janzen. He would be back that afternoon to continue the assault, but first it was time for something to eat. 'I'm really hungry right now,' he said before leaving the compound behind the 18th green. 'I guess it is breakfast time here on the West Coast.'

That afternoon, Woods chewed deeper into the record books. He came back from a triple bogey with birdies at six and seven again, turned in even-par 35. The 71 he turned in doesn't look that impressive as a stand-alone score, but scoring conditions had turned brutal. Jimenez shot 76. Bjorn, paired with Woods, went for an 82 and said of Tiger, 'He's playing every shot as if his life depended on it.' If the U.S. Open makes a man out of you, as Nicklaus said, then this was the round where Tiger grew his whiskers.

Ernie Els was the only player on the leader board to shoot under par, but with opening rounds of 74 and 73 the two-time Open champion had started in 30th place – too far back to cause a stir. Although he picked up three strokes on Woods with a 68, and was alone in second place, Els still trailed by 10 strokes. Tiger now had another Open record: Largest 54-hole lead, previously held and established by Jim Barnes in the 1921 Open.

'It's not like boxing where you give a guy a low blow,' said Paul Azinger. 'We might need Tonya Harding or something.'

Tiger's knees had been chopped out from under him at the third, when his second shot hit a gust of wind and came down in a clump of 6-inch rye just short of the green. Barely able to see his ball, Woods considered taking an unplayable lie drop. Deciding to play it may have been his first and only bad decision of the week. He advanced his third shot a foot, and his fourth came out sideways, into the fairway. A pitch and two putts gave him a 7, but there was no cursing this time. Woods simply smiled at Williams and moved on. 'I smiled just because of the fact I didn't get that bad a [second] shot, and I ended up walking away with a 7,' he said.

It was the attitude he had to have, the attitude needed for an Open. Two holes later he was in the rough twice but walked away with a birdie. When he made 2 at the seventh and 3 at the ninth, it wiped out the triple bogey. Players were now conceding.

'There's nobody who's going to catch him now,' said Rocco Mediate. 'I'd like to see Tiger break the record, to tell you the truth.'

'I stopped looking at his score a while ago,' said Phil Mickelson. 'Nobody has the opportunity to catch him.'

'Tiger is untouchable right now,' said Bobby Clampett. 'Give him the trophy.'

Woods wasn't ready to accept, but did concede the time he spent on the putting green Wednesday night was well worth it. He had taken 28 putts in the third round and was averaging 27 for the tournament.

'I've never had a lead like this, even in fantasy golf,' Woods said. 'It's not necessarily just making putts, it's making putts at the right time. There comes a time in every round when you need to make that big par putt to keep the momentum going. I've been able to make those putts all week.'

Sunday was a victory lap: Tiger against the record, Tiger trying to close out the single most dominating week in golf history. This was the only day he had problems with swing mechanics on the range, but Harmon quickly straightened him out by squaring up Tiger's shoulders at address. 'His shoulders were just a little too open on his takeaway,' said Harmon. 'As soon as we put a club down, everything was perfect. He hit one shot and said, "That's it, I've got it." '

Woods started out with nine straight pars, and when he birdied the 10th and 12th holes, the last bastion of USGA supremacy came tumbling down. Tiger was now at 10-under, but the committeemen and staffers were embracing it. 'I was actually glad that barrier was broken,' said executive director David Fay. 'I don't recall one single conversation [where] people [were] agonizing, frustrated or upset with what Tiger was doing. Clearly the best player in the world playing the best, and that was a wonderful scenario to have.'

What made Tiger's run easier to stomach was that nobody else in the field was under par. Two more birdies at 13 and 14 gave Woods three straight, but more important than the scoring record to Tiger was to play the entire final round without a bogey. When he stood over a 10-footer at the 16th, you would have thought it was the 8-footer at Medinah to stave off Sergio Garcia. Tiger poured it in, and nearly galloped off the green.

In the NBC truck, Roy was turning this into a celebration. The 6 1/2 hours of coverage was up 11 percent over 1999's thriller at Pinehurst, and was the highest for an Open in 25 years. 'I thought going into it we were in for something special because it was the 100th U.S. Open, because it was Pebble Beach, which is such a special place, and even more so because all the top players in the game were playing so well,' said the executive producer. 'Maybe that's what made his performance even more astounding. It speaks volumes for what an unbelievable week of golf he played . . . that's why you can argue it was the best golf tournament ever played. It was great stuff.'

At the par-3 17th, he deliberately aimed at the bunker in front of the green, knowing that he could get up-and-down more easily from there than greenside rough. At the 18th, he took iron off the tee when a birdie would have broken the 72-hole Open scoring record established by Nicklaus (1980) and Janzen (1993) at Baltusrol. 'Why didn't he go for the record?' said Harmon. 'Because the only record he cares about is Jack Nicklaus's [major championship] record.'

At 12 under, Woods had won the Open by 15 strokes. The previous record was 11, set by Willie Smith in 1899. Tiger's accomplishment was compared to Bob Beamon's leap of 29 feet, 2 1/2 inches in the 1968 Olympics, Babe Ruth hitting more home runs in 1927 (60) than any other team in the American League, Secretariat winning the Belmont by 31 lengths. In the 106-year history of the Open, nobody had shot lower in relation to par, or so thoroughly dominated the field.

That it came on Father's Day was somehow fitting. Earl was at home in Cypress, watching on TV. 'I wanted to give him the space to perform and be himself,' he said. 'It was all part of the plan.' Tida, his mother, stood next to him and the Open trophy. He took out three cigars, and handed one of them to his girlfriend, Joanna. There were 32 subpar rounds shot at Pebble Beach. Woods had four of them, finished off by the final-round 67. He had smoked everybody, going around Pebble Beach without a 3-putt in 72 holes. That Wednesday night session on the putting green at Pebble Beach, the work he put in at Butchie's school in Las Vegas, the swing changes he started implementing in 1997, the ability he now had in course management: it was a combination that no human could touch.

'I'm in awe,' said Els, who had the best seat in Sunday's theatre.

'I looked at the scoreboard in total wonderment,' said Padraig Harrington, who finished fifth, 17 shots back.

'He's a freak of nature, worlds apart from the rest of us in every way,' said Michael Campbell, who finished in 12th, 20 shots back.

It was as complete a dissection of a course and a field in major championship history, but it was just the start of golf's greatest summer. As the king of the B Flight, Els thought he had an answer, but quickly realized it was a foolish thought. Tiger's simply in another dimension. After Kapalua, Muirfield Village and now Pebble Beach, nobody knew that better than he did.

'I considered squeezing him in a bear hug, or arm-wrestling him, or just tackling him,' he said. 'But that wouldn't work because on top of everything else, Tiger is getting stronger every day, too. I don't know what we're going to do with him.'

# Thirty Five

# New King at the Old Course

Sir Michael Bonallack, captain and former secretary of the Royal and Ancient Golf Club of St. Andrews, walked the final round with Tiger Woods at the U.S. Open. He marveled at the 'totality' of Tiger's game, how he 'appears to do everything better than anyone else – and he's 40 yards longer.' Sir Michael practically awarded the Claret Jug to Woods one month before his arrival in the Auld Grey Toon. 'If Tiger doesn't win at St. Andrews,' he said, 'there should be a steward's inquiry.'

Gambling guru Angus Loughran certainly hoped that Sir Michael's assessment was spot-on. When the Open was last held at St. Andrews, Loughran put £100 down on Woods to win the Millennium Open at St. Andrews. He was given 100-to-1 odds. That was considerably better than what the London bookies had. At 15 – 8 to win the Slam, not even Woods would make a wager. 'Maybe five quid,' he said. 'Those are bad odds.'

In the four weeks between Opens, Woods had caddied for Jerry Chang at U.S. Open qualifying in Las Vegas, putted 'like I need a seeing-eye dog' at the Western Open and traveled to Ireland for the annual male-bonding golf and fishing trip that serves as an orientation to the British Open. Most of the time was spent with fly rods on the River Liffey, but occasionally the boys would break out the clubs and play a links course. As Woods said before he left Chicago on July 9, 'I won't let the golf get in the way of the fishing.'

St. Andrews was on his radar screen, but there was no need to be anxious about the historical overtones. He would gradually work his way into it, telling the press, 'To have an opportunity to complete the career grand slam at a course where it all started is very symbolic,' while his friends got less of a stock answer. 'He's loving it,' said Stuart Appleby. 'He's pumped about getting the career slam, and he's pumped about doing it at St. Andrews.'

Appleby was on the plane with Woods on the way to the British Open. Also on board that Sunday night after the Western Open were Lee Janzen, Rocco Mediate and David Duval. Mark O'Meara was awaiting their arrival, along with his father, Bob. They would play in a two-day pro-am at Limerick Golf Club in Ballyclough as the guest of John Patrick ('J. P.') McManus, a multi-millionaire who had befriended the golfers through his connection with Joe Lewis, the owner of Isleworth.

The subject of Tiger coming to McManus's pro-am was broached at the Ryder Cup. 'My idea was that he would really drop in as a visitor for one of the days,' explained McManus. 'There was no question of me pressing him to play. He said, "If you're asking me, I'm coming." And so it came to pass.'

McManus made it sweet for them. He and another Irish millionaire named Dermot Desmond put them up at the neo-Gothic Adare Manor Hotel, and helicoptered them to the course. On the first day of the proam, Woods just happened to draw Michael Smurfit, owner of the K Club near Dublin, host of the 2005 Ryder Cup. Tiger shot 12-under and ended up winning the tournament after Appleby was disqualified for using a laser yardage sensor. He donated the £33,000 prize money to McManus's charity.

They checked out of Adare and choppered over to Smurfit's place, where Sean McManmon was waiting. As the estate manager of the club, McManmon knew the fish in the River Liffey by their names. He helped O'Meara catch a 9-1 /2 pound Atlantic salmon just before Woods arrived, and the picture was waiting for Tiger to inspect. Since Tiger has gotten so good on the course, O'Meara likes to joke that he needs 2 shots a side in their bets at home. On the river, Tiger is about a 13 handicap, and determined to reach single digits with a cast that McManmon said was the most natural he'd seen in 35 years of fishing. Typical of Tiger, he was doing reps until he got it perfect. 'He won't go near the water until he gets it right,' McManmon said. 'He has the flow through the line, and the last thing to land on the water is the fly.'

O'Meara first made the fishing trip in 1997. He brought along Duval the next year, and that led to Woods coming in 1999, which was probably the most memorable year. Payne Stewart was along as part of Team Isleworth, and he became legendary for playing his harmonica and piano in the bars, and singing with the locals until 5 a.m. A year later, there was a ceremony at Waterville, where a statue was unveiled and he was named honorary captain.

Later in the week, as it grew closer to the tournament, Woods and O'Meara started hitting balls at the K Club. Although he won at Limerick, he really wasn't hitting it that well. In a trip up to Royal County Down, the wonderful links course at the doorstep of the Mountains of Mourne, Woods reportedly failed to break 80. That's what the townspeople were saying, anyway; most of them were counting as Woods four-putted the first, turned in five over, and never posted an official score.

Back at the K Club, Woods realized it was time to figure it out when O'Meara reminded him of the stakes. 'We were on the practice tee and he wasn't hitting it good,' O'Meara remembers. 'He looks over at me and tells me, "You need to start working on *your* game." I told him no, Bud, you have to work on your game. Next week's important to me, but obviously it's a lot more important to you. He says, "Why's that?" I tell him, "Because my name is already on that trophy." He says, "Yeah, but I've got more majors than you do. I've got you by one." I tell him, "Bud, I wasn't worried about that when you started as a pro. You're going to go so far past me and a lot of other players, it's not even funny." '

O'Meara fixed him. There's nobody who knows Tiger's swing better, other than maybe Harmon – and some say that's debatable. Mark certainly plays more holes with Tiger than Butch, and spotted some flaws right away.

Woods had gotten too narrow from playing in the wind. O'Meara suggested he stand taller, stay back on his right side and hit some high sweepers. That was the shot he would need in the crosswinds at St. Andrews. For the first 10 swings, Tiger couldn't do it. Then he started opening his shoulders and hitting these beautifully shaped high draws that would work anywhere.

The story on the Old Course would be the bunkers, all 112 of them. Some are deep enough to bury an elephant; all had new sod walls, which caused a problem because of their steepness. Players talked about the possibility of sideways paths as the only option of escape.

Woods had played St. Andrews most recently in a Dunhill Cup, but was still learning about its nuances. While it looks like a moonscape, and lacks any grand views of the firth, the Old Course can be a fascinating place. Tiger just loved opening his eyes and discovering what an architectural gem it really is. 'OK,' he said of the fourth hole. 'There is a huge bunker about 350 yards out and normally you never even think about it. But today, with the wind coming down off the right, I hit driver and pulled it a little bit and, even though it was kind of a low-heel pull, it was in the fairway but only 15 yards from the bunker. It comes into play downwind right to left, not straight downwind. It has to be off the right so that as you ride the wind, it rides right into the bunker. But then again, I know that when you're in a howler and you don't quite get it over the slope on the fairway you can be stuck on the upslope of a huge embankment, then blow it up into the wind and get stuck in the same bunker. It's kinda neat to pick up new little things.'

The links had an entrancing effect on Woods, who loved to play shots that required imagination. One of his often-told stories comes from the final round of the 1995 British Open at St. Andrews, where he finished 13 strokes back of John Daly. On the sixth hole, he was 40 yards short of the green. The wind was hard in his face. The ground was so dry, puffs of white dust were kicking up on impact. Rather than risk blading a wedge, Woods took out this putter and got up and down.

The love affair had grown through the years, as Woods came to appreciate the vagaries of the ground game. It was his second-round 66 in 1996 at Royal Lytham that convinced Woods he had the game to turn pro. In 1998, he was just one shot out of the O'Meara – Brian Watts play-off. And at Carnoustie, if his putter hadn't been cold, it would have been his week. He finished T-7, but just four strokes back.

St. Andrews would be a different type of test. At Carnoustie, a course superintendent had gotten carried away and grown rough so deep that it reduced the championship to folly. There was no rough at St. Andrews, but the penalties for finding black holes like Deacon Sime, Hell and the Road Hole bunker could be much more exacting.

'People say to me that all you do is aim left and hit it, but that's not the case,' Woods said. 'I can drive some of the greens depending on the wind. But with the fairways as fast as they are here, you need to position your ball off the tee because it will run. And if you keep it on the left too much, there are pot bunkers on the holes coming the other way that share the fairways. You have to place your ball correctly. The fairways are so fast you cannot get away with any misses.'

His mood in practice rounds and pre-tournament news conferences was extremely relaxed. Butch Harmon had brought out a gutta-percha ball, and used it on the ninth hole to hit a 113-yard 5-iron to set up a birdie. Asked if winning a career Grand Slam would be the highlight of his career, Woods put winning three straight U.S. Juniors and then three straight U.S. Amateur titles ahead of it. Even the three-straight juniors alone would rank higher. 'As anyone knows, there is a dramatic difference between 14-and 15-year-olds versus 17-year-olds physically, mentally, emotionally. There is a huge difference, rather than a person who is 24 and 30. To win at the level three consecutive years, 18 matches in a row, that's not bad.'

Since it was the Millennium Open, an exhibition would be held Wednesday afternoon for all the past champions. Nineteen had accepted the invitation, including 88-year-old Sam Snead. They would play the 1st, 2nd, 17th and 18th holes. Snead would use one of the Callaway ERC drivers, work his way around the loop, stop for pictures one more time on the Swilken Bridge, and then adjourn to the clubhouse for beverages.

Having Snead on the property reminded Tiger of a story. 'When I was 5 o 6 we played at Calabasas Country Club,' Tiger recalled. 'He was playing an 18-hole exhibition where he had a new group of playing partners every two holes. I got a chance to play with him on the last two. There was this little par-3 with a creek in front that I couldn't carry. I was trying to bounce it off the cart path and through the creek. It didn't work, and rolled into the creek. I got in; automatically I was going to play it. The ball was sitting up. From behind me Sam yells out, "What are you doing?" I turn around, like dumbfounded. I'm just going to hit the shot. And he said, "You can't play that. Just pick it up and drop it. Let's go on."

'Well, I didn't really like that very much. I remember just turning around, looking at my ball and I said, "I gotta hit it. I don't want to drop, it is a penalty." So I hit a 7-iron right out of there on to the green. All wet, I two-putted, got my bogey and bogeyed the last. I made bogey, bogey and Sam beat me by two, par, par.'

Tiger had a prime opening-round time and pairing. His playing partners were Nick Price, who is arguably one of the best guys on tour, and David Gossett, the U.S. Amateur champion. The only downside to Gossett was that he had a reputation of playing slow, but with a 9: 30 a.m. time, the 14th match of the day, pace shouldn't be a problem.

Woods started out deliberately, making eight straight pars until he wedged to 3 feet at the ninth and made birdie. Walking up to the green, he described to Price how Butch had broken out a gutta-percha on this hole during the practice rounds, and how he hit 5-iron from 113 to set up a birdie. That seemed to take his mind off of the earlier opportunities he missed, and with an aggressive stroke Woods had made his first move into red numbers.

That set off a nice little run of five 3s in seven holes, which put him at 5-under and in the lead. His best shot of the day may have been the sickle he needed to advance a shot from the hay at 17th to the right front of the green. With three straight closing pars, Woods was in at 5-under 67. The mastery continued: Starting on the weekend at Augusta, he was now 24-under in his last seven rounds of major championship golf.

The lead was taken late in the day by Ernie Els, who went out with David Duval in match 43 and shot 6-under 66. Els had been touted before the tournament by swing instructor David Leadbetter, who was making a comeback with Ernie and trying to bolster the South African's confidence. 'If anyone out of the top 20 can challenge Tiger, then Ernie is your man,' Leadbetter said.

Els didn't seem to be listening. 'Man,' he said. 'you don't know how hard it is for me to win these days. I mean, I have a schedule which is almost exactly the same as Tiger's . . .' With a birdie at 17, Els had taken a first step toward erasing his inferiority complex. That lasted about 30 minutes. After a par at 18, he did television interviews and then walked in the press tent where the very first question by a reporter was about you-know-who.

> Q:     Ernie, I guess a month ago you said in the interview room at Pebble Beach that you basically felt it was an hour's questions about Tiger?

A:    Yes.

Q:    Is that something you don't want to do again?

A:    Well, what's the question? Shall I start talking about Tiger again, or . . . geez! No, not right now, no.

Q:    Put it this way, Ernie, can you imagine being 15 strokes behind Tiger Woods this week after what has happened this day?

A:    Guys, that's a little unfair. I just shot 66. Talk about my round or just get on the phone.

Els had just shot four rounds in the sixties to win the Standard Life Loch Lomond against a strong field that included Tom Lehman, Colin Montgomerie, Phil Mickelson, Jose Maria Olazabal and David Duval. With Lehman and Monty finishing second and third, and Els standing on the 17th tee tied with Montgomerie, the script was almost identical to the U.S. Open finish at Congressional. For the year, he was now 116 strokes under par. The only problem was Tiger. The 67 put him at 152-under for the year.

What was most remarkable about Tiger's first round was his sense of patience. Through eight holes, he was seven strokes off the lead being held by his college teammate, Notah Begay. When he was put on the clock at the 12th and 13th holes because of his partner Gossett, Woods didn't let it bother him. When his ball was waist-deep at the 17th, he thought about where he needed to put his second shot, how to execute the shot by opening the face, holding on with his left hand and swinging hard with his right. Before he hit that shot, cameras caught Woods laughing. What was he laughing about? Just something caddy Steve Williams had told him. When he stood up to hit it, the game face was back on.

'The problem is he's so mature now,' said O'Meara. 'There's an inner calmness about him. Even if he has a couple of bad holes out there, he knows with his talent and his swing, he can rattle off five or six birdies so fast it will make your heart stop. I've never seen anything like it in my life.'

Day Two was the second stage in the transition from the Nicklaus era to the Woods era. This one was more choreographed than the Friday afternoon finish at Pebble, but it had the same historical symbolism: Nicklaus playing the 18th hole in an Open Championship for the final time vs. Woods preparing to tee off at the first, trying to inch closer to his one impregnable record.

As Tiger went on to birdie the first and fourth holes to assume the lead, Nicklaus spent over an hour in the media tent, reminiscing about a tournament he had played for 38 years. The Great Man won the Claret Jug on three occasions, was runner-up seven times, and in some corners of Scotland was referred to as The Great Man Himself. It had been a long and wonderful ride. As appropriate as it was for Tiger to complete his Grand Slam at the Old Course, so, too, was it for Nicklaus to end his era on these same sacred grounds.

When he won the Open at St. Andrews in 1970, beating Doug Sanders in a playoff, Nicklaus said, 'St. Andrews is what the game really means. I wanted to be part of St. Andrews. I wanted to win on the Old Course.' Now, as he prepared to say goodbye, Nicklaus admitted that the Open Championship, more so than the Masters even, was his favorite event. 'There has always been a sense of history that I've enjoyed so much,' he said. 'So many of the great golfers of the past have played on these courses.'

As Nicklaus spoke, perhaps the greatest golfer of all was taking steps toward a three-stroke lead after 36 holes. Els had gone out early and played what looked to be an uninspired round of 72. It was disappointing in that the flags hung limp on the grandstands as he teed off. It was the type of effort that Woods would never accept of himself, and it was the most glaring difference between the two young men. 'Today was my bad round,' Els said glumly. 'I can't see myself playing like that again. I know I can play much better. It was a perfect day for scoring and I knew that before I went out. I just felt that it was going to be perfect. Hopefully the momentum will come my way in the third round. It's very disappointing and I'll need to shoot in the sixties on the last two days.'

Woods had another average-looking day. He caught a good break at the Road Hole, when his second ran through the green but stopped on a patch of grass just short of the pavement. That saved him from bogey and inspired Dai Davies to write this lead in *The Guardian*:

'Tiger Woods yesterday solved the conundrum of whether it is better to be lucky or good. If you want to win golf championships, particularly by massive margins, it is better to be both – and he is.'

Although the halfway lead was half of what it was at Pebble Beach, Woods had a commanding presence over the golfer in second place (David Toms), and two of the three (Steve Flesch and Loren Roberts) tied for third. Of the four players within four strokes of Woods's 133 total, only Sergio Garcia, who was tied with Flesch and Roberts at 137, had been able to push Tiger in a major.

Behind the 18th green, Nick Price was all but telling the engraver to begin his work on the Jug. 'Those guys behind him better pray for the wind to blow hard, because that's the only chance they have,' said Price, who won the Open in 1994 at Turnberry. 'I said to my caddy when I won the PGA at Southern Hills in 1994, I only did that once in my life [run away from the field]. He's done it four or five times and he's going to do it another 24 or 25 times. I had that feeling once and that was at that PGA. You put the ball in the right spot, and when you miss the green you're in a position where you can up and down it. Seventeen was a perfect example. Most of us would have ended up in the asphalt, and he ended up in the grass and made 4. It's going to be a very interesting weekend for Tiger.'

Price made another good point. The way St. Andrews is laid out allowed Woods to go about his business with less of the usual dust and hassle that is a byproduct of his fame. With parallel holes, and then the loop, all of the spectators and media are gathered to the periphery of the course. Price, who had played as many tournament rounds as anybody with Woods over the last five years, had just missed the cut. Yet, unlike Els, talking about the phenomenon was not a hassle.

'He's on cruise, man,' Price said. 'I'm telling you, he hasn't even tried any shots yet. You look at the holes. The two par-5s are par-4s for him, and the 10th hole is a par-3 for him. It should be. The 12th hole is a par 3 for him. With the right wind, 18 is a par-3. I've only seen him miss hit three shots this week. He's playing very intelligently.'

At the 17, Price busted his best drive of the day. Woods took out his 3-wood and cut it one yard past Nick's ball. 'It's a different game,' Price said. 'He's hitting 2-irons, 3-irons, even 4-irons off some of these tees. The height he hits the ball is such an advantage, and then he has the ability to hit it low, too. He's got it all.'

Woods put the tournament out of reach on Saturday with another 67 that was once again almost workmanlike in nature. When he missed a 4-footer for par at the second, his streak of 64 straight holes in a major championship without a bogey came to an end. Typically, though, Woods came right back with a birdie at the third and made seven for the day to take a six-stroke lead over Duval (who shot 66) and Denmark's Thomas Bjorn.

As Hugh McIlvanney noted in *The Times*, the balance between Tiger's inspiration and pragmatism had been nearly flawless. Self-indulgence had not been allowed to show its face. 'I just tried to play as smart as I could, getting myself into positions to execute the shots,' Woods said. 'There were very few mess-ups, but overall it was pretty good.'

Duval had at least made it interesting by birdieing the last and then issuing somewhat of a challenge in the press tent. He wanted the chance to look Tiger in the eye. 'It will be a circus. It will be exciting. It will be a slugfest, whatever you want to call it,' Duval said. 'I wanted to make sure I gave myself a chance to be there.'

The downside to Duval's situation was the first twinge of a back spasm that would sidetrack him for the next four months. Whether he traumatized it lifting weights, mountain biking or hitting balls, Duval was in such bad shape that he conducted his post-round interviews while standing. Tom Boers, the back expert who had worked in the past with Fred Couples and Davis Love III, was at the British Open, and worked some of the problem out. But how it would react overnight was the question.

Woods looked forward to the challenge, and was glad to see that Duval was ready to take him on again. Although they were cold around one another at first, their friendship had grown through the trips to Ireland, and the vacation they took together with their girlfriends in Las Vegas. Duval and Julie MacArthur were even scheduled to fly home to Florida on Tiger's plane.

The coronation commenced at 2: 40 p.m., when starter Ivor Robson said in his distinctive, high-pitched voice, 'On the tee, Tiger Woods.' There was reserved applause as Woods, wearing black pants and a red sweater, began his day of work with an iron shot down toward the Swilken Burn.

Duval made a game of it early, making four putts in the first seven holes and lipping out two others. Knowing there were driveable par-4s ahead, Woods had played it conservative, making birdie at the 464-yard fourth with a 9-iron second shot to 12 feet. The sense of drama ended with Woods hitting a driver onto the 10th and 12th greens and two-putted for birdie. He moved to 19-under par, two strokes clear of the 72-hole Open scoring record established by Nick Faldo with another two-putt birdie, this one at the 581-yard 14th.

It was now just Tiger against the record. He made a bogey at the 17th, but that was overshadowed by the problems Duval had in the Road Hole bunker. Taking four strokes to get out, Duval made quadruple bogey 8 to literally limp home.

In the chaos that followed, Woods continued to keep his head. As the gallery followed in behind him, some overzealous marshals began pushing people back into the Swilken Burn. As he reached the green, an exotic dancer from a local club ran to the flagstick and posed for the cameras. Woods tried not to notice either distraction. By now, he had assumed the dual roles of ultimate warrior and ultimate sportsman. He was about to win the Grand Slam, but it seemed to be an afterthought to what Tiger deemed at that moment to be more important. When they both made pars at the 18th, Woods made a point of walking off the green with Duval, and telling him 'Walk off like a champion, because you are a champion.' With an inward nine of 43, Duval had finished 12 strokes back and in a tie for 11th place.

'If it wasn't a major, I probably wouldn't be here,' Duval said. 'It's disappointing, because I feel I'm starting to play better. I didn't want to make a big deal about this, and still don't, but there have been so many rumors around. I figured I'd try to set things straight. The back thing probably has affected my scores a bit, but that's no excuse, by any means.'

The second-place medal was won for the third-straight major by Els, who threw a catch-up 69 on the board to finish at 11-under, eight shots back of Woods. In the *Washington Post*, Tom Callahan would later refer to it as the Bridesmaid Slam. In a world without Tiger he would have at least three, maybe four majors. But that may be the Big Easy's legacy.

'The guy's 24 years old,' Els said. 'and he's lapping us in the majors every time, it looks like. I'm supposed to be getting to my prime. I'm 30 years old but I'm going against a guy who's fearless and with so much confidence that it's going to be tough to beat him. We just have to hope he's off. At the moment, he's streets ahead of us.' There were 47,000 spectators at St. Andrews on Sunday, which pushed the attendance for the week to a record 230,000. There were no steward's inquiries. Woods made £500,000, or U.S. $759, 150. The bookies took a bath. Angus Loughran took his reported 10,000 quid in a check.

The sky was the color of steel when they finished, and as he stood on the 18th green once again for the trophy ceremony, Woods felt the history come up through his feet. He was now an indelible image cast in the consciousness of St. Andrews, as much a part of its lore as Old Tom Morris, Bobby Jones and yes, even Jack Nicklaus. Unlike the Seve Ballesteros victory over Tom Watson in 1984, there was no triumphant series of fist pumps when it was over. This was just one pump, a hug with Steve Williams, and his hat was quickly off to shake everyone's hand. As John Hopkins would write in The Times '[Tiger's] victory by eight strokes was only marginally more emphatic than his conduct off it.'

At the trophy ceremony, Woods was just as reserved, talking in reverential tones about the Old Course, and the special meaning of his Grand Slam being clinched at the Home of Golf. In his post-round interview, columnist Art Spander of the *Oakland Tribune* asked Woods if he had stepped foot in a bunker all week. Woods, who knew Art from his days in junior golf, flashed his customary smile and joked that yes he had, every day – on the practice ground.

It was hard to say what was more improbable: No three putts at Pebble Beach or no bunkers at St. Andrews. In either case, it was sterling, as in silver.

Afterward, back at the Old Course Hotel, Woods and his entourage packed for the flight home. Harmon had left early. Over at Leuchars Royal Air Force Base, a Gulfstream V was fueled and ready for the Atlantic crossing. After he kissed his mother in the valet parking area of the hotel and told her that he loved her, Woods stepped into a courtesy van and headed toward the airport with Joanna, the Claret Jug, and 10 pieces of luggage. (There's no baggage limit on Air Tiger.)

Once airborne, Duval and Woods sat facing one another, talking about their day, how it turned out, and how it was fitting that they could share the moment together. In the three years since he had won the Masters, Duval was the only golfer on the planet to pass Tiger and ride the No. 1 ranking.

As he looked at Tiger's name on the holiest grail in competitive golf, Duval was inspired. 'I got to see where his name was placed, and it made us both realize what a great, great achievement just happened,' he said. 'Tiger just didn't win a golf tournament that Sunday. He placed himself in history with four other folks. It's hard to report about that enough.'

Later, they talked about fishing, and how they'd have to do Ireland again in 2001. Like Nicklaus and Palmer, they had grown closer together through mutual respect, and when Tiger took a stand on the Ryder Cup issue, that solidified their friendship.

Duval would like to return the favor someday, both as a stand-up friend and as the guy who took Tiger down in competition. He knows that Woods would have no problem with that, because Tiger's measure of greatness has also been defined by his ability to both win and lose with grace and dignity.

'We were in a spot where we were talked about in the same sentence,' acknowledged Duval. 'There's been a lot of different circumstances that we've been in. Friendships grow.'

So do rivalries, and leaving St. Andrews, golf definitely needed one.

## Thirty Six

# REVERSE SPIN

After Tiger Woods won the U.S. Open, the editors at Time magazine wanted an exclusive interview. They approached Mark Steinberg to pitch the idea. 'No cover, no interview,' Steinberg told them. The deal was struck. Assistant Managing Editor Dan Goodgame flew from New York to St. Andrews to follow Tiger during his pre – British Open practice rounds. Staff writer Romesh Ratnesar flew from London to New Orleans for a Tiger Woods Foundation clinic. Photographer Herb Ritts flew from Los Angeles to shoot Woods while Ratnesar interviewed him. Tiger got the cover on August 14, 2000, the week of the PGA Championship.

This is how it worked now. Tiger did Time He didn't do the *Louisville Courier-Journal*. And when he does *Time* and not the *Louisville Courier-Journal* he gets ripped for living in his own little world.

'The new millennium's Michael Jordan is wealthy enough, powerful enough and driven enough to veto intrusions with impunity,' wrote *Courier-Journal* columnist Pat Forde, whose interview request for a PGA preview was denied. 'That is the contradiction of the 24-year-old Tiger Woods: He's the king of the world but he keeps to a very small, private parcel of it. He's the most alluring presence in sport, but he keeps the attracted masses at a steely arm's length . . .

'His image is as carefully manicured as the greens at Augusta

245

National. Nike and the International Management Group, two of the most powerful and savvy forces in sports, are zealous curators of their Ming vase of a client. IMG has detached six people to Team Tiger alone, headed by agent Mark Steinberg.

'When asked about the percentage of requests for Tiger's time that are greeted with a "yes," Steinberg said, It'd be tough to put a number on that. One percent might very well be accurate. Things come in all the time, every day . . . The dynamics are very complex, but we try to keep it as simple as possible around him, so a crazy world could seem simple and organized to Tiger.'

Woods was educated – the hard way – about interview requests and his responsibilities as a spokesperson for the game. The first lesson occurred in 1997, in the back of a limousine while riding to a photo shoot in Los Angeles. The second lesson came at Congressional CC in Bethesda, Md. after the opening round of the U.S. Open. One thing about Tiger, though: He never makes the same mistake twice.

In the winter of1997, Woods was convinced by his management teams at IMG and Nike that it would be good for his career to participate in an interview with *GQ*, the men's fashion magazine. The deal was similar to the *Time* deal: By granting exclusive access, Tiger would get the cover. The difference was editorial control. The writer of the *GQ* piece, Charles Pierce, is brilliantly gifted but belongs to Hunter S. Thompson Gonzo-style school of journalism. IMG would have known that had it done its homework. Instead, it bowed to pressure from Nike executives who felt the *GQ* interview and cover would be tremendous exposure for the swoosh brand and for their $40 million investment. If the IMG braintrust in Cleveland had read Pierce's work, they would have known this wasn't going to be a puff piece.

The ground rules were that Pierce would get three hours of one-on-one time with Tiger. Pierce then took it upon himself to use anything that was said or observed in those three hours. Tiger was 20 at the time, just out of college and acting like life was a big frat party. Pierce heard him use cusswords and tell racist, sexist and homophobic jokes to a limo driver and a make-up artist. When Tiger asked Pierce not to use the material, Pierce said, 'Too late.' Most golf writers probably would have cut a deal with the kid, knowing it would mean greater access in the future. Pierce was not a golf writer; this was his one crack at Tiger and he wanted to paint a real-life picture of what he felt Woods was all about.

The *Sports Illustrated* Sportsman of the Year bonus piece by Gary Smith was still fresh in everyone's minds. In the article, entitled 'The Messiah,' Smith quoted Earl as saying his son would have an impact on this world far greater than golf. Greater than Gandhi and Mother Teresa? Greater, Earl said.

Pierce's *GQ* feature came out in mid-March, about four weeks before the Masters. The Woods Camp went ballistic, but most of the public shrugged. While it wasn't good for Tiger's corporate image, the piece endeared Woods to many, showing that he was no different than most college kids with $100 million in the bank. At the same time, the *GQ* article portrayed golf's new golden boy in an unfavorable, politically incorrect light and made him look like a hypocrite to critics of the first Nike commercial. Women's rights groups, gay rights activists and members of the Moral Majority also jumped on the anti-Tiger bandwagon.

IMG brought in a public relations consultant to handle damage control and attempted to discredit Pierce by attacking his reporting techniques, alleging he paid a limousine driver to secretly tape his conversation with Woods. Whether or not the allegation is true (and Pierce vehemently denies it), the result was disastrous in Tiger's relationship with the media. The relationship was strained anyway because of his father's background in the military and later as a public information officer in New York. Earl had taught Tiger to keep his answers short, to not elaborate and to make points. It was a 'name, rank and serial number' mentality. The *GQ* article, coupled with some negative articles that were written after Tiger hosted a media outing at Isleworth, created a somewhat hostile working environment.

Woods showed up for his first Masters news conference with an attitude. When questions were asked that had been asked on the West Coast and Florida, Woods rolled his eyes and gave half-hearted answers. The interview session was such a bomb that the hostility was now working both ways. IMG and Nike blamed the media. The media blamed IMG and Nike for Tiger's smart-ass demeanor. It took years and Steinberg to bridge the gap, and even then writers like the *Courier-Journals* Forde were excluded.

The list for interview requests after winning the career Grand Slam and the back-to-back Opens victories had grown to include *60 Minutes*, Oprah Winfrey and Montel Williams. When a respected golf writer like the *Washington Post*'s Len Shapiro wanted a sit-down to preview the Presidents Cup, Steinberg and IMG's Bev Norwood told him it probably wouldn't happen but to keep checking with them.

Shapiro, one of the hardest-working, fairest and most ethical writers covering any sport, compared it to the scene involving the Washington press corps and political candidates. He saw a big improvement in Tiger. He'd just like to see more of the real Tiger. 'I think he now recognizes more people, feels a little more comfortable, knows people who cover the sport are not looking to ambush him,' said Shapiro.

'I think he's mature with it, gotten better with age; I just wish he'd tell us a little more about himself and not rely on stock answers all the time. I think he's extremely bright, and he knows how to handle certain questions . . . but Tiger doesn't always tell you everything he knows. How many politicians do? He keeps a lot to himself. We know very little about the way he lives other than the few snippets about Isleworth. He's very private, which is fine, but he's gotten to the point where people want to know more about him. Maybe if he writes his own autobiography he'll reveal it. But in general he keeps us at arm's length, which most politicians in Washington do with the exception of John McCain. He'll tell you want you want to hear, but really good reporters go deeper if they can.'

Shapiro was covering the U.S. Open at Congressional in 1997 when Woods was presented with his second test in dealing with the media. Tiger had arrived that June as the Masters champion, which meant that he was now obligated to issue a few comments following every round, and to go through the highlights and lowlights on his scorecard. Nobody on his management team explained the protocol to him.

Nicklaus and Palmer talked after every round. Tiger would be expected to as well – no matter what he shot. At Congressional, Woods was on the leaderboard early on Thursday, but ran into trouble on the inward nine, made two double bogeys coming in to shoot 74, and tried to blow by the media assembled in an interview area by the clubhouse. Melanie Hauser, a board member of the Golf Writers Association of America, served as a pool reporter and followed Woods to the parking lot. The scene was intense. Slamming his Walkman on the dashboard, he glared at Hauser and said, 'OK, what do you want?'

Hauser kept her poise. She calmly and professionally explained that she needed some quotes, and Woods gave her a few perfunctory answers before driving off. Sensing what would be written, Harmon talked to Woods that night, and when he came into the media tent the following day, Tiger halfheartedly admitted he was wrong. His reasoning was that since he shot 74, and wasn't on the leaderboard, there was no need to stop and talk. Then he saw that Nicklaus had weighed-in on the subject and the following spring, at the Golf Writers Dinner in Augusta, Tiger issued a formal apology. Accepting the GWAA's Player of the Year Award, Woods took the high road and said it would never happen again.

'I just feel like I can handle things a little bit different than I used to,' he said. 'It's just because I understand how it all works now. I've been out here for a few years. It's like starting a new job. You don't really know what to expect. When you guys were first writing you probably didn't know what to expect, and after a while you start getting comfortable. You start to understand the people you're working with, your environment, what's expected of you. Eventually, you start to feel where almost – I won't say "at home," but at ease, not only with yourself, but with people around you.'

A noticeable change occurred when Steinberg took over in 1998. Along with Harmon, Norwood, Mark O'Meara and Lee Patterson (a media official for the PGA Tour), Tiger had encircled himself with five men who knew how the game worked outside the ropes. These men knew that the media could be your ally, not your adversary, if you chose to cultivate working relationships with key individuals who covered the sport on a regular basis.

The attitude that noted author John Feinstein once wrote about ('When Tiger spoke to the media, it was clearly a struggle for him not to roll his eyes when he answered questions.') was gone. Woods approached his news conferences with a good attitude. There might not be a slew of great one-liners, but his answers to good questions were insightful and he was giving it 100 percent, especially to the local writers who asked him the same questions he's been asked for four years. He didn't make many eagles, but rarely did Tiger double bogey an answer.

At the 1999 NEC Invitational, Woods was asked what advice he'd give to the next superstar golfer about the media. It was a good question considering his early bitterness, but Woods showed just how far he'd come in four years by gliding through the answer like he was gliding down a fairway.

'For one thing, you've got to always be yourself,' he said. 'I understand that you're going to make mistakes. You're going to have your ups and downs. Basically, what my father has always taught me is that if you come from truth, everything will be OK. What I found is that out here, you have to always tell the truth, but you can also be diplomatic, too, because I've been ripped before for telling the truth. And now I've kind of changed my position and kind of softened it, but still get my point across. Just learning how it all works out here, that takes some time.'

With Steinberg's coaching, Woods made it a point to learn names, and address questioners at news conferences by some sort of identification. It was an old Jack Nicklaus technique. He also began hanging around on the stage after his news conferences were over to handle any follow-up questions and to participate in what David Begg, the former press officer at the British Open, described as 'scrums.' By being more proactive, and participating in these scrums that Nicklaus, Palmer and Greg Norman made part of their routines, Woods got to know writers better and he also lessened his load for one-on-one interview requests. Members of the electronic media also commented on how much more cooperative Tiger was, how he was giving them 100 percent when the cameras and microphones were turned on.

'I kind of sit back sometimes and give him a big picture view,' said Steinberg. 'Deep down, there are some people in the media he likes. Are there some people in the media he doesn't like? Of course, there are some people on the golf course he doesn't like, some people in the business world he doesn't like. It's not a fairy tale here. It's just so much easier to kind of get through everything and do it with a smile, rather than say no and have those same people chase you for the next two or three months and then have to do it.'

From his position at Tiger's news conferences, you can see Steinberg beam every time Tiger calls Mel Hauser (Golfweb. com), Doug Ferguson (AP), Mark Soltau (*CBS Sportsline*), Cliff Brown (*New York Times*), Ron Sirak and John Hawkins (*Golf World*) or Jeff Babineau (*Golfweek*) by their first names – even sometimes a pet name (Mel, Dougie, Soltie, Cliffie, Ronnie, Hawk and Babs, respectively).

'I like to stay more out of things than in things,' said Steinberg, 'so if I'm in the back row or a press conference and Tiger calls somebody by their name and smiles at them or jokes with some of the questions, it makes me feel good. I know that warmth that he's conveying to the media will get conveyed to the world.'

In the old days, Woods also said that he never read anything that was written about him (which wasn't true), whereas at the end of 1999 he started talking about passages in specific articles, going after writers good-naturedly if he disagreed with their opinions. Tiger has even come to develop a working relationship with one of his old whipping boys, Jeff Rude of *Golfweek*. Rude writes a lot of tongue-in-cheek stuff, especially in his 'Spraying It Off The Tee' column, but Tiger sometimes doesn't get the humor. He reveled in blowing off Rude after he traveled all the way to Thailand in early 1997 to cover the Asian Honda Classic.

Rude doesn't want to be called 'Jeffie' in news conferences. He just wants Tiger to lighten up and give him thoughtful answers to his questions. 'It's just him feeling his way,' said Rude. 'He's matured before our eyes, as a person and as a golfer. He's growing up.'

The one writer Woods really has a problem with is the ubiquitous Feinstein, the *Golf Magazine* columnist and author of the best-selling book *A Good Walk Spoiled*. In 1996, Feinstein wrote a cover story for Newsweek in which he compared Earl Woods to Stefano Capriati and classified him as golf's equivalent to the overbearing tennis father who lived vicariously through his daughter. Feinstein further buried himself with Team Tiger by writing an 88-page Library of Contemporary Thought book entitled: *Tiger Woods, Master or Martyr?* The book was well reported, but delved into one of Tiger's most sensitive subjects: The Blow-off of the Fred Haskins Dinner; The Dissing of President Clinton and the wife of Jackie Robinson at Shea Stadium in New York following his Masters victory; the racist comments Fuzzy Zoeller made at Augusta regarding Tiger's choices for the champions' menu, and the way in which Tiger refused to sign a golf ball for the Billy Andrade – Brad Faxon charity tournament in Rhode Island. As big a hitter as Feinstein is in sports journalism, Tiger will never forgive him.

Conversely, Feinstein hasn't backed off in his opinion of Earl. 'He's no different than Stefano or Richard Williams or any of the pushy, obnoxious parents who inhabit sports,' said Feinstein in

September. 'He just happened to win the lottery and get the kid with extraordinary talent who is also bright enough and tough enough to handle all that has come at him. I don't think it's a coincidence that Tiger has matured more and more as he has spent less time with Earl.'

Woods and Feinstein sat down to dinner in 1998, when Feinstein was working on his book *The Majors*. He told Tiger he understood his anger. He also told Woods, 'that he was smart, if not smarter, than any athlete I'd ever met, and one of the smartest people I've met in any walk of life.'

'I think that's what separates him from everyone else at least as much as his physical ability,' Feinstein said. 'He figures things out; he doesn't make mistakes twice – on and off the golf course. He's done a great job with the media in the last year, learning how to give articulate, lengthy nonanswers to most questions. He says plenty, reveals little – that's a skill, and I mean that as a compliment.'

Just the fact that he sat down to dinner with Feinstein reveals how hard Woods is trying with the media. Another more public example occurred when Tiger was watching *Viewers Forum* at his Isleworth home on a Sunday night in mid-August of 1999. He had returned home the night before after missing the final-round cut at the International. A Golf Channel viewer asked on the call-in show why the media criticizes Woods for his emotional outbursts on the course while Sergio Garcia seems to get popularized for the same behavior.

Craig Dolch, the golf writer at the *Palm Beach Post* answered: 'Because sometimes Tiger goes too far. At this week's International, Woods broke his driver and had to replace the one he used to win the PGA Championship.' Dolch had seen a story on *CBS Sportsline* detailing the incident.

Woods immediately grabbed his phone and called the Golf Channel's VIP line. Lee Siegel, the show's executive producer, took the call. Within minutes Woods was on the air with Dolch. 'Hey, Craig, I don't know where you get your information from,' Woods said, 'but that's not true. I've never broken a club on the golf course in my life.'

Dolch told him he had seen the story on the CBS Website, but Woods insisted it didn't happen. Instead of being angry, a calm Woods then stayed on the phone for 10 minutes and answered questions from other callers. He had turned a potentially negative situation into a positive one.

Ten weeks later, Dolch approached Woods after he won the Disney event. 'I just wanted to tell you I appreciated the way you handled that call,' he said. 'You could have been real combative, but you were very professional.'

Woods flashed his familiar smile and said, 'No problem.'

Dolch was one of the regular beat writers who cover golf in the United States, so he had a built-in credibility factor working. Woods found it hard dealing with some of the columnists in Chicago during the 1999 PGA, the reporters from non-golf publications, and the British tabloid press who were always trying to trap him into a controversial answer. The best example came with the final question on Sunday night in the press center at St. Andrews. A British writer chose to conclude the news conference with a reference to an interview Earl did with *Icon* a bi-monthly men's magazine in which he was quoted as saying, '[Scotland's] for white people. It sucks as far as I'm concerned. It has the sorriest weather. People better be happy that the Scots lived there instead of the soul brothers – the game of golf would have never been invented. We wouldn't have been stupid enough to go out in that weather and play a silly-ass game and freeze to death. We would have been inside listening to jazz, laughing and joking and drinking rum.'

It was an awkward time to being up that issue, but Woods was quick on his feet and handled it with just the right touch. Looking the questioner in the eyes and smiling that smile of his, Woods responded, 'I don't think he actually said that, but I know you wrote it though.'

Woods is only superguarded on three subjects: his playing schedule, his workout program and his girlfriend, Joanna Jagoda. His schedule had always been kept secret for two reasons: One, for security reasons. Two, because if he waited until the Friday deadline to commit, he could avoid getting ripped for withdrawing from an event. The reason he didn't want to talk about Jagoda was out of respect for her. He especially didn't want the paparazzi following her, or tabloid coverage of their relationship showing up at supermarket checkout lines. 'She's young, and she hasn't gone through this enough yet,' he said of Jagoda.

The secrecy of his workout program was especially guarded, almost to the point of being comical. Asked about it at Kapalua before the 2000 Mercedes Championship, Tiger would answer only what he wanted to answer, and playfully pull back on information that he felt was classified.

> Q:   Somebody said when you won the PGA, you
> lifted before every round, is that right?
> A:   Maybe [laughter].
> Q:   Why are you being coy?
> A:   Why not?
> Q:   Can you talk about your regimen?
> A:   No.
> Q:   Do you lift three, four times a day?
> A:   No.
> Q:   Trade secret?
> A:   No, it's just what I do. What I do is what I do.

Despite the frustrations with Tiger's secrecy on some topics and his programmed response to others, he was now generally getting good press. *The New Yorker*'s August 21 & 28, 2000, issue featured an article written by essayist David Owen. The story, entitled 'The Chosen One,' was based in Oklahoma City, were Owen attended a Tiger Woods Foundation dinner and clinic, and observed a sermon given by Earl Woods at the St. John Missionary Baptist Church. Owen never received special access to Tiger, but didn't expect any going in.

'It was probably better that way,' said Owen. 'I had this horrible fear of suddenly being granted an hour with Tiger, and then not being able to think of a question that he hadn't been asked a thousand times before.'

On the first page of his 9,000-word piece, Owen wrote, 'The night before, at a fund-raising dinner for the benefit of the foundation, I had stood glumly for half an hour at one end of a corridor with a group of other glum reporters, to observe Woods's arrival at the dinner (but not, we were reminded several times, to ask any questions). As it turned out, he arrived by a different route. Later, we were offered a chance to look down upon the evening's festivities in silence from a steel catwalk high above the crowd, a hugely unappealing prospect. I avoided that fate by managing to pass for non-media – I had had lunch at a barbecue joint earlier that day with several people from the foundation, and they arranged for me to fill an empty seat at a table at the actual dinner – but I never shook the slightly shameful feeling that I was unwanted and didn't belong.'

The Time 'exclusive' didn't break any new ground, but it hit a hot button. In one of his paragraphs, Ratsenar wrote, 'Just before the 1997 Masters, an article in *GQ* quoted him [Tiger Woods] telling a stream of off-color, racist and homophobic jokes. Woods thought the remarks were off the record.'

Pierce fired back in a letter to the editor that appeared on Jim Romanesko's Media News Website:

As the author of the above-mentioned (*Time*) story, I guess I ought to be happy that Tiger's no longer lying about my having wiretapped him, a marginally slanderous – to say nothing of transcendently nutty – accusation made publicly on several occasions not only by young Mr. Woods, but also by his fractious daddy, Earl. Now, apparently, he's content merely to accuse me of unethical professional conduct. I guess he is maturing, just like they say he is.

'As Tiger Woods knows good and goddamn well, and as he knew good and goddamn well at the time, nothing that was said in the two hours we spent together ever was going to be off the record. He knew that good and goddamn well for a number of reasons.

'First, he knew it good and goddamn well because he's been dealing with the media since he was three.

'Second, he knew it good and goddamn well because that particular two hours was the result of weeks of careful negotiation between his people and my magazine – the tobacco settlement took less fuss and bother – the upshot of which was that anything that was said or done in those two hours was mine to use. That two hours included the limo ride to the photo shoot, the photo shoot itself, and the limo ride back. And not one second more. Or, as Tiger himself put it, and as I quoted him in the story: "The key to it is to give them a time and stick to it. If they say I'm there for an hour, I'm there, on time for an hour. If they ask for more, I say, 'Hell, fuck no.' and I'm out of there." I never asked for more.

'And, finally, he knew it good and goddamn well because, after he told the joke at the photo shoot about the Little Rascals – the one that ends with Hey, Darla, how my dick ta'te? – he said to me, Hey, you can't write this. And I replied, Too late, which it was. Nothing goes off the record retroactively. The subject never came up again, not even on the limo ride home, when Tiger enlivened the last of my carefully negotiated interview time wondering why so many good-looking women hang around baseball and basketball. Is it because, you know, people always say that, like, black guys have big dicks? I quoted that, too. It happened during my time.

'I hardly want to make this my life's work. However, the Woods camp – and its various camp followers in the media – have been trafficking in this rot for three years now. It has been argued that I shouldn't have quoted him the way that I had, which is plainly a request to ignore the pig in the parlor. (Some more refined journalistic sense than my own must be required to know what to ignore. What if, during my carefully negotiated interview time, Tiger Woods had pulled out an axe and chopped up a busload of nuns? What if he just talked about it?) It also has been argued that this was merely the way that a 21-year-old talks. That may be true, if we are talking about a bunch of Stanford kids leaning on a keg, Metallica blaring out the dorm windows. I do not know many 21-year-olds who, upon walking into a group of strange adults, turn first to revolting homophobic quippery as small talk.

'All that aside, however, what Woods and his acolytes have said about the way I do my job is precisely the same as if someone accused Woods of shaving strokes on his scorecard, or kicking the ball out of the rough. Tiger Woods said the things I reported that he said. That ought to have been an end to it. And, if you're listening up there at Time it would've been nice at least to have gotten a phone call.'

The response to Pierce's letter from a Martin Cassavoy was the best indication of just how bulletproof Woods had become. When you're the Chosen One in 21st century culture, it's OK to talk a little dirty.

'Charlie,' Cassavoy wrote, 'in twenty years, when Tiger Woods is in his mid-40s and at the end of his brilliant career, are you still going to scream into the wind about how the young Tiger really did tell a few tasteless jokes? Get over yourself. You sound like Bob Dole at that famous 1988 debate. "Tell Tiger Woods to stop lying about my record!" '

# Thirty Seven

# MAY DAY SIGNAL

In the Old Course Hotel on the Saturday night of the British Open, Butch Harmon had dinner with a man who always seems to have a full table with him whenever and wherever he dines, the redoubtable golf agent Chubby Chandler. Harmon teaches Darren Clarke, who is one of Chandler's clients, and thus they talked not only about what a great performance Tiger Woods was putting on, but what his domination meant to the future of the game. It was Chandler's opinion that the long-term Tiger effect could destroy golf's growing popularity, that other players needed to step up the way Clarke did in the Andersen Consulting Match Play Championship the previous February at LaCosta. Chandler, it should be added, wasn't alone in this belief.

Jack Nicklaus also weighed in on the subject before he departed St. Andrews on Friday. When Jack Nicklaus weighs in, golf people tend to listen. Nostalgia-tripping a little bit, he went back to the days when there was always someone out there to be his foil. Heck, he *was* a foil, to the legendary Arnold Palmer. After that palace revolt, Jack had to withstand the bull rushes of Lee Trevino, Johnny Miller and Tom Watson before abdicating. Don't forget, he finished runner-up in the majors 18 times. Somebody had to beat him, because Jack Nicklaus never beat himself.

Tiger had no one to challenge him, and that irritated Nicklaus. It was always the competition that made the game, always the uncertainty that no one, not even a Nicklaus, could count on a 'W' every time out. Tiger was kind of reaching that point, winning six times in 2000 and 13 of his last 23 starts. 'Right now everybody has run up a white flag and surrendered,' Nicklaus said. 'I always had somebody challenging who knew how to win major championships. Tiger doesn't have that now, but he will. He's certainly not going to get off the next 15 years with a free run. He's good for the game, but he needs challengers.'

Where would this challenger come from? As Jesper Parnevik said at the U.S. Open, the only thing that can stop Tiger from winning is Tiger. But right now Tiger wasn't beating himself, and nobody among the top five players in the world were taking it upon themselves to throw down the gauntlet. They all seemed and sounded defeated before they even arrived in Louisville for the 82nd PGA Championship.

This was not Tiger's problem. He would be gunning for his third-straight major at Valhalla, and it didn't matter if the course didn't stack up to Augusta National, Pebble Beach or St. Andrews: His power was now so great that a win by Woods would validate it, place it as a milestone at the end of golf's greatest year. A win by Woods in the PGA would be the first step toward his second Grand Slam – Nicklaus had gone around the horn three times – and give him four wins in his last five majors. On top of all that, only one other professional in history had won three majors in the same year, that being Ben Hogan in 1953. These were the milestones that Woods would shoot for in Kentucky, but the big picture would only become clear if he could take it the way he did at the U.S. and British Opens.

'It's like going to the British Open and worrying about completing the Grand Slam.' Woods said. 'I think that is just a by-product of winning the tournament.'

Woods knew the PGA would be his toughest test for several reasons, the first reason being the golf course. While he had won twice on Nicklaus designs, capturing the Memorial in 1999 and 2000, Valhalla was still the type of layout that could bunch the field. If somebody was having a career week, Woods could have his hands full.

There was also the letdown factor: Even Woods had to feel a loss of urgency after back-to-back wins at Pebble Beach and the Old Course. If he didn't, he wasn't human, and there were people who were saying he wasn't. 'I'm definitely mortal,' said Rocco

Mediate at the U.S. Open. 'I think we all are. But he's not.'

There was now this larger-than-life quality to him, as if he had entered legendary status in 97 career tournaments. People were starting to go crazy for him, and it was more than just the kids. There was an infatuation with his talent, a respect for the way he handled it, and an uncertainty about just who he was. Tiger had become insanely popular despite having a killer instinct the likes of which no star athlete in this country has ever displayed. Surprisingly, that did not come from Earl, the grizzled Vietnam vet. It came from his mother, Tida, who told S.L. Price of *Sports Illustrated* that she had told the young Tiger, 'Go after them, kill them. When you're finished, now it's sportsmanship. Before that, go for that throat. Don't let your opponents up.'

And for the most part, Tiger hadn't. There were a few who had bowed up, starting with Ed Fiori and ending with Lee Westwood in May at the Deutsche Bank Open. Since then, a whole lot of nobody. It had really become just Tiger and the golf courses. They were his only opponent now, and even *they* were losing.

Television didn't seem to care, because each televised tournament kept posting record ratings numbers. One of the best examples of the yearning to get Tiger on TV was posted by the Golf Channel at the Buick Open. While it was less discreet than Dick Ebersol's decision to air the Saturday morning of the U.S. Open, the call made by TGC executives on August 10 was a near classic. In the end it was the right call, just poor execution.

Tiger played in the morning on this day, the opening round of the Buick Open. The Golf Channel had the afternoon window free, and Woody Austin was on his way to a career day. A decision was made, a gutsy one, to show Tiger instead. It was his first round back after the British Open, and Woods had been keeping a low profile since St. Andrews. He had been in New Orleans (for a Tiger Woods Foundation benefit), Toronto (for the filming of a Buick commercial for the Olympics), and the Bahamas (scuba diving with Joanna). When he added the Buick to his schedule, tickets immediately sold out.

The decision was made to tape Tiger's back nine and air it. Rather than tape a highlights package, which would have suited the tour, the Golf Channel went with full-metal Tiger. The problem in Ponte Vedra, where the tour is headquartered, is that it wasn't fair to Austin or the other players who had afternoon times in Grand Blanc, Mich. Rather than show Austin shooting

63, Paul Azinger 65 and Hal Sutton 67, the Golf Channel went with the guy who shot 70.

Golf Channel spokesman Dan Higgins said his network simply 'got caught up in the Tiger frenzy,' and while ratings for that slot set a record, the PGA Tour front office, and some of its players, went ballistic. 'We always try to deliver what the viewer wants,' Higgins said. 'I think we probably went too far this time,'

A terse statement was issued from Ponte Vedra, saying it was 'disappointed' in the Golf Channel's decision. Azinger intimated the players might start thinking twice about making guest appearances on *Golf Talk Live* and *Viewer's Forum* 'My mother was watching and thought there was a rain delay,' said Sutton. 'Then she looked online and saw us playing and couldn't figure out what was going on.'

Whether it was right or wrong politically, the Golf Channel was simply reacting to the story. The story in suburban Detroit, as it had been all summer, was not the PGA Tour, not Woody Austin, not Paul Azinger, and not Hal Sutton. It was Tiger Woods, and if this were basketball they'd be calling him the Swoosh Doctor. At Warwick Hills CC, galleries had doubled from previous Buick Opens and Tigermania was raging in full force. Doug Ferguson, the AP golf writer, went out to the course at 7 a.m. Wednesday morning to watch Tiger tee off in the pro-am. He saw that the gallery lined both sides of the fairway, 200 yards down. He saw sons sitting on their father's shoulders, and a flurry of strobe lights going off to capture Tiger's swing. 'It looked like a disco,' Ferguson told friends.

Cursing under his breath on his takeaway, Woods ripped one down the middle and transformed into the public Tiger, smiling, signing autographs, and posing for photos with the tee marshals and their disposable cameras. It was golf as we've come to know it, inside the ropes during the summer of 2000.

Woods wouldn't say it, but it was understood that he was playing the Buick as practice for the PGA. At the end of the year, that's different; that's when every tournament means something because there's nothing to peak for. Now he would take events like the Buick Open to shape shots in competition that would come up the following week, to get the bad habits out of his game and peak just at the right time. His Augusta timetable was two days off, but he had nailed Pebble Beach and St. Andrews almost to the minute.

His goal was to do the same at Valhalla, so he ducked down to Louisville early in the week for an afternoon of practice. Butch Harmon flew in from Las Vegas, and they started closing down the range with those hit high 4-irons that come down like pillows. Ten strokes back after 36 holes, Woods finished 67 and 68 to tie for 11th. He was there on Sunday, trying to hit a shot through a root because, he told Peter Kostis of CBS, 'I was trying to make birdie.'

As Jaime Diaz of *Sports Illustrated* noted, this was his way of peaking for majors. 'I just think he has a governor,' said Diaz, who has chronicled the Woods story for the *New York Times*, *Golf Digest* and *SI* for a decade. 'He knows now when to be really real intense, and when to just come and play. Ultimately his purpose is to be ready for every major, and to do that he knows he can not be focused on every stroke, every swing. At tournaments like the Western Open and the Buick Open, he's more concerned with the way he's hitting it, his ball shape, than he is winning. He's come to realize the focus he needs to make putts in majors is different; he knows he can't have it all the time. That doesn't mean he's not trying. There's just two levels. He's trying hard not to give it total passion, knowing he's only got a few bullets in the gun for that. Like a marathoner, you can't run a marathon every week.'

That was certainly the way it was for Woods since the previous summer, when he took some downtime after the British Open before winning the PGA. That's why, when asked at the Western Open if he was worried about his putting, Woods just shrugged it off, reminding everyone, 'I was pretty bad going into the U.S. Open, and that turned out all right.' Woods then took it to St. Andrews and responded with one of the best ball-striking weeks of his life. 'That's what's so great about him,' said Harmon. 'He loves the pressure. Like he says, he can still win four majors in a row. When the time comes that he wins the first three in a year, he is the one guy who will be able to handle the pressure heading into the PGA. He is perfectly happy being Tiger Woods.'

That observation by Harmon came into focus on the first round of the PGA. Paired with Nicklaus and Masters champion Vijay Singh, Woods played Valhalla like it was his own personal jukebox stocked only with sixties music. By throwing a little 66 on the board, Woods had now taken it under 70 in six straight major championship rounds. Taking it back all the way to

Saturday at the Masters, he had now gone sixty-something in 10 out of 11 rounds in a major. Nobody could touch that kind of streak, although on that opening day at Valhalla one career journeyman had a piece of it.

By shooting 66 himself on Thursday, Scott Dunlap was only one-tenth of the way there. With no career victories, nobody expected him to hang around for long, but there he was on Friday with a 68. When the field was repaired for Saturday, there was Scott Dunlap and Tiger Woods in the final group.

Woods spent the first two days walking the final steps of Jack Nicklaus's last summer in the major championships. It was Jim Awtrey's idea for the pairing, and when he approached Jack, the PGA's CEO could see the great man liked the concept. He didn't want to go out there with Tiger and shoot a pair of 80s. He wanted to show the kid just one final time – show himself one more time – that his tired body could still drag out a respectable performance.

Nicklaus threw all he had at it, and he was tapped out by one of the most emotional moments a man can endure, that being the loss of his mother. Helen Nicklaus died on the Tuesday night before the tournament; she was 90 years old and did not want to go, at least until the PGA was over. Her greatest fear was of dying while Jack was playing in a major. They saw each other the night before, when Jack stopped at Muirfield Village after the Canadian Senior Open. He knew it wouldn't be long, but it still hit him hard. There were those who thought he should have withdrawn from the tournament, but he played because that's what Helen would have wanted him to do.

The Thursday round was played in oppressive heat. With his shirt totally sweat-stained, Jack stood to the left of the 17th green, on top of a rock wall. When he designed Valhalla, Nicklaus looked at that wall and thought it was so far out of play, nobody would ever hit it there. Now he was up there, trying to figure out how to save par, when the standard bearer had a _ next to his name.

Woods watched this from the green, with a par-saving putt of his own. Although he played well, there were some chances he left out there. This was a day when Tiger could have taken it real low, but the putter let him down.

Now, though, Tiger was just watching Jack in one of his classic grind modes, trying to figure out how to get a sand wedge on his ball, how to get the ball on the green somewhere where he could make a putt and show the kid a thing or two. It didn't surprise Woods to see Nicklaus wedge it to 10 feet, although it surprised Nicklaus.

The par putt should have been conceded, because everybody knew Jack was going to make that one – which he did. That little show made Tiger bear down even more and make his downhill slider. As they stood off to the side, waiting for Singh to putt out, you could read Jack's lips say, 'It is a par-4.'

On Friday, Tiger and Jack knew what it was about. So did everybody. It reminded Nicklaus of the 1971 PGA Championship, when he was paired for the only time in his career with Gene Sarazen. Jack, who was beginning to deal better with his mother's death, seemed at times to be 10 years younger than his 60 years. With birdies at the first two holes, Jack was even thinking about the cut; when he missed a short birdie at the third, it seemed to commit him even more. Bogeys at the 12th and 14th holes cost him, as did the missed birdie putts at 15 and 17. But with a near hole-out for eagle at the last, there was no better way to draw the curtain.

Tiger had the best seat for it, a panoramic view that made him appreciate the moment even more. Said Woods, 'Walking off the tee on 18 I said, "It's been an honor and privilege playing with you, Jack, I've enjoyed it, now let's just finish off on a correct note." He says, "You got it, let's go." ' And they both made birdie, Tiger's for 67 and a two-day total of133, Jack's for 73 and a total of148.

Making his first appearance in the press tent on this day was Bob May. Nobody thought much of him as he went through his card, although his recent form indicated that he could be dangerous. With a runner-up finish in Memphis and a win on the European Tour in 1999 over Colin Montgomerie, this former southern California hotshot was finally playing up to his junior golf record. The best stat on his computer printout was driving accuracy: 13-for-14 in fairways hit. In the papers, he was nothing more than a Hollywood footnote, primarily because his first sponsorship group at Bel Air Country Club in Los Angeles included actor Joe Pesci and disc jockey's Rick Dees.

Woods had his hands full on Saturday. The crowd was beered-up and people were openly rooting for Dunlap and pulling against Woods. There was the feeling that somebody would say something stupid at any minute, but it never happened. Woods got off the course with a 70, which kept him heading toward the PGA's 72-hole scoring record. It did not, however, shake Dunlap, who also shot 70 and was doing what no man in the previous two majors had been able to do.

May, who had somehow gone from footnote to sidebar, had produced his second-straight 66 and was now one stroke off the lead. It was discovered that as a junior golfer in southern California, it was his records that Tiger Woods had first chased. Schooled by Eddie Merrins at Bel-Air, he went on to Oklahoma State, got out in 1991, and spent eight years knocking around until the European Tour gave his career a rebirth. Because he was first to post at 12 under, that earned him final pairing status with Woods. He didn't seem to be worried. 'Everyone is asking, "How are you going to feel playing with Tiger tomorrow?" ' he said. 'Well, it's going to be fun.'

Woods and May grew up 20 minutes from each other in Orange County, that mass of urban sprawl south of Los Angeles. May, seven years older than Woods, was a middle-class kid who grew up in La Habra and whose father owned a service station and later worked on high-performance boats. It was enough to earn a way into Merrins's heart at Bel-Air, and the legendary 'Li'l Pro' worked May into his lesson book at 7 a.m. every Sunday morning. May was a dutiful, if not a particularly gifted, athlete. At 16 he qualified for the Los Angeles and became the youngest competitor in that tournament's history. By the time he was out of college and struggling to find a pro game, Woods was also playing in his first L. A. Open at 16 through a sponsor's exemption. 'I just wanted to hopefully one day win as many tournaments as he did,' Woods said.

Woods and May. It looked like a total rout. It turned out to be what many called the most exciting final round in major championship history, in a class with the Nicklaus victory at Augusta in 1986 and the Watson win over Nicklaus at the 1982 U.S. Open. While May lacked star power, he didn't lack game. In fact, he brought *all* of his game, shooting a final-round 66 that ended with his 270th stroke of the tournament taking a last-minute surprise turn to the left and dropping in the hole for birdie.

That put it all on Woods. As always, he came up bigger than big by making one of those will jobs down the hill, left-to-right, with the certainty of a Delta Force marksman. When he made that, Tiger let loose his first real fist-pumping spectacular in a long while. 'That's why he's Tiger Woods,' said May afterward.

May had fought valiantly. Three closing 66s will usually win any major, but this wasn't any major. He had let Tiger back in the game by misreading a downhill 5-footer at the 15th. Walking off that green, all Tiger had to hear was Steve Williams saying, 'The ballgame's on now!' At that point, Woods could have fallen three behind with three holes to play. With that new life he tore back into the tournament with a wedge to 4 feet at the 17th for birdie.

The way May was running on fumes, it looked like Tiger would take the Wanamaker Trophy in regulation. Right after he missed the 5-footer at 15, May whipped his drive into the woods at 16 and made a miraculous par, went bunker-to-bunker at 17 and saved par, and then played the 18th commercially until that last putt. When they got to 16 again, the longest par-4 on the back side, Woods could hit 2-iron while May had to crack his best drive. It just wasn't in him, and he went left rough to right rough short of the green while Tiger was pin high and looking for his third straight.

May then hit a wedge shot that had Tiger laughing in amazement. The ball landed front right, rolled all the way across the green and up and down two plateaus, until it died at the cup for a tap-in par. Tiger loved this stuff. May had a putt on his same line in regulation, and Woods remembered it breaking quite a bit back up the hill in the last 4 feet of its roll. He played it two more balls out, judged the speed better than May did, and followed it to the hole, finger-wagging at it and grabbing it almost before it hit the bottom of the cup. The celebration was new to his repertoire, at least on tour, and it sent the gallery charging up to the 17th in hysteria. When he's playing O'Meara at Isleworth and makes one of those for a 'Benji,' (that's Tigerspeak for a $100 bill), Tiger has actually caught the ball as it rolls in.

His shot at the 17th sort of gets lost in the list of unbelievable things that happened that day. On a degree-of-difficulty scale, it ranked with Larry Bird's jumper through the window, off the ceiling, and into the net in the famous McDonald's commercial. With his drive in the right rough, he punched a low screaming 8-iron that skipped off the cart path, missed a patch of deep rough that would have swallowed his ball, and chased through the back of the green. May was again having problems, but Tiger was only halfway to par. He still needed to putt up the back of a buried rhino and make a par putt, which he did.

The 18th was a chapter unto itself. All Woods had to do was hit the fairway. He pulled his drive so far left it missed all the trouble, hit a cart path, bounced straight up into the trees, came back down, and then took a mysterious ride toward a near perfect lie in trampled-down grass. Woods saw none of this from the tee, but he heard about it afterward. Advantage May, but he couldn't capitalize on it. That 'Swing the Handle' swing that Merrins taught him had one too many hitches on the 18th tee, and he pulled one into the deep hay.

As the players walked to their balls, CBS was showing a replay taken from its blimp camera. From that angle, it looked like a spectator had kicked Tiger's ball from what would later be called 'golf's Grassy Knoll.' All Tiger saw was a ball he could advance back up toward the fairway.

May had almost no shot, and he near-shanked his second down toward the water hazard. From there he was lucky not only to avoid a penalty stroke, but to have a decent lie. His third came up shot right on a green that Dennis Paulson described in one of the earlier rounds as 'being shaped like a toilet seat.' Woods was having problems of his own, when his third shot dropped from the sky and into a deep bunker.

From behind the green, Woods's black Nike hat disappeared as he stepped in to play his fourth shot. All that could be seen was the sunlight hitting his wedge, and then a ball coming out in line with the cup. When it stopped 18 inches from the cup, Woods all but had his third straight major. May still had one more scare in him, rolling his 60 footer to the edge of the cup, but he needed 4, not 5, to push the playoff to sudden death. Tiger Woods had proven to be tougher than Richard on Survivor And Bob May had addressed the concerns of golf's cognoscenti, who were worried about the game lacking a rival for Tiger Woods.

'This was one memorable battle,' Woods said. 'It was a very special day to have two guys competing at a level you don't see unless you have the concentration heightened to where it was.'

A stretch limousine was waiting for him in the parking lot at Valhalla and the jet was waiting at the airport. It had been a long day, a long summer. The kid was tired. He had done it all, yet there was more work to do.

# Thirty Eight

# ENCORE PERFORMANCES

On Monday afternoon August 21, less than twenty-four hours after he survived the PGA Championship at Valhalla, Tiger Woods was on the practice tee at Isleworth Golf Club in Orlando, grinding for two hours in the broiling Florida sun. It wasn't enough for Woods to set the PGA's 72-hole scoring record, to win his third-straight major of the year, to conclude what many considered the greatest golf season ever: Those last two drives he hit in the playoff at Valhalla were disconcerting.

It had already sent the wrong message. 'Tiger is by far the best player in the world, and does things nobody else can do,' said Thomas Bjorn at the NEC Invitational, 'but he won't keep going. He'll run into trouble and start losing tournaments. Blowouts like Pebble Beach and the British Open, those are things he's going to do from time to time. The PGA shows more the way it's going to be. When the pressure was on, Tiger wasn't as impressive as he was in the other majors. It's easy when you're leading by seven or eight. In the PGA, he hit a lot of poor shots down the stretch.'

Woods did hit a few loose shots down the stretch at Valhalla, but he did shoot 18 under, and he did set the PGA scoring record, and he wasn't exactly slapping it around. Words like Bjorn's would serve as inspiration. He would lodge those words in a steel-trap memory bank and remember them the next time he and Bjorn were in the same pairing. In the meantime, he would go back to the range the way he did at Isleworth – the way Jordan went back into the gym the morning after scoring 63.

The last person in the world surprised by Tiger's post-PGA practice session was Butch Harmon. He also knew that Tiger had a new set of Titleist irons that he would be putting in play that week at the NEC. The kid had worn out the grooves on the old blades. 'That's just him,' Harmon said. 'That's his desire.'

By the time he arrived at Firestone Golf Club on Wednesday morning, Woods had recovered from the grueling week at Valhalla and almost had his game where wanted it for the NEC. This $5 million annuity for Ryder Cup and Presidents Cup participants was the first of two World Golf Championship events that Woods won during his torrid run in 1999, and was scheduled to be his final tournament of his blockbuster summer. He would do a corporate outing for American Express on Monday, fly from Akron to Palm Springs for the Battle of Bighorn TV match with Sergio Garcia, and then take his much-deserved annual fall vacation. 'I need some downtime,' he said. There was no better way to do that with another seven-figure paycheck on the pile of earnings that could reach $10 million by year's end.

For the relentless Woods, there is no such thing as a letdown, and as his gutting of the field and the tournament scoring record at Firestone's South course proved, his incredible season was far from being over at the PGA. With rounds of 64 – 61-67 – 67, Woods wanted to send a further message that the closeness of his win at Valhalla was an aberration, that his double-digit victories were not as much as his close calls. In shooting 259, and winning the NEC by 11 strokes, Woods took this campaign to another realm.

This wasn't so much an encore performance as it was an addendum to what the PGA Tour commissioner called 'the list of incredulousness.' Woods just shrugged at the notion that he couldn't get up for another fight just four days after the PGA. He didn't let anybody know of his flu until the final day, when he collapsed in a chair after his final interview, and took home with him eight bottles of water. 'You've got to give it all you've got,' said Woods. 'Jack (Nicklaus) was probably best at that. I always remember reading that quote from him where he used to say, "I've never turned the switch on and off. I've always had it on." '

There are occasions when Woods renders both the competition and his sport totally helpless, and Firestone was one of those weeks. He started out Thursday with a 30 on the front side, but finished with two bogeys on the last three holes and went straight to the driving range for work with Harmon. It was like the day at Muirfield Village when he shot 63 but knew it wasn't a clean 63. The next day he was eight under through 12 holes before backing off. The 15-under par total of 125 established a new 36-hole PGA Tour scoring record.

His opponents now seemed resigned to the fact that Tiger was playing a different game, none more so than Phil Mickelson, who shot 66, lost five shots to the lead and still found himself paired with Tiger for the third round. 'I think that people watching on television or people asking these questions are looking at it in relation to the leader, and that's not how I'm looking at it,' said Mickelson, who eventually finished tied for fourth. 'I look at how I'm compared to the course and what I expect out of myself score-wise.'

On Saturday, Woods started birdie-eagle-birdie and made it look like 59 was a lock. A sloppy bogey at the fourth broke his momentum and he finished with 14 straight pars. As Finchem said, 'He shot 67 and listening to the television announcers, you would have thought he shot 87.' His Sunday round, completed with cigarette lighters flickering in the dark after a three-hour rain delay, was punctuated as only Woods can punctuate: with an 8-iron from 168 yards to 2 feet for a closing birdie. Asked to rank it, Woods had to shrug. 'I don't know,' he said. 'I couldn't see it. But I could hear it.'

Woods's toughest opponent for the week was a wasp that stung his left ring finger on the 15th green Saturday. Justin Leonard and Phillip Price of Great Britain tied for the B Flight Trophy. Americans Jim Furyk, Phil Mickelson and Hal Sutton were tri-medalists in the C Flight. And where was Thomas Bjorn in all this? Fifteen strokes back, at 274.

'Phenomenal,' said Colin Montgomerie. 'I can only see that gap widening, and good luck to him,'

With eight victories, Woods had already equaled the win total he established last year. His goal now? Take the win total as deep as possible. His schedule included the Presidents Cup and then his second season, a stretch run Tiger looks at as his playoffs. Beginning October 26 at the National Car Rental Classic, he would go from Walt Disney World to the Tour Championship at East Lake, and then crank up the G-V for his around-the-world tour to Valderrama (American Express Championship), Thailand (Johnnie Walker Asian Classic), Hawaii (PGA Grand Slam), Los Angeles (Williams World Challenge) and Buenos Aires (World Cup). 'Nelson won eighteen tournaments in one year,' Woods said. 'That's not a bad year.'

Since the PGA, Montel Williams, Oprah Winfrey and the producers of 60 Minutes have all called, trying to book Woods for their shows. He has put them all off, for now, wanting to focus on a job that is not yet complete. Sunday marked the four-year anniversary of the day he turned pro, and he celebrated with his 23rd career win. When he was out there, playing in the dark, it reminded him of the surreal nights he finished up at the Navy course with his father, calling shots that he couldn't see, imagining the flight based on the feel in his hands of club meeting ball.

That is the essence of Tiger Woods, a young man who knows his history, who loves the art of his profession, and who is determined to outwork everybody in his field. Whether or not there have been better years is an incomplete story. But with five majors, and the scoring records in all of them, with every misstep scrutinized, with everybody wanting a piece of him, the past four years have sometimes felt like an eternity. That's why when he's out there, either on the range at Isleworth with a new set of irons, or inside the ropes closing out another blowout victory, the kid comes out in him. 'Like I told my friends, I feel like I live in dog years,' he said. 'It feels like I've been out here for a long time.'

He would do the clinic the next morning, sick as one of those old dogs he talked about. He would fly to Palm Springs for the Battle of Bighorn, losing under the lights on the final hole to Garcia, drawing better ratings than the first three Monday Night Football exhibition games that featured the debut of Dennis Miller. And then, in a surprise move, he added the Canadian Open to his schedule and was back out on September 7, doing it all over again.

The reason he added the Canadian tournament to his schedule was some contractual obligations that required him to play twenty PGA Tour events. He also had a chance to become the first person since Lee Trevino in 1971 to win the U.S., British and Canadian Opens in the same year. And on top of all that, he wanted to bridge the eight-week gap between the NEC, which ended on August 28, and the Presidents Cup, which began October 19.

When Woods committed to play at Glen Abbey on September 1, it touched off a gasp of expectation. You would have thought it launched a national holiday. From the tournament selling out immediately, to ramped-up television coverage by Canadian TV, to the Church of Incarnation on Abbey Road in Oakville, Ontario (which made $10,000 by opening its parking lots to overflow traffic), the Tiger Effect had a huge impact not only on Toronto, but the entire country.

Woods did not disappoint his Canadian following. With Grant Waite playing the role of Bob May, Tiger went down to the final scene before out fighting yet another course, and out doing another inspired opponent. On Friday he hit a 380-yard drive at the 18th hole that was part of an birdie-eagle-birdie-eagle stretch that started at the 15th hole and ended at the clubhouse. On Sunday he blasted a 218-yard 6-iron from a fairway bunker on the 72nd hole to set up the clinching birdie. There was no topping that.

'It was a shot that obviously won him the tournament,' said Waite. 'To have the mind-set, the poise, the calmness inside his body to be able to make that swing to hit that shot, just shows you that he's got such an advantage on the rest of the players.'

Woods definitely got off on it, as he did being pushed by Waite. He wants more of Bob May and Grant Waite. He knows that's the only way he'll get better. 'I think that when the pressure is at its peak,' Woods said later, 'that's when your concentration level is heightened, too. Guys pull off some of the best plays or best shots when the pressure is the most intense because that's when they concentrate the hardest. It builds to a crescendo. Everything is heightened to the point where you execute shots at a higher level.'

It gave him nine victories for the year, just two shy from matching Sam Snead's best year (1950). And it made him only the second player in history to complete the Triple Crown, winning the National Opens of the United States, Great Britain and Canada in the same year.

One could only imagine what he would do to finish out the year, and in 2001, for an encore.

'He is an incredible man that's played golf like nobody in the universe has ever played,' Waite said. 'Maybe out there in some other universe some guy can do this. But in this one, where we are, nobody has ever stepped into a pair of golf shoes and played the game like he has.'

There is a Bernard Darwin observation of Ben Hogan that applied. Of Hogan, Darwin once wrote, 'If he had needed a 64 on the last round, you were quite certain he could have played a 64. Hogan gave you the distinct impression he was capable of getting whatever score was needed to win.' That was Woods at Valhalla, Woods at the Canadian Open. He needed 67 on Sunday at Valhalla for a playoff, and with that closing birdie at the 72nd hole, 67 was what he shot. He needed 65 in the final round of the Canadian, and with that closing birdie at the 72nd hole, 65 is what he shot to beat Waite.

'The game is not as easy as Tiger is making it look right now,' said Nick Price, leaving the implication that it will not last forever. Well, Price is right. It won't. The deal is, however, that the window on Tiger Woods has only really cracked itself open. We are only getting the first glimpses of what is to come. 'He's the best who's ever played,' said Mark Calcavecchia. 'And he's only 24.'

David Agnew of Charleston, South Carolina, was in the gallery on Sunday for Tiger's British Open win at St. Andrews. He had positioned himself behind the fifth tee box and was there when Woods and David Duval came through. 'He swung with such power, such unbelievable power, and struck the ball so hard, that the crowd gasped,' said Agnew. 'We went down the fairway to see where the ball ended up, and it appeared to outdrive David Duval by 100 yards or more. I read in the paper the next day it was 428 yards. You could feel the crowd's astonishment with how hard he swung the club. The thought that someone [could] swing that hard under pressure and hit it down the middle every time was astounding.'

Woods kissed major championship silver three times in 2000, bussing the U.S. Open Trophy in June, the Claret Jug in July and the Wanamaker Trophy in August – then bringing home the hardware to Isleworth in the greatest collection of precious metal since the King Tut Exhibit.

He outdrove, outputted, outwilled, outfinessed, outworked, outcompeted and outgolfed all but a few, and for those few, it was just a moment in the sun. Woods was there every time he put a peg in the ground. If his sport were basketball or hockey, they'd say he came to play every night. 'He's just better in all aspects of the game, period, especially mentally,' said Rocco Mediate. 'A lot of people have trouble with the truth is the truth. Yeah, he can be beat. But he's going to win more times over a ten-or twelve-year haul and we've got no chance. The guy is better than everyone else.'

The debate now was not whether he was better than Jack Nicklaus. The debate now was whether Nicklaus was better than Woods. In almost every evaluation, pound for pound, mind for mind, the Bear was finishing runner-up. 'I told Johnny Miller that Jack Nicklaus is the greatest player of all time recordwise, but by what I've seen, I find it hard to believe there's ever been a better actual player than Tiger Woods – ever,' said Mark O'Meara.

Even Nicklaus had acquiesced. The only test that Woods hadn't passed was the test of time, and that, in Jack's estimation, seemed like an eventuality. 'I've been in a funny position,' he said. 'I'm not going to sit there and say, "He can't break the record." I think he probably will, but it's not a foregone conclusion by any means. I've done the best I can. I hope Tiger challenges my record. It would be good for golf. And if he breaks it, I hope he does it during my lifetime. I'd like to witness it and be part of it.'

There was a power to Tiger Woods that went beyond the strike of the golf ball David Agnew heard behind the fifth tee at St. Andrews. He signed a $100 million contract with Nike, and his father called it 'chump change.' And when asked at a stockholder's meeting if Nike had a better way to invest its money, Phil Knight boldly stood up and told his audience, 'No, it couldn't.'

Earl Woods always knew this day would come, and from that same house on Teakwood where Tiger was raised, he would answer the phone and tell everybody I told you so. 'No matter how others try, they don't have the God-given talent like he does,' Earl told *Golfweek*'s Jeff Rude. 'Talent is going to win out in the long haul. What can they do now? Nothing. Work hard, fine. Get in better shape, fine. But you can't outwork him, you can't outcondition him, and they certainly can't outthink him on the golf course. So, where is there to improve?'

Tiger Woods knows. And that's why he was out on the range at Isleworth the day after the PGA. He was out there, improving.

# Thirty Nine

# RETROSPECTIVE

It was the middle of September, just after Tiger Woods ripped through the majors, and Greg Norman was in his office, talking about the sacredness of golf's Grand Slam, and the machine who was programmed to attain it. Norman is a great student of the game. He has known Tiger for almost a decade. Mentally and physically, he has taken Tiger apart and put him back together again. He thinks he knows what's inside. 'He is one of those athletes, who, if you use him as a case study, you'd have to say that he was groomed at a young age to do what he's doing,' Norman said. 'If you look at any other world-class athlete like that, they've all done other sports, Tiger was groomed to be in this position. Of course it's a lot easier said than done. I couldn't take this red pen and make this red pen black.'

Norman grew up on the beach in Queensland and developed his golf muscles surfing and playing Aussie rules football. Woods was literally trained in the high chair to do what he's doing. Either Earl Woods had a good swing, or Tiger was sneaking a peak at his dad's *Golf Digests*.

'You've got to give credit to the people who were around him when he was ten to fifteen years old,' said the Shark, putting his red pen down. 'I played with him at Old Marsh. He was definitely focused on where he wanted to be in life, and all the credit to him; you don't see it very often. You could tell he had grown up fast and young.'

They played the day after Tiger's sixteenth birthday. Tiger had won the Orange Bowl Junior Classic in Miami. Butch Harmon had just walked into Norman's life. It was New Year's Eve on December 31, 1991, and Woods was driving with his father up to Orlando, where they had a game scheduled with Mark O'Meara and Ian Baker-Finch at Isleworth. It was an IMG recruiting trip, organized by Hughes Norton. Woods weighed 140 pounds. Norman weighed 180, and was second on the PGA Tour in driving distance that year at an average of 282. 3. Tiger busted it past him all day. Today he's got him by twenty when he's at 85 percent, as much as he wants when he cranks it up. 'Tiger is not a big guy,' said Norman, meaning big by linebacker standards. 'But he's got body speed and rotation, and the technique to do it. If you look at evolution of teaching techniques, they're totally different now than they were twenty years ago. Now it's your body speed that controls your accuracy and gives you more distance. I played with Adam Scott in a practice round at the International, and I couldn't believe how far he hit the ball. He's not a physically strong guy, but it's mind-boggling what these kids are doing. You can put a lot on equipment, but you also have to put a lot of that on anatomy. It's been studied so much more in depth, that we now know what muscles to fire. Now a kid ten, fifteen years old know which ones to fire first. If you're targeting someone who is five years old, you figure by the times he's seventeen or eighteen, he'll be there once his body develops. Tiger is so technically correct, and when you're technically correct you can stand up there and fire. That's why he's allowed to be so free in his swing. With a training routine and a coaching routing, the whole adaptation is so finely tuned. You can see it in him as an athlete and a player.'

Norman is 45 now, more competitive in business than he is in golf, at a stage in his life when carrying the Olympic Torch across the Sydney Harbour Bridge is a priority over tournament golf. In 1986, he led all the majors after 54 holes and came away with only one of the titles. The Saturday Slam had become his cross to bear until Tiger came along to cast it in a different light. There is a better appreciation now for what Norman did do that year than what he didn't do. Tiger Woods was eleven at the time, chasing down Bob May's legacy in southern California junior golf. It was a different time in golf, a different place.

There was no Jack Nicklaus shooting 65 on Tiger the way there was at the Masters, no Bob Tway holing out a bunker shot on the 72nd hole of the PGA at Inverness. There were also no 75s on Sunday at Shinnecock. As gifted as he was as an athlete, as dedicated as he was as a worker, Norman just didn't quite have it, at least not the way this young man Woods has it. 'I was right there,' Norman said. 'I've thought about that many times. What if? What could I have done differently? I reflected on it. How close it was, what it would have meant to me and what it would have done. It's hard to answer that. I would have loved to say I won the Grand Slam. From an athlete's perspective, it's the ultimate of Holy Grails.'

For Tiger Woods, there were no 'What ifs,' no looking back on that opening round at the Masters, that small block in time from the big picture where he didn't capture the moment. There was flawless precision in his two Open victories, and fortune in the PGA when May missed a putt on the 15th hole that could have locked it up. And yet, when it was over, when he had taken it two steps further than Norman, when he had reached the Ben Hogan level and carved a new face on golf's pantheon, there was no looking back. He would leave that to the golf writers. He was too busy moving on, thinking about next year's Masters rather than the one he left behind.

Out of the 1,095 shots that Tiger Woods hit in major championships last year, there were only two that separated him from the Grand Slam. Two swings out of 1,095 from the quadrilateral, the impregnable quadrilateral, the Holy Grail.

Two swings.

A 7-iron into the 10th at Augusta National that flared out to the right and buried in a greenside bunker. An 8-iron at the 12th that was back-handed by an invisible wall of wind and was buried in the depths of Rae's Creek along with the balls of Tom Weiskopf, Dan Forsman, Greg Norman, Tom Kite and all the others who have lost the Masters tournament on that hole.

Two good passes on those shots and Tiger Woods is no worse than tied on Sunday with Vijay Singh. Instead he's exactly five shots back, the difference between two pars and two double bogeys.

That is golf.

And that is what makes the victories by Tiger Woods in the three remaining major championships of the 2000 season even more remarkable. He won by 15 at the U.S. Open. He won by eight at the British Open. And he won by a stroke at the PGA Championship. In all of those cases, he made the breaks and he got the breaks. He had good tee times at both Opens – and the PGA. But no three putts at Pebble, no bunkers at St. Andrews and no doubt at the PGA? That says it all about Tiger Woods, yet it only scrapes the surface.

Woods has become so big that he knocked the NFL Preview off the cover of *Sports Illustrated* for the first time in that magazine's forty-four-year history. He has made such an impact that the SI editors were also trying to figure out whether Woods deserved to be its first repeat Sportsman of the Year. All this from the most powerful sports magazine in the world, and the Woods Camp was privately seething over not getting the cover after the British Open.

'I wouldn't tell Tiger to change his underwear right now,' says Harmon. 'The only thing I'd change right now if I were Tiger is the route I took to the bank.'

Nick Price tells us that the game isn't as easy as Tiger makes it look. Tom Watson makes it sound like Tiger's raised the bar so high, it would take Greg Norman's helicopter to scale it. Even Jack Nicklaus concedes that this kid has got him beat. It's been a telling year.

Now we get to see if he can do it again, and again. If three majors a year isn't asking too much. If he can be inspired by Southern Hills and Royal Lytham the way he was the 'the most felicitous meeting of land and sea in the world' and the 'Home of Golf.' If he'll be going for seven-straight majors at the Atlanta Athletic Club in September. Unheard of? So was going 4-for-5.

How could he keep this going? Many reasons, none more so than this: Tiger Woods is a grinder. He is the most talented grinder golfer has ever seen, but make no mistake about it: he is a grinder like no one else is a grinder. He will fight you to the last drop of blood has been spilled. He will play every stroke, as Thomas Bjorn observed, 'as if his life depended on it.'

The first weekend Tiger turned pro, Curtis Strange interviewed him for ABC. It was at a hotel in Milwaukee, and Tiger was still a kid back then, still saying 'second place sucks.' While it sounded crude, the kid meant it.

Curtis respectfully disagreed. 'You'll learn,' he said. Tiger Woods hasn't learned yet. He still thinks 'second place sucks.' He just won't quite say it that way anymore.

Early on, we compared him to Nicklaus and Arnold Palmer. Now he is more like Ben Hogan. He is the most relentless ll of practicer in the game. He knows immediately why a swing went wrong, and what to do to correct it. Either he 'got stuck' or he didn't 'arc the plane,' the catch phrases from his sessions with Butch Harmon. He also knows that on the days when it's right, watch out. There is no one less afraid of going deep than Tiger Woods.

Even with the governors he's put on his swing and his battle plan, there is not a more explosive force in the game. At the same time, there is not a golfer more in touch with the clubhead. Randy Reifers, the two-time Ohio amateur champion, was watching him warm up before the final round of the Memorial on a Monday morning at Muirfield Village. If Tiger swung the club fifty times, he only dug up turf twice. Every other divot drew nothing but brown roots, the truest sign that a ball striker is not too steep, and on plane.

Ed Sabo, a 51-year-old teaching pro at Bear Lakes Country Club in West Palm Beach, saw this warming up on the range before the PGA Championship. He also heard it when Woods started hitting shots. It was a different sound than all the rest. And then he noticed something he'd never seen before: Tiger's caddy, Steve Williams, taking out a pin sheet. 'Okay, first hole, back right,' says Williams, and Tiger hits a high cut into an imaginary first green. 'Okay, second hole, front left,' says Williams, and Tiger hits a drawing 3-iron into the par-5. He goes through the golf course at Valhalla this way, and then he ends the session with the drive he needs off the first tee. Not only does he practice harder than everybody, he practices *better*.

With modern technology, golf is supposedly no longer a game about shot making. Golf is now a game of power, and Tiger has taken it there. The expression 'Tigerproofing' is a universally understood word in the golf world. Yet, there's also nobody with more shots than Tiger Woods. He's got the ability to dial in the stinger, the sweeper, the bomb, the three-finger hit and check, the 3-wood chip, the suck-back wedge. Rick Burton, general manager at East Lake Golf Club in Atlanta, was the rules official assigned to Tiger's group during the 1999 PGA Championship at Medinah. He'd see Tiger take out a 3-iron and shape a low cut. Then he'd see Tiger take out the same club and hit a high draw over trees, around a dogleg. A year later, he was at Valhalla and saw Tiger, in the playoff against Bob May, take an 8-iron and punch it under the trees, off a cart path, over the rough, and through the green, where he took out a putter and played a Dornoch wedge to save par. Stuff like that should be illegal. With Tiger, it's become routine.

Tiger has also supplanted Ben Crenshaw as the most ardent student of the game. Living close to the Golf Channel, he'll get in his white Porsche and take a cruise over to the studios in Orlando, where he'll find a quiet room, and watch tapes of the majors, the old Shell Matches, and the Big Three Challenge competitions that are black-and-white classics. He is even dressing in a more traditional sense. Like Hogan, you see him more in grays and blacks, less of those Nike zippers that were circa 1997.

The indications are that he is built to last, that his father has moved into the background, that this is about Tiger Woods now, that he takes advice from his support group but makes the big decisions himself. We'll never know whether Earl was told to move into the background, if his health contributed to it, or, as he has said, it was part of 'the plan' to cut the strings. What we do know is that Tiger didn't need a golf scholarship to be accepted at Stanford, that he was a sharp young mind who just needed some maturity and polish, that he was responsible for the integrity of the game, that he was entrusted with a code of values that defined golf.

Arnold Palmer no longer has to tell him: Take your hat off in the clubhouse and quit slamming the clubs. By repositioning himself, changing his image, becoming more likable to all of America, Woods had become the highest-paid athlete of all time, blowing by Norman and even Michael Jordan. How much is he worth? Depends on whose money it is.

In Phil Knight's case, the dollar has never been stronger. In May, after he finished 4 – 1 in his first two tournaments with the Tour Accuracy ball, Tiger made a surprise visit to Nike Headquarters in Beaverton, Oregon. The occasion was a quarterly sales meeting, and Tiger dropped in to rouse the troops. He brought with him a glove and a ball used to win the Memorial Tournament, presenting it to Bob Wood, president of Nike Golf. 'To Nike Golf,' it said. 'The first of many.'

Wood was speechless, but talked a good game at the negotiating table and re-signed Tiger to a five-year, $100 million deal that made him the highest-paid athlete in the world. 'We're psyched, we're really psyched,' Woods said.

Not as psyched as Woods. According to *Golf World*'s Ron Sirak, Tiger would be paid a minimum of $54. 6 million in 2001. That would not include a $2 million appearance fee to play in Dubai, and $1 million appearance fees for the Deutsche Bank SAP Open and the Johnnie Walker Classic.

Yes, Tiger Woods can be bought – but you better bring a bunch of zeros.

British billionaire Joe Lewis paid $1. 7 million in a charity auction to play 18 holes at Isleworth – and this is the man who owns Isleworth. At that same auction, Irish business tycoon Dermot Desmond paid $1. 2 million for an autographed Pebble Beach flag that Woods signed. By those standards, the $204,000 winning to play with Woods in an Internet auction on ultimate bid. com seem like a bargain.

What's he doing with all that money? Building an empire, which brings us back to Norman. Greg met his wife on a flight from Detroit, had a family, raised a family, moved to Jupiter Island, started hanging around the right people, and soaked up all the knowledge he could from the likes of Nelson Pelz, Jack Welch and some of the other icons who comprise the winter Palm Beach crowd. His golf course design business let to a turf grass business. He moved off into wines, the Internet, clothes, land development, restaurants and the staging of golf events.

Sooner or later, Woods will have to make a decision in all these areas. There was no question the American Express outing and Showdown at Sherwood on the same day, one day after the PGA and NEC Invitational, was a result of being tugged in too many directions. It's easy to say that he's young and can handle it. But when Tiger gets run down he gets sick, and that's what he's got to watch out for. Long term, that's what will lead to the burnout. It's so intense simply being Tiger Woods, the golfer. Throw all those corporate layers on his life, and Tiger might get blurred vision when it comes to his golfing goals.

Finally, there are the issues of health and family. Norman pounded balls and paid for it in his late thirties and early forties. As fit as he was, the shoulder and hip sockets couldn't handle the stress. Woods goes at it harder, but is more supple and arguably stronger – although it would be interesting to see who would win the arm-wrestling match. The weight-training campaign has him looking like a world-class athlete, not just some skinny kid. You hear Woods talking less about physical ailments now that he's buffed.

Where will all this lead? As the veterans like Nicklaus, Norman, Byron, Nelson and Gary Player say, it's not a lock that Woods will continue his march unimpeded. Golf does not exempt anyone from hardship. Woods would be the first. His only 'slump' was the famous self-imposed swing change. He has walked on by trouble, either by design or luck. His errant tee balls, like the ones he hit on the last two playoff holes at Valhalla, end up with a good lie and a shot to the green.

That's all Tiger Woods asks for. A chance. Destiny is calling. He'll take care of the rest.

# Forty

# THE MASTERS

It was mid-March, and Tiger Woods just moved into a new house just off the south end of the driving range at Isleworth County Club in Orlando, Florida. There was no furniture in the home to speak of, but on the mantle above the fireplace were trophies that Woods had collected in his assault on the game of golf. Lined up, side-by-side was the U.S. Open trophy, the Wanamaker Trophy given to the U.S. PGA champion, and the oldest trophy in golf, the Silver Claret Jug given to the winner of the Open Championship. His goal for the year: Not give any of them back and add a second green jacket to his collection.

'Three are lined up,' Woods said. 'Put another one up there, and it would look pretty good.'

There is no letup in Tiger Woods, and no worries either. At the time, he was in the throes of what had been labeled a slump – but a slump by Tiger's standards simply meant not winning. Woods tried to tell the media that he wasn't that far off, but starting late in the West Coast swing, the S-word kept coming up in every news conference. When he made double bogey on the 72nd hole of the Dubai Desert Classic and lost to Thomas Bjorn, *Golf World* magazine ran a cover headline that asked the question: What's Wrong with Tiger? *Sports Illustrated* called it The Choke of Araby. And at his news conference that week at the Bay Hill Invitational, tournament host Arnold Palmer acknowledged that he, too, went through several lulls in his career. 'I agree, Tiger's in a slump,' Palmer said. 'But he may win the next six tournaments he plays, too.'

If Tiger was frustrated by the lack of respect he was getting in print and on the airwaves, he wasn't showing it that afternoon at Isleworth. Kicking back in his own golf cart, listening to rap artist Shaggy on the stereo speakers, Woods talked about the rumored comeback to basketball by Michael Jordan and flexed his triceps for a friend. Then, with a persimmon driver he took from Mark O'Meara's garage, he showed off by crushing drives that had Palmer staring high into the air, mouth agape, incredulous not only at the sight, but the sound of Tiger's supernovas. 'He hit it as good as the real stuff,' said Palmer, referring to the new titanium drivers.

It was only five days later that Woods began to prove Palmer right by defending his title at Bay Hill. With birdies on the 70th and 72nd holes, Woods held off a final-round charge by Phil Mickelson to win for the 24th time in 96 appearances on the U.S. PGA Tour. One week later, he captured the one important tournament that had eluded him, the Players Championship. He had, in the words of Germany's Bernhard Langer, gone from vulnerable to venerable in a span of eight days. 'He has that aura about him again,' said Langer, who finished third.

Just three weeks earlier, the quotes coming out of Dubai suggested that the indomitable stranglehold Woods had over his competition was history. Even Colin Montgomerie, who had been the first to concede Bay Hill to Woods in 2000 after the opening round, was now talking smack. 'He hasn't dominated the way he did,' Monty had said. 'There is certainly a feeling of being less afraid of Tiger. People have beaten him, so the thinking is, "Why can't I?"'

Bjorn, who shot 82 while paired with Woods in the third round of the 2000 U.S. Open at Pebble Beach, came away from the Dubai victory with a sense that he could now look Woods in the eye. That said, he wanted to warn everyone not to get carried away with the results from Emirates Golf Club. 'It doesn't make him anything but the greatest player in the world,' said the Dane. 'He's by far better than anybody. Don't forget that.'

There were some American tour pros who noted Tiger's frustration and adopted an I-told-you-so attitude. Their point was that golf is a humbling game and that even the great ones struggle. They had forgotten just how tenacious Woods can be with his game-face on.

The Players was a quick reminder. Even without his vaunted A-game, Woods hit enough good shots to play his way into the last group on Sunday with Jerry Kelly, a pugnacious former hockey player who had assumed the Bob May role in the PGA Tour's version of Europe's Volvo PGA Championship. The putt that will forever be a trademark of Tiger's win at the TPC-Sawgrass was the 60-foot snake that Woods made for birdie on the 17th green Saturday. It was described by John Hopkins in *The Times* as like a putt between London and Bristol with stops in Birmingham and Bournemouth. Mark Rolfing was there for NBC-TV, and described the scene for *Golf World*.

Said Rolfing: 'When people talk about great shots rarely do they use a putt in that context. But to me that was one of the great shots even through it was a putt. It was so far away and so much going on, in terms of the speed and the break at the atmosphere. It was late in the day and it was noisy down there. When it went in, I said it was the loudest noise I'd ever heard. What was interesting was, there were three other players who saw it, and everybody froze. Phil [Mickelson] who was getting ready to putt, but the two players on the [16th] green were mesmerized also . . . I looked over there and everything came to a surreal halt, because nobody could believe it.'

It was, as Johnny Miller described from the broadcast booth, 'Another Tiger moment.' In a final round that was stretched out over two days before because of rain and lightning, Woods played near flawlessly, shooting 68 to win by a stroke over Singh. He was back on schedule again, ready to take on the majors without answering the slump question.

Although he was thinking Grand Slam again, Woods began the season giving special priority to two events. The first target on his radar screen was the Masters, a tournament he won by 12 strokes in 1997. A win at Augusta would give him an unprecedented four straight majors, and while that could not officially be considered a Grand Slam, it would constitute yet another in a series of record-breaking accomplishment that have defined the game since 1996, the year he turned professional. Beyond that stop in Georgia, Woods had targeted Royal

Lytham and St. Annes as a venue that was high on his priority list.

It was at Royal Lytham in '96 that Woods realized he had the game to compete on the major-league level. After an opening 75, he made eight birdies in 11 holes and shot 66 in the second round. With two closing rounds of 70, he finished tied for 22nd at 281, and captured low amateur honors. 'I really enjoyed playing there,' Woods said before the Mercedes Championships at Kapalua in Maui. 'I enjoy running the ball up along the fairways, playing a different game.'

We have come to associate Tiger Woods with playing a different game anyway, sort of the way Bobby Jones once described Jack Nicklaus. It is a game with which we are not familiar, yet one of the many ways that Woods has separated himself is his ability to adapt. Links golf, played as much on the ground as in the air, with its unpredictable bounces, and howling winds, is a game that some American touring pros disdain to the point of skipping the trip.

Woods relished the challenge, and grew to appreciate not only the style of golf, but also the history of the event. The deep rough got him at Royal Troon in 1997, where he tied for 24th, but only a stroke kept him from the playoff between Brian Watts and close friend Mark O'Meara at Royal Birkdale in 1998. In 1999, he was four strokes out of the three-way playoff between Paul Lawrie, Jan Van de Velde and Justin Leonard at Carnoustie.

St. Andrews, the home of golf, was destined to be his week. He knew that all the great ones had won there, and had yearned to put his name alongside Jones, Nicklaus and all the Open champions who had hoisted the Claret Jug over the Old Course. Riding the momentum of a 15-stroke win at the United States Open, playing a course that was tailor-made for his game, and going for the career Grand Slam, there was no way of stopping him. In many ways, it was the crowning moment in what is considered the greatest season ever.

'I honestly think this is just the beginning,' said Peter Kessler, the Golf Channel host and historian. 'I think he's getting better, and as good as he is, his confidence is never misplaced on the golf course. Shots that no one else would consider sound look like good course management decisions for Tiger.'

Woods had developed an almost computerized mind when it

came to making the right decisions – and then executing them. He studied courses and had almost instantaneous recall of every nook and cranny. The putt he made on the 72nd hole at Bay Hill was a perfect example. It was only because of a spectator that Tiger's ball had not hooked over the out-of-bounds fencing. After sticking a 5-iron to 15 feet, Woods remembered that the north wind which turned Bay Hill into Bay Chill had dried the moisture out of the greens. By playing a little more break, Woods read the line and buried the putt.

In America, the phrase 'Raising The Bar' had become synony-mous with Woods's exploits. With the advent of new golf ball technology, average length hitters now felt capable of looking – as Bjorn said – Tiger right between the eyes. But as Woods proved, when he really needed it, there was no one who could stand in his way.

The 65th Masters was predestined as Tiger's tournament to lose. At the Players Championship, he was practicing pitch shots that he would use around the green at Augusta. Two days after that event, he was at Augusta National at 6:50 a.m. to check out the course changes made since the 2000 tournament that he lost by six strokes to Vijay Singh. At his news conference the Tuesday before the event, he was asked how long he had been practicing specifically for the Masters. 'Probably since the beginning of the year,' he said. Later, he was asked, 'Would you bet on yourself at 5-4 [odds]' Woods looked impassively at the questioner. 'Would I bet on myself?' he said. 'I believe in myself.'

The key would be the opening round. In 1997, Woods opened with a 70, but needed a back-nine 30 to stay in the golf tourna-ment. In 2000, a double bogey at the 10th, and a triple bogey at the 12th, led to a 75 on Thursday. Asked if he replayed those holes in his mind, Woods coldly dismissed the question. 'I guess probably the only time I replay it is when people ask me,' he said. 'That's about it.' Scoring conditions were ideal, with 14 players shooting in the 60s. Chris DiMarco, playing in his first Masters, led the pack with a 65. Woods hit his tee shot on the first hole into the trees on the right and made bogey, but navigated around the course with a 70 and was tied for 15th place. 'Any time you start in the red [under par] the first day of a major, you're in good shape,' he said.

Day two brought a sense of déjà vu to proceedings. With birdies on his last two holes, Woods shot 66 to match the first two scores he posted in 1997. Two three-putt greens from above the hole at Nos. 9 and 16 cost Woods a share of the lead, but he wasn't complaining. Two back of DiMarco was a perfect position going into the weekend. He stiffed shots at 17 and 18, did his hour with the media, and went straight to the range. 'After [the bogey at] 16, I just wanted to get back to at least where I was,' he said. 'To get two back was a bonus.' Tied for second with Woods was Phil Mickelson, who recovered from a double bogey at 12 with three closing birdies to shoot 69. David Duval matched Tiger's 66, and was tied for fourth. The makings were there for a weekend shootout with the three best young players in the game.

On Saturday, Woods shot 68 to take his first lead at Augusta since 1997. He did this by shooting 33 on the back nine with birdies at 13, 14 and 15. In Tiger's words, there wasn't 'anything special' about the round other than the curling 30-footer he made for birdie at No. 11. He two-putted both of the back nine par-5s, reaching the 13th with an 8-iron and the 15th with a 7-iron. 'He hits it so far, par is literally 68 for him,' said DiMarco, who shot 72 in the Woods pairing. 'The par-5s are just long par-4s for him. The reason he's so good is it doesn't look like he does anything and he shoots 68.'

Keeping pace was Mickelson, who finished birdie-birdie for his second-straight 69. They would be paired in the final group on Sunday, the Nos. 1 and 2 players in the world. Mickelson was 0-for-35 in major championships, but had been the only player to consistently give Woods trouble. Although they weren't paired together, the left-hander beat Woods twice in 2000, at the Buick Invitational of California and the Tour Championship, and again at the Buick Invitational in 2001.

The previous November, at East Lake Golf Club in Atlanta, Mickelson shot 66 in the final round to prevent Woods from winning his 10th tournament of the season. Tiger closed with a 69, but bogeyed the 71st hole and saw his 19-tournament winning streak snapped where he either led or shared the lead after 54 holes. 'I have a lot of respect for Tiger as a player and a person,' Mickelson said. 'With that being said, I've been able to go head-to-head with him and come out on top a few times. I do have confidence that I can prevail. I'm looking forward to the challenge.'

The challenge was too much for Mickelson or any of the

challengers to handle. When Tiger is chasing history, and locked into the moment, you have to play air-tight golf. Mickelson and Duval both were victims of their own mistakes, some physical, some mental.

Mickelson set a Masters record with 25 birdies, but he made crippling bogeys from just off both par-3 greens on the first nine, and when he really needed to stick a 7-iron tight at the 16th, he pulled the shot and three-putted. One stroke back at that point, with honors after Tiger three-putted for par at the 15th, Mickelson surely had his chance, but didn't step up. 'He made birdie and put it right back in Tiger's face,' said swing coach Rick Smith. 'It was time to stuff it in there, but Phil didn't.'

Mickelson's ball landed only inches from where Tiger's 8-iron pitched, but the hook spin kept his ball on the top ledge, where the best he could have hoped for was seven feet for par. Had he made that par save and shot 69 instead of 70, Mickelson would have been the first player in Masters history to shoot all four rounds in the sixties. In the final piece of irony that shows the demanding nature of the competition, he still would not have won. It would have taken a closing 67 just for a playoff.

'If I'm going to win with Tiger in the field, I can't make the mistakes I've been making,' Mickelson said. 'Mentally, I'm not there for all 72 shots. I'm slacking off on two or three, and it's costing me.'

Duval opened with birdies on seven of the first 10 holes and pulled even with Woods at 12 under. They would exchange the lead seven times in the last nine holes, the last time when Duval stepped to the 16th tee at 15 under.

With the wind quartering in his face, and the pin in its usual back left position, Duval selected a 7-iron and blistered a shot that flew the entire green. It was a shot that will always haunt Duval, who had 183 yards to the flag and a body juiced with adrenaline. 'I don't have an explanation,' he said. 'I can't hit an 8-iron there. The minimum carry is 176 yards over the bunker. I hit it so solid I didn't even feel the shot. To be honest, I thought I might have made a 1. The shot I equate it to is the 5-iron I hit on the last hole in Palm Springs when I shot 59.'

From behind the green, Duval had a dangerous chip shot to a green that was running away from him. He did well to leave himself seven feet for par, but the putt never had a chance. It wasn't until the 17th green that curiosity got the better of him and he looked at a scoreboard. Coincidentally or not, he missed the hole from twelve and five feet with the two birdie opportunities that were there coming in. The putter that was so hot early in the round had gone cold and the worst possible time.

Some of the sting was taken out of those last two misses when Tiger birdied 18 to finish at 16 under, but for Duval, it was still the same sad story driving down Magnolia Lane. In his last four Masters tournaments, he had shot 31 under par, which was nine strokes better than Tiger in the same span. He had finished second, sixth, third and second, but there are no green jackets for cumulative stroke average at Augusta. 'It's hard to be upset when it's Masters Sunday and you shoot 67,' he said. 'I played well; it just wasn't enough. I believe I'll win this thing. I love this place and can't wait to get back. The only thing I don't like about this tournament is that it happens only once a year.'

Woods could tell by the sound of the gallery that Duval was unable to get it done. There were six golfers within three strokes of the lead at the start of the day, but in the end it was a three-man, and then a one-man tournament.

He turned in 34, overcoming a bogey at the first with birdies at the second, seventh and eighth. At the 11th, he hit the most breathtaking shot of the tournament, chipping an 8-iron from 145 yards that landed pin high, and spun left, nearly into the cup for an eagle. After a tactically safe bogey from the back bunker at 12, he birdied 13 by curving a 3-wood around the corner with his best drive of the week. The high sweeper flew Mickelson's drive, and left him an 8-iron into the green. 'I've practiced on the range all week just in case I might need it,' Woods explained afterward. 'I had to pull it out. I had to step up and aim another 15 yards farther right and hit that big slinger around the corner to give myself a chance.'

Going for the knockout punch at 15, Woods three-putted from twelve feet, straight up the hill. All it did was add a brief moment of suspense to the drama. He then played 16 the way Michelson and Duval should have, hitting a towering 8-iron that caught the ridge and rolled to safe two-putt range. After a par at 17, he stood on the 18th tee and sent one final message about his strength and superiority. With a high cut around the dogleg, Woods left himself 78 yards into the green. He chipped a wedge to fifteen feet, drained the putt, and in a rare show of emotion, hid his face inside the Nike cap. It was at that moment that he realized the size of his achievement.

'I started thinking, I don't have any shots left to play,' he said. 'I just won the Masters.' The first hug came from Steve Williams, his faithful caddy. Just off the green, Earl and Tida were next in the receiving line. Then, just outside the scoring hut was Butch Harmon, his instructor.

He was now eight green jackets shy of the 10 Jack Nicklaus once predicted he would win, and 12 major championships from tying the Golden Bear's 18. Only 11 other players had won more grand slam events, and at 25, with his best years yet to come, it only seemed like a matter of time before Tiger Woods had passed them all.

'When I won in '97, I hadn't been a pro a full year yet," Tiger said at his news conference. 'I was a little young, a little naïve, and I probably didn't understand what I had accomplished for at least a year or two after the event.

'This year I understand. I've been around the block. I've witnessed a lot of things since then. I have a better appreciation for winning a major championship, and to win four of them in succession, it's just hard for me to believe, really, because there's so many things that go into it.'

Under the oak tree behind the clubhouse, Earl held court. 'To me,' he said, 'it's like when a scientist discovers a star. He discovers it, he gets his name on it. Nobody has ever done this before, so Tiger should get his name on it.'

And so it came to be known as the Tiger Slam.

'One of a kind' was the headline the next morning in the Atlanta Constitution. Sports Illustrated put 'Masterpiece' on their cover. In a house at Jones Creek, John Hawkins stayed up all night trying to capture it for the readers of Golf World.

'Call it what you want,' he wrote. 'A Grand Slam. An Impregnable Quadrilateral. The Monopoly To Which Others Contributed So Sloppily, or better yet, simply refer to it as the greatest stretch of dominance in golf history. Let the glory echo the accomplishment, not the corny labels attached to it, for if there's one thing we should remember about the 65th Masters, it's that action speaks louder than words.'

Tiger was long gone. After a dinner at the clubhouse, he boarded his jet and was back at Isleworth, too exhausted to celebrate. He had all four major championship trophies laid out on the coffee table, plus the crystal for the Players Championship.

'From what I understand, I have to give back my U.S. Open trophy pretty soon,' he said before departing Augusta.

The message was clear: With wins in five of the last six majors, the USGA would have a hard time getting it back at Southern Hills. Tiger was going for the clean sweep.

# AFTERWORD

There's no bigger fan of Tiger Woods than me. Jack Nicklaus won the most majors and I would never deny that he's the greatest player who ever lived, but nobody's ever dominated like Tiger Woods. He is without question the best golfer the world has ever seen at age 24. I could not say the greatest golfer ever, until his record proves it.

I played with them both, and if you can compare apples with apples – Jack Nicklaus in his prime, next to Tiger Woods in his prime, both of them using the exact same equipment – then there would be very little difference in length. I think Tiger is a better iron player from a 4-iron down to a wedge. Nicklaus was a better 1-iron and 2-iron player. They are both equally good putters. Tiger Woods hits bunker shots better than Nicklaus. I think Tiger Woods's chipping is better than Nicklaus. Mentally, I think Jack was better. But if you put all the comparisons together, I can't separate them. Jack Nicklaus still won 18 major championships. Tiger Woods has won five. Now, 13 more is a hell of a long way to go!

How many major championships can Tiger roll off? One must be very careful when you start making predictions. We have seen some very strange things in golf. Look at what happened to a superstar like Tom Watson and Johnny Miller. Look at Seve Ballesteros. Look at Nick Faldo. Golf is a very strange, a very fickle and a very humbling game. It is a puzzle without an answer. It's one little vertebra in your back. It's your nerves, your eyesight. It's picking the right woman to be your wife. I always said that about Jack, myself and Arnold Palmer. Our wives were the real Big Three. Tiger hasn't reached that stage in his life yet.

Let me say if he stays healthy, and all things remain normal, there's no telling what he could do. I hope Tiger does go on to reach great heights, because he is so good for the game, so good for all of us. He's putting money in all of our pockets, but what impresses me the most is the way he's handling it. He's bringing manners back into the game, taking his hat off in victory and making compliments about his opponents in defeat. That is far more important than the way he's playing. He is the role model to millions of young people, the biggest golf role model in the world, and the biggest role model in sports if he continues in this spirit. More people will know Tiger Woods in the next few years than the president of the United States and the prime minister of Great Britain combined.

The golf he's played is really of genius standard. These are scores and margins of victory that we've never seen. I was with my son, Wayne, at a press conference earlier this year and I was commenting that I thought Tiger Woods would win the Grand Slam someday. Wayne raised his hand and said, 'Dad, if I may interrupt, I believe he'll win it this year.' I said, 'Well, possibly so,' and sure enough, Tiger did.

Jack always pretended that the Grand Slam didn't mean anything to him, but I was different. When Jack won the Open Championship at Muirfield in 1966, he tried to act like it was something the golf writers created. I, on the other hand, was obsessed by it. It was always an ambition that I had.

I won the first leg of the Grand Slam by winning the Open Championship at Muirfield in 1959. I won the Masters in 1961 and the PGA Championship in 1962, and I thought, 'I haven't won the U.S. Open. I've still got one to go.' Sam Snead never won the Grand Slam. Arnold Palmer never won the Grand Slam. Neither did Raymond Floyd or Tom Watson. I wanted to be the first modern player, after Gene Sarazen and Ben Hogan, to win it.

The 1965 U.S. Open was played at Bellerive Country Club in St. Louis. Jack said to me, 'If you want to win the Open, come practice with me.' Jack had a lot to do with it; it shows what a wonderful person he is. I was so focused that week. I went back o my hotel every night to meditate in my room. I never went to dinner. I'm not superstitious, but I washed the same black shirt every night. I went to the gym and I worked out to the exact same routine every day.

I went to a church. I didn't go pray for a win. I didn't say, 'God, let me win.' I prayed for courage. And I prayed for patience. And to be really focused. I went to the scoreboard every day at the club and I stood in front of that scoreboard, that big USGA scoreboard, and I saw Ken Venturi's name as the defending champion. I just stood right there and visualized the name: *Gary Player, U.S. Open Champion.*

When I look at Tiger, I see that same intensity and focus. You've got to be obsessed. You've got to have a hunger. You've got to have a desire. You've got to have a passion. Tiger has it. It's something you hopefully never lose.

– GARY PLAYER